A Division of
Penton Technology Media
221 E. 29th Street • Loveland, CO 80538 USA
(800) 650-1804 • (970) 663-4700 • www.29thstreetpress.com

RPG IV
Jump Start
Fourth Edition

*Your guide
to the new RPG*

By Bryan Meyers

Library of Congress Cataloging-in-Publication Data

Meyers, Bryan, 1948-
  Rpg IV jump start : your guide to the new RPG / by Bryan Meyers.-- 4th
ed.
        p. cm.
Previous ed. has subtitle: Moving ahead with the new RPG
  ISBN 1-58304-092-7
  1. RPG IV (Computer program language) I. Title.
  QA76.73.R2 M48 2001
  005.2'42--dc21

                                    2001005768

29th Street Press® is a division of
Penton Technology Media
Loveland, Colorado USA

This book was printed and bound in Canada.

ISBN 1-58304-092-7

2004 2003 2002 WL 1 10 9 8 7 6 5 4 3 2

This one's for my daughter,
Lindsey,
with this reminder:

Whether in a game or in life,
you're going to miss 100% of the shots you don't take.

Take the shot!

Acknowledgments

Over four editions of this book, many people have provided information, encouragement, advice, and correction; thanks especially to Hans Boldt, Paul Conte, George Farr, Susan Gantner, Jon Paris, and Roger Pence.

When a book tries to stay current with a moving target, such as RPG IV, time becomes the enemy. Katie Tipton gallantly fought the enemy, editing the galleys even on weekends. Thanks, Katie. Thanks also to Martha Nichols for the sharp new look and for her timely production work, to Mike Friehauf and Matt Wiebe for the cover, and to Kathy Wong for her administrative support.

Table of Contents

[*Italic type* indicates a *sidebar*.]

Chapter 1 Introduction to RPG IV **1**

Why a New RPG? 1
Fear Not! RPG IV Is Not That Different 2
What Changed? 2
    Name Changes 3
    Blank Lines and Comments 4
    Pushing the Limits 4
    Summary of Specification Changes 5
Was IBM Successful with RPG IV? 6
What's It Really Called? 7

Chapter 2 Header Specification Redesign **9**

Control Keywords 9
    Date Formats 12
    Time Formats 13
Specifying NOMAIN in an H-Spec 13
Using a Standard Control Specification 13

Chapter 3 File Specification Changes **15**

File Keywords 17
Plan to Exploit Longer Field Names 21

Chapter 4 The Definitive D-Specification **25**

Definition Keywords 26
Defining Standalone (Work) Fields 29
Defining Named Constants 30
Defining Data Structures 32
Learn the D-Spec Quickly 33
    Defining Special Data Structures 36
    Mapping Indicator Data Structures 37
    Defining Externally Described Data Structures 38
    Defining Arrays and Tables 39
Coding Long Field Names 42

Chapter 5 Input Specification Changes **43**

New Data Types 46
Field Renaming: New Perspectives 46

Chapter 6 Calculation Specification Changes **49**

Maintaining a Legacy 51
New Opcodes 51
Renamed/Deleted Opcodes 52
Using the Extended Factor 2 52
Using the Operation Extender 58
Error Block Watch in Force 59
The Free-form (R)evolution 60
Specifying Array Elements 62

Chapter 7 Free-form Expressions **65**

Using EVAL to Assign Numeric Values 65
Make Friends Quickly with Free-form Expressions 66
Using EVAL with String Expressions 68
Using EVAL with Arrays 69
Using EVAL with Indicators 69
Using EVAL to Avoid Work Fields 71
Using EVAL to Avoid "Column Cram" 72
Numeric Overflow with EVAL Expressions 72
Improving EVAL's Precision 73
Free-format's EVAL Twin: EVALR 74
EVAL Imprecision: The Details 75

Chapter 8 RPG Built-in Functions **77**

Learn to Use BIFs 79
String Manipulation Using BIFs 80
    Stripping Blanks with the Trim BIFs 80
    Using the %SUBST Function 81
    Performing a String %SCAN 82
    Using the %REPLACE Function 83
Functions for Program Self-Examination 84
    %SIZE-ing Up a Field 84
    Using the %LEN Function 85
    Using the %ELEM Function 86
Using Functions to Eliminate Indicators 87
    Checking for End-of-File Using %EOF 87
    Eureka! The %FOUND Function 88
    All Things %EQUAL 89
    Using %LOOKUP*xx* Instead of LOOKUP 89

Error Handling with Built-in Functions 91
 %ERROR Checking 91
 What's Your %STATUS? 91
 This File Is %OPEN for Business 91
Data-Conversion Functions 92
 Converting to Packed Decimal with %DEC*x* 92
 Using %INT*x* and %UNS*x* 93
 Using the %CHAR Function 93
Editing Expressions with Built-in Functions 94
Pointing Toward %ADDR and %PADDR 94
Detecting Null Database Values 96
Using Variable-Length Fields 96

Chapter 9 Using Date/Time Operations in RPG IV **99**
Defining Date and Time Data 99
Formatting Date and Time Data 100
Initializing Date and Time Fields 103
How OS/400 Stores Date/Time Data 103
Using Date Fields in Calculations 105
Take Advantage of the New Date, Time, and Timestamp Data Types 106
 Date Arithmetic in Free-form Expressions 106
 What's the %DIFFerence? 108
 Using the %SUBDT Function 109
Maintaining a Legacy: ADDDUR and SUBDUR 109
 Using the TEST Operation 111
Using Date Operations with Legacy Data 114
Using C to Convert Dates 116
Maintaining a Legacy: MOVE Operations 117
Miscellaneous Date/Time Topics 119
Supporting Dates in Display Files 121

Chapter 10 New Data Types **123**
Indicator Data Type 123
Using Variable-Length Fields 124
New Numeric Data Types 125
 Using Floating-Point Numbers for Scientific Notation 125
Pointer Support 126
 Defining Pointer Data Types 127
 RPG IV Pointer Manipulation 128
 Using Pointers with APIs 131
 Using Pointers to Process Lists 132

Chapter 11 Output Specification Changes 135

Chapter 12 Converting and Compiling Programs 139

Changes in Source File Members 139
Using the CVTRPGSRC Command 140
  CVTRPGSRC Parameters 142
Solving Conversion Problems 144
Compiling RPG IV Programs 146
Nested /COPY and Conditional Compiles 147

Chapter 13 RPG and ILE 149

Calling Programs in ILE 149
Implementing Bound Procedure Calls 151
ILE Activation Groups 153
Separate ILE from RPG IV 155

Chapter 14 Procedures, Subprocedures, and Prototypes 157

What Is a Procedure? 157
From Subroutine to Procedure 157
  Declaring Prototypes 159
Prototypes Provide Compiler Rules 160
  Coding a Subprocedure 160
How to Use Procedures 162
Compiling Procedures 163
Why Prototypes? 163
  Parameter-Passing Methods 164
  Additional Parameter-Passing Options 165
The Last Word on Procedures 165
Other Uses for Prototypes 166

Chapter 15 Rethinking RPG Standards 169

Use Comments Judiciously 169
Centralize Declarations 169
Expand Naming Conventions 171
Write Indicator-less Code 172
Structured Programming Techniques 173
Modular Programming Techniques 173
Hone Your Modular Programming Skills 174
Free the Factor 2 175
Character String Manipulation 175
Avoid Obsolescence 176
Miscellaneous Guidelines 177
Final Advice 177

Appendix A RPG IV Operation Code and Function Summary **179**

Appendix B Status Codes **247**

Appendix C DATECALCR Sample RPG IV Program **255**

Index **263**

Chapter 1

Introduction to RPG IV

Ever since IBM introduced Report Program Generator in the early 1960s, the RPG language has been largely responsible for bringing programming to "the masses" in the IBM midrange computer world. From the start, RPG exhibited certain characteristics that made it unique among computer languages. The three most obvious attributes are

- its fixed-logic cycle, which hides many processing steps from the programmer
- its columnar orientation, which requires that each element of a source code specification appear in a specific location in the source line
- its special class of built-in Boolean variables, called indicators

Early on, programmers stretched RPG beyond its original purpose as a quick means of generating business reports, using the language for complex computations, complicated file updates, and complete business applications. Far from being limited to batch processing, RPG found its way into interactive applications and complex data-management processes. As the popularity and power of midrange computers (especially the System/3) grew, IBM kept enhancing RPG to try to adapt it to changing data-processing trends.

All the while, however, RPG doggedly maintained its defining characteristics, and IBM kept adding functions into the limited space that the 80-column specification allowed. As computer professionals became concerned about issues such as increasingly complex applications and structured program design, RPG's bulging seams became greatly strained. In 1994, 30-some years after the birth of RPG, IBM introduced the latest and most dramatic iteration of RPG: RPG IV.

For the first time in the history of the language, the columnar syntax has been challenged. All the specifications have changed: Some vestigial specifications from an earlier era have been eliminated and new specifications and data types have been added. The language's basic underpinnings have been enhanced to keep pace with other modern computer languages, with support for such things as free-form expressions, built-in functions, and modular procedures.

Why a New RPG?

We've already touched on some of the reasons IBM introduced RPG IV; they all boil down to the fact that the old RPG syntax was no longer able to accommodate the requirements and enhancements that would help it keep pace in an increasingly interoperative computer world. The original input specification (I-spec) was acting out many roles that had nothing to do with file input to the program, including data structure definition, variable initialization, and redefinition of memory areas. The calculation specification (C-spec) was so crowded that IBM's language designers couldn't squeeze in more function. Limitations on the lengths of fields were beginning to hamper RPG's utility in its prime arena: business programming.

Specifically, IBM had the following objectives in mind when it set in motion the plans for a new RPG:

- reformat and simplify the RPG specifications
- raise or remove arbitrary language limitations
- add new features and improve existing ones
- enable RPG's participation in the Integrated Language Environment (ILE)
- position the language for further enhancement

Fear Not! RPG IV Is Not That Different

At first glance, RPG IV code looks quite different from RPG III. RPG IV's more expressive, longer identifiers, its new D-spec, free-form coding, and subprocedures certainly change the way RPG looks. However, once you spend the time needed to grasp a handful of major changes, RPG IV — even though parts of it look foreign — is no harder or more complex than RPG III. Any proficient RPG III programmer can easily learn at least the rudiments of RPG IV in half a day.

One of IBM's major goals was to make RPG IV quick and easy for RPG III programmers to learn. To help ease you over the speed bump from RPG III to RPG IV, IBM ships RPG IV with a conversion utility. Running a familiar RPG III program through IBM's conversion facility, or one of several available from other vendors, is a good way to quickly ramp yourself up on RPG IV differences.

What Changed?

With RPG IV, everything you've always known about RPG's syntax has changed. These are the major changes to watch for:

- wider columns to accommodate new limits
- keyword notation in many specifications
- limited free-format specifications
- new definition specification
- date data-type support
- pointer support
- integer data-type support
- new built-in functions
- new subprocedures

Here's an overview of other changes you will find as you become more acquainted with RPG IV.

Name Changes

RPG IV raises or practically eliminates many arbitrary limits that earlier versions of RPG imposed. The most obvious increase is probably the least impressive: longer names.

☑ **File names can be 10 characters long. Variable names can be 4,096 characters long.**

File names can now be up to 10 characters long, compared with the old limit of eight characters. Other data item names (e.g., for variables, data structures) can extend to a whopping 4,096 characters (although 14 characters is probably the practical limit to fit within some columnar specifications).

Two less obvious improvements to naming rules are probably more significant:

- You can mix uppercase and lowercase characters to improve readability.
- You can now use the underscore character (_) in variable names.

☑ **RPG IV allows mixed-case characters.**

Lowercase characters can now be used almost everywhere in RPG IV — in file names, field names, data structure names, array names, labels, operation codes, and reserved words. Unlike some other languages, however, RPG is not case sensitive. The RPG compiler accepts lowercase letters in symbolic names but translates them to upper-case names during translation. Thus, the following variable names are all considered to be the same field:

```
EMPLOYEE_ID
employee_id
Employee_Id
```

The RPG compile listing will show the fields as you type them, complete with mixed-case characters. In the cross-reference portion of the compile listing, all the characters will be in upper case.

The compiler will not translate comments, quoted literals, or compile-time tables or arrays. Nor will it change currency symbols, decimal edit values, or date/time edit values or separators. You can still use lowercase comparison values in the record identifier entries of the I-spec without fear of the compiler changing them.

The new freedom to use mixed-case characters brings with it a caveat. The dollar sign ($), number sign (#), and at sign (@) characters have heretofore been "safe" to use in RPG names. Although these characters are still allowed in RPG names, in some character sets they are uppercase versions of other national characters. If your RPG application will cross national boundaries, you run the risk of introducing invalid or duplicate field names into your program if you use $, #, or @ in your field names.

Blank Lines and Comments

Other changes in RPG IV help you improve the readability of your code and give you new options for documenting it.

☑ **RPG IV allows blank lines.**

Not only can you use RPG IV to enhance the readability of program source by allowing mixed-case characters, but you also can include completely blank lines in your RPG source. The syntax checker and the compiler will ignore them.

☑ **Version 5 introduces // characters to begin comments.**

Beginning with Version 5, RPG IV adds a couple of new options for comment lines, joining some other languages in using double slash characters (//) to signify the beginning of a comment. Any specification that starts with // in any column is considered a comment (columns from 6 up to the // must be blank). Free-form C-specs can include comments "inline" with other specifications, beginning the comments with // anywhere on the line. The third comment option, coding an asterisk (*) in column 7, also works, as it has from RPG's first days.

The following examples illustrate the new comment options.

```
*.. 1 ...+... 2 ...+... 3 ...+... 4 ...+... 5 ...+... 6 ...+... 7 ...+... 8
 // This is a valid comment line anywhere in an RPG program

        // Comments can begin anywhere, as long as the line starts with '//'

RegPay = RegHrs * Rate              // This is a valid inline C-spec comment

  * This is a traditional RPG comment, still valid
```

Pushing the Limits

In addition to allowing the use of lowercase characters in names, RPG IV raises or eliminates many other artificial boundaries that previous versions of the language have imposed over the years. Figure 1.1 summarizes the changes to character and other size limits.

FIGURE 1.1
Comparison of Old and New RPG Limits

	RPG III	RPG IV
File name	8	10
Number of files in program	50	No practical limit
Record format name	8	10
Field name	6	4096
Character field size	256	65535
Numeric field size, decimals	15,9	30,30
Data structure name	6	4096
Named data structure size	9999	65535
Unnamed data structure size	9999	9999999
Array name	6	4096
Number of array elements	9999	32767
Named constant size		
Character	256	1024
Numeric	15,9	30,30
Number of subroutines in program	256	No practical limit
Size of program	Varies	No practical limit

Summary of Specification Changes

As mentioned, all RPG specification types have been changed. Some have been eliminated, and new ones have emerged. The number of specification types has been reduced to seven:

H   Header (control) specifications provide general information about the program to the compiler.

F   File description specifications describe the files in the program.

D   Definition specifications describe the data used by the program.

I   Input specifications describe file input records and fields.

C   Calculation specifications define the program's logic and calculations.

O   Output specifications describe file output records and fields.

P   Procedure specifications mark the beginning and ending boundaries of procedures.

Each specification type is optional, but the specifications must appear in your program in the order listed above.

The extension (E) and line counter (L) specifications have been removed, and their functions have been incorporated into keywords in the F-specs and D-specs. Record address files are now defined in the F-specs instead of in the E-specs. Arrays and tables are now defined in the new D-spec instead of in the E-spec. Form length and overflow line specifications have moved from the L-spec to the F-spec.

Was IBM Successful with RPG IV?

Did RPG IV meet IBM's goals? Here are some general observations; after you've mastered the new RPG, you can be the judge.

✓ **RPG IV combines columnar layout with a keyword format in most specifications.**

In many ways, IBM succeeded in simplifying the specifications by making them more consistent from one specification type to another. Although most of the specifications still require specific information in certain columns, they also incorporate a keyword syntax into the specification to accommodate today's new functions and to facilitate future features without forcing them into irrelevant columns. At Version 5, the C-specs are free-form from column 8 to column 80.

✓ **Most RPG III boundaries have been stretched or eliminated.**

✓ **RPG IV features new functions and data types.**

Most of the existing limitations in the language have been effectively removed — or at least raised to reasonable ceilings. Certainly RPG IV features many new functions as well as improvements on existing ones. Support for procedures, built-in functions, pointers, date and time data types and operations, and free-format expressions stand out as welcome additions to the language. Some strange-looking operation codes, such as LOKUP, REDPE, and OCUR, have been renamed to take advantage of stretched columns (LOOKUP, READPE, and OCCUR).

✓ **RPG IV participates in ILE.**

The major rationale for changing RPG's syntax was to allow participation in the Integrated Language Environment (ILE). Although it's unclear exactly why the old syntax could not take part in this strategic change in AS/400 architecture, as long as IBM was making major changes anyway, the timing for an entirely new syntax was serendipitous. Undoubtedly, the language developers were growing increasingly frustrated by RPG's narrow limitations and were feeling that the original RPG just couldn't handle one more major role in such cramped quarters.

In its new, wider digs, RPG can breathe easier for the near future. With the new support for keywords, the developers are no longer entirely dependent upon finding room in existing columns to further enhance the language. In the recent past, they have resorted to unnatural means to crowd more function into columns, using hard-to-read colon (:) delimiters between factors, transforming I-specs into a mongrel means of defining data other than file input, and overloading the C-spec's half-adjust function to implement a number of varied, but unrelated, new features.

Although RPG IV falls short of a revolution, it bears little resemblance to the RPG that first crawled onto dry land in the 1960s. At the same time, you'll find that RPG IV is a comfortable "step up" from the RPG you have been using.

In this book, we'll show you the "new" RPG from the perspective of a programmer who already knows the old RPG. We'll point out the differences between the two and demonstrate how to take advantage of the new syntax and function. When you're done with this guided tour, you'll be well on your way to effectively using RPG IV in your everyday programming tasks.

What's It *Really* Called?

IBM provides several different versions of the RPG compiler with the AS/400.[1] This bounty of software has led to a great deal of confusion about what to call the new RPG.

There are now three major dialects of the RPG language. *RPG II* is the variation of RPG used by the System/36 and earlier machines; it most closely matches the original RPG specifications (there was an original RPG — with no numerals — but it's long dead). *RPG III* is the syntax most often associated with the System/38 and the AS/400. Its distinguishing features are support for externally described files and support for full-procedural (non-cycle) file processing. By and large, it maintains the same column definitions as RPG II. The new RPG language, with its extended columns, new specifications, and ILE support, is called *RPG IV*.

Positioning of RPG Dialects	
RPG II	System/36-compatible RPG
RPG III	System/38-compatible RPG
	Original Program Model RPG/400
RPG IV	ILE RPG/400

The official name for IBM's RPG compiler is ILE RPG/400. This program product includes compilers for all three RPG dialects: RPG II, RPG III (versions for both AS/400 and System/38), and RPG IV. Most of these compilers include not only support for the current release of the operating system but also a copy of the compiler from one or more previous releases, so that you can maintain downward compatibility with previous releases.

1 In October 2000, IBM relaunched its AS/400 product line and gave its AS/400 systems a new name, iSeries. Because this book covers the RPG of yesterday as well as today, we use the name "AS/400" throughout this book, even in sentences, such as this one, that apply to systems now known as the iSeries.

Chapter 2

Header Specification Redesign

The control specification (more commonly called the header specification, or H-spec) has fallen into disuse with RPG III. With RPG IV, it finds new life. In addition to its previous functions of providing general information about the program (e.g., program name, currency symbol) to the RPG compiler, the H-spec now includes defaults for date and time formats and lets you create an RPG module without a main procedure. Its free-format keyword orientation facilitates the addition of new features, including compiler options in the source. Figure 2.1 illustrates the layout for an H-spec.

FIGURE 2.1
Control Specification Layout

```
*.. 1 ...+... 2 ...+... 3 ...+... 4 ...+... 5 ...+... 6 ...+... 7 ...+... 8
HKeywords+++++++++++++++++++++++++++++++++++++++++++++++++++++++++++++++++++++++
```

Columns	Description
1–5	Sequence number
6	H
7–80	Control keywords
81–100	Comments

Control Keywords

Figure 2.2 lists the keywords and values the new H-spec supports.

FIGURE 2.2
Control Specification Keywords

Keyword	Description
ACTGRP(*NEW|*CALLER|'name')	Specifies ILE activation group (valid only with the CRTBNDRPG compile command).
ALTSEQ{(*NONE|*SRC|*EXT)}	Specifies an alternate collating sequence.
ALWNULL(*NO|*INPUTONLY|*USRCTL)	Specifies processing for null-capable fields.
AUT(*LIBCRTAUT|*ALL|*CHANGE|*USE| *EXCLUDE|'auth-list')	Specifies authority for users without specific authority to compiled object.
BNDDIR('{libr/}name' {. . .})	Specifies binding directory (or directories) to use when binding object.
CCSID(*GRAPH|*IGNORE|*SRC|number| *UCS2:number)	Specifies default graphic character set identifier.
COPYNEST(1–2048)	Specifies maximum nesting level for /COPY members.
COPYRIGHT('string')	Provides copyright information to include in module.

continued ...

FIGURE 2.2 CONTINUED

Keyword	Description
CURSYM('symbol')	Specifies character to use as currency symbol, enclosed in apostrophes (').
CVTOPT(*{NO}DATETIME *{NO}GRAPHIC *{NO}VARCHAR *{NO}VARGRAPHIC)	Specifies compiler conversion options for date, time, timestamp, and graphic data types, as well as variable-length data.
DATEDIT(format{separator})	Specifies numeric field format for the Y edit code: *MDY, *YMD, or *DMY. Optional separator character defaults to a slash (/); an ampersand (&) indicates a blank separator.
DATFMT(format{separator})	Specifies format for date literals and default format for date fields. Defaults to *ISO (see "Date Formats" section of this chapter for more values).
DEBUG{(*NO|*YES)}	Enables DUMP opcode.
DECEDIT(*JOBRUN|'value')	Specifies character used for decimal point for edited numbers, enclosed in apostrophes ('). Also indicates whether to print a leading zero for absolute numbers less than 1. Valid values are '.' (default) ',' '0.' '0,'
DFTACTGRP(*YES|*NO)	Specifies whether to force a program to run in the default activation group (valid only with the CRTBNDRPG compile command).
DFTNAME(rpg_name)	Specifies default name for RPG program or module.
ENBPFRCOL(*PEP|*ENTRYEXIT|*FULL)	Specifies whether performance collection is enabled.
EXPROPTS(*MAXDIGITS|*RESDECPOS)	Specifies precision rules to be used when evaluating expressions.
EXTBININT{(*NO|*YES)}	Specifies whether to process externally described files with binary (no decimal place) fields as if the fields were integers.
FIXNBR(*{NO}ZONED *{NO}INPUTPACKED)	Specifies compiler options to fix invalid decimal data.
FLTDIV{(*NO|*YES)}	Specifies whether to use floating-point representation for division.
FORMSALIGN{(*NO|*YES)}	Specifies whether to prompt for first page (1P) forms alignment on printed forms.
FTRANS{(*NONE|*SRC)}	Specifies whether file translation is to be performed, using a translation table in the source.
GENLVL(0–20)	Specifies maximum error level to allow when compiling object.

continued ...

FIGURE 2.2 *CONTINUED*

Keyword	Description
INDENT(*NONE|'char-value')	Specifies indentation character for source listing.
INTPREC(10|20)	Specifies integer precision.
LANGID(*JOBRUN|*JOB|'lang-id')	Specifies language identifier for some SRTSEQ options.
NOMAIN	Indicates that there is no main procedure in this module.
OPTIMIZE(*NONE|*BASIC|*FULL)	Specifies optimization level for compiled object.
OPTION(*{NO}XREF *{NO}GEN *{NO}SECLVL *{NO}SHOWCPY *{NO}EXPDDS *{NO}EXT *{NO}SHOWSKP *{NO}SRCSTMT *{NO}DEBUGIO)	Specifies compiler options to use for this object.
OPENOPT(*{NO}INZOFL)	Specifies open printer file option.
PRFDTA(*{NO}COL)	Enables collection of profiling data.
SRTSEQ(*HEX|*JOB|*JOBRUN|*LANGIDUNQ| *LANGIDSHR|'name')	Specifies sort sequence table to use when compiling object.
TEXT(*SRCMBRTXT|*BLANK|'description')	Specifies text for compiled object.
THREAD(*SERIALIZE)	Specifies multithread environment.
TIMFMT(format{separator})	Specifies format for time literals and default format for time fields. Defaults to *ISO (see "Time Formats" section of this chapter for more values).
TRUNCNBR(*YES|*NO)	Specifies whether to ignore numeric overflow (not valid for expressions).
USRPRF(*USER|*OWNER)	Specifies the user profile under which to run the compiled object (valid only with the CRTBNDRPG compiler command).

The H-spec has no strict columnar requirements; the keywords can appear anywhere in columns 7–80. Columns 81–100 offer space for comments. You can include more than one keyword on a specification line, and a single keyword can span more than one line. Figure 2.3 illustrates a multiple-line H-spec.

FIGURE 2.3
Sample Multiline Control Specification

```
*.. 1 ...+... 2 ...+... 3 ...+... 4 ...+... 5 ...+... 6 ...+... 7 ...+... 8
HKeywords++++++++++++++++++++++++++++++++++++++++++++++++++++++++++++++++++++
H DFTNAME(Cust_Updat)
H CURSYM('$')
H DATFMT(*MDY/)
H TIMFMT(*ISO)
H COPYRIGHT('Copyright 2001, Bryan Meyers')
```

Date Formats

Figure 2.4 shows the valid RPG IV formats and separator characters for date literals and date fields. You use these options with the DATFMT keyword. Note that the RPG default is DATFMT(*ISO); you *cannot* specify *SYSVAL.

FIGURE 2.4

Valid RPG Formats and Separator Characters for Date Literals and Date Fields

Option	Description	Format	Valid separators	Edited field length	Example
*MDY	Month/day/year	mm/dd/yy	/ - , . & (blank)	8	12/31/01
*YMD	Year/month/day	yy/mm/dd	/ - , . & (blank)	8	01/12/31
*DMY	Day/month/year	dd/mm/yy	/ - , . & (blank)	8	31/12/01
*JUL	Julian	yy/ddd	/ - , . & (blank)	6	01/366
*ISO	International Standards Organization	yyyy-mm-dd	-	10	2001-12-31
*USA	IBM USA standard	mm/dd/yyyy	/	10	12/31/2001
*EUR	IBM European standard	dd.mm.yyyy	.	10	31.12.2001
*JIS	Japanese industrial standard	yyyy-mm-dd	-	10	2001-12-31

Time Formats

Figure 2.5 shows the valid RPG IV formats and separator characters for time literals and time fields. You use these options with the TIMFMT keyword. Note that the RPG default is TIMFMT(*ISO); you cannot refer to any system values. The edited length of the field for each of these formats is eight bytes.

FIGURE 2.5

Valid RPG Formats and Separators for Time Literals and Time Fields

Option	Description	Format	Valid separators	Example
*HMS	Hours:minutes:seconds	*hh:mm:ss*	:	19:30:00
			,	
			.	
			& (blank)	
*ISO	International Standards Organization	*hh.mm.ss*	.	19.30.00
*USA	IBM USA standard	*hh:mm XM*	:	07:30 PM
*EUR	IBM European standard	*hh.mm.ss*	.	19.30.00
*JIS	Japanese industrial standard	*hh:mm:ss*	:	19:30:00

Specifying NOMAIN in an H-Spec

If you include the NOMAIN keyword in an RPG module's specifications, the compiler omits any code related to RPG's fixed-logic cycle. Including this keyword indicates that there is no main procedure in the module and that the module cannot be an entry-point module. If you use keyword NOMAIN, you must bind the module either to a module that *does* have an entry point or to a service program. The topics of binding and service programs are related to the Integrated Language Environment (ILE), which is discussed briefly in Chapter 13. When a module specifies NOMAIN, the module will consist only of F-specs, global variable declarations, and subprocedures (as discussed in Chapter 14). A module with NOMAIN cannot include primary or secondary files, detail or total output, or executable C-specs.

Using a Standard Control Specification

You can use three methods to provide control information to the compiler:

- H-specs in the source
- *LIBL/RPGLEHSPEC (user-defined data area)
- QRPGLE/DFTLEHSPEC (IBM-supplied data area)

The most direct way to provide control information to the compiler is by using H-specs in your source. If your source contains no H-specs, the compiler will generate H-specs using keywords and values stored in the data areas.

The three sources of H-specs are *not* cumulative: If your program contains H-specs, no data areas will be checked; if data area *LIBL/RPGLEHSPEC exists, QRPGLE/DFTLEHSPEC will not be checked; if the compiler finds no control specification information in any of the source areas, it will use default values for the keywords.

To provide a data area for standard H-specs, use the CRTDTAARA (Create Data Area) CL command. Specify the desired keyword entries as the initial value for the data area (free-format, without an H in position 6). The data area must be long enough to contain the keywords.

For example, you could create the following data area for a default H-spec:

```
CRTDTAARA  DTAARA(QGPL/RPGLEHSPEC)                    +
           TYPE(*CHAR)                                +
           LEN(26)                                    +
           VALUE('DATFMT(*YMD/) TIMFMT(*HMS)') +
           TEXT('Default RPG H-spec')
```

This data area would be equivalent to including the following H-specs in a program:

```
*.. 1 ...+... 2 ...+... 3 ...+... 4 ...+... 5 ...+... 6 ...+... 7 ...+... 8
HKeywords++++++++++++++++++++++++++++++++++++++++++++++++++++++++++++++++++++
H DATFMT(*YMD/)
H TIMFMT(*HMS)
```

Chapter 3

File Specification Changes

The file is the key AS/400 component for all I/O operations; in RPG, you use the file specification (F-spec) to declare (i.e., define) files to be used by a program. The F-spec has gained a great deal of new function in RPG IV, primarily through the implementation of a hybrid column/keyword specification layout, as well as through the stretching of several columnar fields, such as file name.

You'll find the keyword format easier to read and understand than the column-only format, and it certainly will make it easier for IBM to add new functions to the F-spec in future releases. The keyword format also makes it possible for the F-spec to take over a few definitions previously handled by the now-defunct extension specifications (E-specs) and line counter specifications (L-specs). The keyword format also has effectively eliminated the file continuation specification; instead of using a separate format, you can continue a file definition simply by including in subsequent lines as many file keyword specifications as you need for any file. Figure 3.1 describes the new F-spec layout.

FIGURE 3.1
File Description Specification Layout

```
*.. 1 ...+... 2 ...+... 3 ...+... 4 ...+... 5 ...+... 6 ...+... 7 ...+... 8
FFilename++IPEASFRLen+LKLen+AIDevice+.Keywords+++++++++++++++++++++++++++++++
```

Columns	Description
1–5	Sequence number
6	F
7–16	File name
17	File type: C Combined (input/output) I Input O Output U Update
18	File designation: (Blank) Output F Full procedural P Primary R Record address S Secondary T Array or table
19	End of file: (Blank) Allow LR before all records are processed E All records must be processed before LR

continued ...

FIGURE 3.1 *CONTINUED*

Columns	Description
20	File addition: (Blank) Do not add records A Allow record adds
21	Match field sequence: (Blank) Ascending A Ascending D Descending
22	File format: E Externally described F Program-described
23–27	Record length (1–32766, blank)
28	Limits processing: (Blank) Sequential or random processing L Limits processing
29–33	Length of key or record address (1–2000, blank)
34	Record address type: (Blank) Non-keyed processing A Character keys D Date keys F Float keys G Graphic keys K Externally described key P Packed keys T Time keys Z Timestamp keys
35	File organization: (Blank) Non-keyed program- described I Indexed T Record address
36–42	Device: DISK Disk file PRINTER Printer file SEQ Sequentially organized SPECIAL Special device WORKSTN Workstation file
43	(Reserved)
44–80	File keywords
81–100	Comments

In RPG IV, the old limit of 50 files per RPG program has been eliminated. There is now no practical limit to the number of files you can include in a single RPG program. File names can be up to 10 characters long.

The file type no longer requires specific operation codes in the calculations. For example, you can define a file as an update file (with a U in column 17) but never include an UPDATE opcode in the calculations. The reverse is not true, however — if you include an UPDATE opcode, you must define the file as a consistent file type.

File Keywords

The F-spec supports the keywords and values shown in Figure 3.2. Many of these keywords implement functions that programmers could use by coding specific columns in RPG III. Some, however, represent new or enhanced functions.

FIGURE 3.2
File Specification Keywords

Keyword	Description
BLOCK(*YES|*NO)	Allows user control over file record blocking.
COMMIT{(rpg_name)}	Commitment control. Optional rpg_name is an indicator to control commitment control at runtime.
DATFMT(format{separator})	Default date format and separator for program-described files (see "Date Formats" section in Chapter 2 for values).
DEVID(field_name)	Field to contain name of device that provided record.
EXTFILE(file_name)	Name of file to open.
EXTIND(*INUx)	File open conditioned by external indicator.
EXTMBR(member_name)	Name of file member to open.
FORMLEN(number)	Form length of PRINTER file.
FORMOFL(number)	Overflow line number of PRINTER file.
IGNORE(recformat{:recformat...})	One or more externally described record formats to ignore. Mutually exclusive with INCLUDE.
INCLUDE(recformat{:recformat...})	One or more externally described record formats to include. Mutually exclusive with IGNORE.
INDDS(data_struct_name)	Data structure to contain INDARA indicators from workstation or printer file.
INFDS(data_struct_name)	Data structure to contain file feedback information.
INFSR(subr_name)	File exception/error subroutine.
KEYLOC(number)	Beginning position of key for program-described index files.
MAXDEV(*ONLY|*FILE)	Maximum number of WORKSTN file devices.
OFLIND(*INxx)	Overflow indicator for PRINTER files.
PASS(*NOIND)	Do not pass indicators to data management on output, and do not receive them on input.

continued ...

FIGURE 3.2 *CONTINUED*

Keyword	Description
PGMNAME(program_name)	Program to handle support for SPECIAL file.
PLIST(plist_name)	Parameter list to pass to PGMNAME for SPECIAL file.
PREFIX(prefix_string{:number})	Prefix for field names in file. If second argument is used, prefix replaces that number of characters in field names.
PRTCTL(data_struct{:*COMPAT})	Data structure for dynamic printer forms control information and line count. *COMPAT for RPG III-compatible layout.
RAFDATA(file_name)	File containing records for record address file.
RECNO(field_name)	Relative record number.
RENAME(Ext_format:Int_format)	Rename record format from Ext_format to Int_format.
SAVEDS(data_struct_name)	Data structure saved and restored for each device.
SAVEIND(number)	Indicators up to specified number are saved and restored for each device.
SFILE(recformat:rrnfield)	Subfile record format and relative record number field.
SLN(number)	Display file starting line number.
TIMFMT(format{separator})	Default time format and separator for program-described files (see "Time Formats" in Chapter 2 for values).
USROPN	Explicit open of file, using OPEN opcode.

✓ **You can now specify which files/members to open at runtime.**

The EXTFILE and EXTMBR keywords let you code the specific external names of files and/or members that you want to open for a file specification; you can also specify library names. The EXTFILE keyword values can be literals or variables, in the form *filename*, *library/filename*, or **LIBL/filename*. The EXTMBR keyword values can be *membername*, '*ALL', or '*FIRST' (with apostrophes). The values must be in the correct case, and if you use variables, you must set the values before attempting to open the file. If you've previously issued an override for the external file, the override will be in effect when your program opens the file.

Here are some examples of using the EXTFILE and EXTMBR keywords:

```
*.. 1 ...+... 2 ...+... 3 ...+... 4 ...+... 5 ...+... 6 ...+... 7 ...+... 8
FFilename++IPEASFRLen+LKlen+AIDevice+.Keywords++++++++++++++++++++++++++++++
FInput     IF   E          K DISK    USROPN
F                                     EXTFILE(DataIn)
FMaillist  UF   E          K DISK    USROPN
F                                     EXTMBR(MailMbr)
FSales     IF   E          K DISK    EXTMBR('*ALL')
```

Here, if the variable DataIn contains the value MYDATA/KEYDATA, that file will be opened when the RPG program opens file Input. The variable MailMbr will have a value naming the member to process when Maillist is opened. Finally, all members of the Sales file will be processed.

Typically, files that you code using EXTFILE and EXTMBR with variables will be opened under user control (USROPN keyword) instead of being opened automatically, but you can also provide the name by passing it as a parameter to the program, by using *INZSR or INZ to give the variable an initial value (see Chapter 4), or by using EXPORT/IMPORT to share the variable from another module (see Chapter 15).

✓ Use PREFIX to rename all the fields in a file.

In RPG IV, the PREFIX keyword provides a way to globally rename all the fields in an externally described file. Rather than having to rename the fields individually in the I-specs, you can attach a prefix to the external field names; your program then refers to the field names that include the prefix. Your RPG program will refer to a field using the field's full, prefixed name. In the following example, all the fields in the Customers file will be renamed to include a prefix of CU:

```
*.. 1 ...+... 2 ...+... 3 ...+... 4 ...+... 5 ...+... 6 ...+... 7 ...+... 8
FFilename++IPEASFRLen+LKLen+AIDevice+.Keywords++++++++++++++++++++++++++++++
FCustomers UF    E          K DISK     PREFIX(CU)
```

If file Customers includes a field called NAME, this RPG program would refer to that field as CUNAME.

An alternate syntax for the PREFIX keyword lets you overlay one or more of the characters naming a variable. In the following example, all the fields in the Customers file will be renamed with an overlaid prefix:

```
*.. 1 ...+... 2 ...+... 3 ...+... 4 ...+... 5 ...+... 6 ...+... 7 ...+... 8
FFilename++IPEASFRLen+LKLen+AIDevice+.Keywords++++++++++++++++++++++++++++++
FCustomers UF    E          K DISK     PREFIX(CU:2)
```

If Customers includes a field named GGNAME, this RPG program would refer to that field as CUNAME. The overlay option is useful when you may already have assigned prefix names to fields but you need to rename those prefixes within a program. The number of characters in the prefix need not match the number of characters to overlay.

✓ The INDDS keyword helps eliminate numbered indicators.

RPG IV is slowly but surely eliminating the need for the 99 traditional numbered indicators that have always been one of its identifying characteristics. But Data Definition Specifications (DDS) still use numbered indicators as the primary means of setting conditions. RPG IV now lets you map the numbered indicators coded in the specifications for a workstation or printer file to a data structure in the RPG IV program. You can then assign names to the indicators and refer to them by name instead of number. The F-spec keyword INDDS names the data structure to associate with these numbered indicators. To use INDDS most effectively, you must also specify the INDARA keyword in the DDS for the file; INDARA tells data management to return a 99-byte data structure to the RPG IV program instead of passing individual indicator states. Chapter 4 shows an example that uses INDDS.

☑ The L-specification no longer exists.

The FORMLEN, FORMOFL, and OFLIND keywords consolidate printer form functions that previously were shared by the F-spec and the L-spec (which no longer exists). The following code would describe a typical report in an RPG IV program:

```
*.. 1 ...+... 2 ...+... 3 ...+... 4 ...+... 5 ...+... 6 ...+... 7 ...+... 8
FFilename++IPEASFRLen+LKLen+AIDevice+.Keywords++++++++++++++++++++++++++++++++++
FTransRpt  O   E           PRINTER FORMLEN(66)
F                                  FORMOFL(60)
F                                  OFLIND(*INOF)
```

☑ The INCLUDE keyword now complements the IGNORE function in F-specs.

RPG III's file continuation specification supported the IGNORE function, which let you ignore a record format from an externally described file. RPG IV goes one better by adding an INCLUDE function to include only the format (or formats) you specify. For either keyword, you can specify one or more formats, separating them with a colon (:). You cannot use both keywords for the same file (IGNORE and INCLUDE are mutually exclusive). In the following RPG III/RPG IV comparison, we assume that a logical file includes three formats: USA, CANADA, and FOREIGN. If the program were to include only USA formats, we would use the IGNORE function in RPG III, while in RPG IV we could use either the IGNORE or the INCLUDE keyword:

RPG III

```
*.. 1 ...+... 2 ...+... 3 ...+... 4 ...+... 5 ...+... 6 ...+... 7 ...
FFilenameIPEAF....RlenLK1AIOvKlocEDevice+......KExit++Entry+A....U1.*
FMAILLISTIF  E          K        DISK
F              CANADA                          KIGNORE
F              FOREIGN                         KIGNORE
```

RPG IV

```
*.. 1 ...+... 2 ...+... 3 ...+... 4 ...+... 5 ...+... 6 ...+... 7 ...+... 8
FFilename++IPEASFRLen+LKLen+AIDevice+.Keywords++++++++++++++++++++++++++++++++++
FMailList  IF  E          K DISK     IGNORE(CANADA:FOREIGN)
```

or

```
FMailList  IF  E          K DISK     INCLUDE(USA)
```

☑ You can now activate commitment control at runtime.

The COMMIT keyword now lets you activate commitment control for a file *optionally* at runtime, when the program opens the file. Commitment control lets you group file updates into an all-or-nothing group; if any of the updates in the group fails, none of the updates will take place. Commitment control requires journaling to be active. You can name a field (one-byte character) that the program will evaluate when it opens the file. If the field contains a 1, the file will be opened with commitment control; otherwise, COMMIT and ROLBK operations will be ignored. You can pass the field to the program as a parameter or set it in the program before the file is opened.

In the following example, the program will explicitly open the Customers file, using the OPEN opcode. If the value of field CmtCust is 1, commitment control will be active for the file.

```
*.. 1 ...+... 2 ...+... 3 ...+... 4 ...+... 5 ...+... 6 ...+... 7 ...+... 8
FFilename++IPEASFRLen+LKLen+AIDevice+.Keywords+++++++++++++++++++++++++++++++
FCustomers UF   E           K DISK     USROPN
F                                      COMMIT(CmtCust)
```

Plan to Exploit Longer Field Names

One of the most ballyhooed features of RPG IV is its support for longer identifiers (e.g., field names, subroutines, format names). Having additional length lets you assign CL-command–like names to subroutines and assign more meaningful field names.

For externally described files, the effect of the longer field name is less direct, at least for the millions of pre-existing files that contain six-character field names. RPG IV offers two ways to provide more meaningful field names for old, six-character fields, the first of which is the new PREFIX keyword provided by the F-spec.

RPG IV retains the ability to rename an externally described file using the I-spec, in a syntax similar to that used by RPG III. Although this approach is not as convenient as the PREFIX method and seems a little old-fashioned, you could write, for each file, an I-spec /COPY member that gives the fields longer, more meaningful names. You could then include this /COPY member in any RPG IV program that uses the file, thus providing effective, painless migration to long field names.

Even with free-form calculation specifications, you may still encounter "column cram" in some specifications when you try to use extra-long field names, especially those longer than 14 characters. IBM alleviates this difficulty by letting you continue a field name onto a subsequent line by using an ellipsis (...) as a special continuation character. If a specification contains an ellipsis as the last three nonblank characters in a line, the specification will continue to the next line. You can thus include field names up to the 4,096 character limit in D-specs and C-specs.

☑ Rename record formats with the RENAME keyword.

The F-spec keywords we've discussed thus far have been new or enhanced functions in RPG IV. Several routine functions, however, are neither new nor enhanced — they're just different. In many cases, F-spec continuation lines previously handled these functions; now, a keyword serves the purpose. For example, to rename a record format within a file, you use the RENAME keyword. The following example shows corresponding RPG III and RPG IV code:

RPG III

```
*.. 1 ...+... 2 ...+... 3 ...+... 4 ...+... 5 ...+... 6 ...+... 7 ...
FFilenameIPEAF....RlenLK1AIOvKlocEDevice+......KExit++Entry+A....U1.*
FMAILLISTIF E        K        DISK
F          MAILFMT                            KRENAMEMAIL2
```

RPG IV

```
*.. 1 ...+... 2 ...+... 3 ...+... 4 ...+... 5 ...+... 6 ...+... 7 ...+... 8
FFilename++IPEASFRlen+LKlen+AIDevice+.Keywords+++++++++++++++++++++++++++++
FMailList IF   E        K DISK    RENAME(MAILFMT:MAIL2)
```

☑ The SFILE keyword describes subfiles.

To describe a subfile in RPG IV, you use the SFILE keyword, which replaces the SFILE continuation line. Keyword SFILE has two parameters separated by a colon: the subfile record format name and the relative record number field name. The following code compares RPG III and RPG IV:

RPG III

```
*.. 1 ...+... 2 ...+... 3 ...+... 4 ...+... 5 ...+... 6 ...+... 7 ...
FFilenameIPEAF....RlenLK1AIOvKlocEDevice+......KExit++Entry+A....U1.*
FMNTCUST CF  E                   WORKSTN
F                                SFLRRNKSFILE CUSTSFL
```

RPG IV

```
*.. 1 ...+... 2 ...+... 3 ...+... 4 ...+... 5 ...+... 6 ...+... 7 ...+... 8
FFilename++IPEASFRlen+LKlen+AIDevice+.Keywords+++++++++++++++++++++++++++++
FMaintCust CF   E             WORKSTN SFILE(CustSfl:SflRecNo)
```

☑ Keywords INFDS and INFSR enhance file error processing.

To name a file's information data structure and error-processing subroutines, you also can use F-spec keywords. In RPG III, these functions required file continuation lines. The following examples show corresponding RPG III and RPG IV code:

RPG III

```
*.. 1 ...+... 2 ...+... 3 ...+... 4 ...+... 5 ...+... 6 ...+... 7 ...
FFilenameIPEAF....RlenLK1AIOvKlocEDevice+......KExit++Entry+A....U1.*
FMAILLISTIF E        K        DISK
F                                     KINFDS DSMAIL
F                                     KINFSR ERMAIL
```

RPG IV

```
*.. 1 ...+... 2 ...+... 3 ...+... 4 ...+... 5 ...+... 6 ...+... 7 ...+... 8
FFilename++IPEASFRlen+LKlen+AIDevice+.Keywords+++++++++++++++++++++++++++++
FMailList IF   E        K DISK    INFDS(InfDS_Mail)
F                                 INFSR(Error_Mail)
```

☑ **Record address files don't use the E-spec anymore.**

RPG IV also uses an F-spec keyword to support record address files, which can contain limits records to process a file sequentially within limits or relative record numbers to process a file by relative record number. In RPG III, a record address file required not only an appropriate F-spec but also an entry in the E-spec to link the record address file to the main file being processed. Because the E-spec no longer exists, you use the RAFDATA keyword to name a record address file. The following example shows the difference between RPG III and RPG IV:

RPG III

```
*.. 1 ...+... 2 ...+... 3 ...+... 4 ...+... 5 ...+... 6 ...+... 7 ...
FFilenameIPEAF....RlenLK1AIOvKlocEDevice+......KExit++Entry+A....U1.*
E....FromfileTofile++Name++N/rN/tbLenPDSArrnamLenPDSComments+++++++*
FLIMITS  IR  F     6  3        EDISK
E   LIMITS  MAILLIST
```

RPG IV

```
*.. 1 ...+... 2 ...+... 3 ...+... 4 ...+... 5 ...+... 6 ...+... 7 ...+... 8
FFilename++IPEASFRLen+LKLen+AIDevice+.Keywords+++++++++++++++++++++++++++++
FLimits     IR  F   6    3  DISK     RAFDATA(MailList)
```

Miscellaneous F-spec keywords include USROPN (instead of specifying UC in columns 71–72) to explicitly open files in a program and EXTIND to condition file opens based on the status of external indicators U1–U8.

Chapter 4

The Definitive D-Specification

The RPG IV definition specification (D-spec) consolidates into one specification all the data-definition requirements for arrays, data structures, work fields, data areas, named constants, procedure prototypes, and procedure interfaces. With RPG II and RPG III, you can describe data in several ways (e.g., in the E-specs, I-specs, and C-specs); the D-spec replaces some of these methods and provides a single area in the RPG program for data definition.

The D-spec eliminates the E-spec for defining arrays and tables. Likewise, RPG IV strips the I-spec of its role in describing named constants, data structures, and data areas. Although you can still define fields in the calculations of an RPG IV program, the D-spec provides the preferred program section for all data definition — except for file input (which is described by the I-spec). Your code will be easier to maintain if you avoid defining data in the C-spec and use only the D-spec for this purpose. Figure 4.1 illustrates the specification layout for the D-spec.

FIGURE 4.1
Definition Specification Layout

```
*.. 1 ...+... 2 ...+... 3 ...+... 4 ...+... 5 ...+... 6 ...+... 7 ...+... 8
DName++++++++++ETDsFrom+++To/L+++IDc.Keywords+++++++++++++++++++++++++++++++
```

Columns	Description
1–5	Sequence number
6	D
7–21	Data item name
22	Externally described: (Blank) Program-described E Externally described
23	Data structure type: (Blank) Miscellaneous definition S Program status data structure U Data-area data structure
24–25	Type of definition: (Blank) Data structure subfield C Constant DS Data structure PI Procedure interface PR Prototype S Standalone field, array, or table
26–32	From position or reserved word
33–39	To position or length

continued ...

FIGURE 4.1 CONTINUED

Columns	Description
40	Internal data type:
	(Blank) Character if blank decimal positions entry; otherwise, packed numeric for standalone field or zoned numeric for subfield
	A Character
	B Binary numeric
	C Unicode
	D Date
	F Float numeric
	G Graphic
	I Signed integer numeric
	N Indicator
	O Object
	P Packed-decimal numeric
	S Zoned numeric
	T Time
	U Unsigned integer numeric
	Z Timestamp
	* Basing pointer or procedure pointer
41–42	Decimal positions (0–30, blank)
43	Reserved
44–80	Keywords
81–100	Comments

Definition Keywords

Like many of the new RPG IV specifications, the D-spec uses a hybrid column/keyword orientation to enhance readability and ease the implementation of new functions in the future. The D-spec supports the keywords and values shown in Figure 4.2.

FIGURE 4.2

Definition Specification Keywords

Keyword	Description
ALIGN	Aligns data structure subfields of integer or float data type on word boundaries.
ALT(array_name)	Names a main array for use with this alternating array.
ALTSEQ(*NONE)	Definition ignores alternate collating sequence, if any.
ASCEND	Specifies that array or table entries are in ascending order.
BASED(pointer_name)	Names a pointer to the address of the data item.
CCSID(number|*DFT)	Specifies a character code set identifier.
CLASS(*JAVA:class_name)	Names a class for an object definition.

continued ...

FIGURE 4.2 *CONTINUED*

Keyword	Description
CONST(constant)	(1) Specifies the value of a named constant (optional). (2) Indicates that a parameter is passed by read-only reference.
CTDATA	Specifies a compile-time table or array.
DATFMT(format{separator})	Specifies a default date format and separator (see Chapter 2 for values).
DESCEND	Specifies that array or table entries are in descending order.
DIM(numeric_constant)	Defines the number of elements in an array or table.
DTAARA{(data_area_name|*LDA|*PDA)}	Associates the data item with an external data area.
EXPORT{(external_name)}	(1) Allows the data item to be accessed by another ILE module, using the IMPORT keyword. This ILE module allocates the storage. (For information about ILE, see Chapter 13; for information about using EXPORT and IMPORT to share data items, see Chapter 15.) (2) Allows a procedure to be accessed by another ILE module (for more information, see Chapter 14).
EXTFLD(field_name)	Renames a subfield in an externally described data structure.
EXTFMT(code)	Specifies an external data type for compile-time and pre-runtime numeric arrays and tables: B Binary C Unicode F Float I Signed integer L Left sign P Packed decimal R Right sign S Zoned decimal U Unsigned integer
EXTNAME(file_name{:format_name})	Names a file containing field descriptions used for subfields in a data structure.
EXTPGM(program_name)	Names an external program whose prototype is being defined (for more information, see Chapter 14).
EXTPROC({proc_type{:class}:}proc_name)	Names an external procedure whose prototype is being defined (for more information, see Chapter 14). Normally takes the format EXTPROC(proc_name), but can be any of the following: • EXTPROC(*CL:proc_name) for ILE CL procedures that require special data type handling • EXTPROC(*CWIDEN|*CNOWIDEN:proc_name) for ILE C procedures that require special data type handling • EXTPROC(*JAVA:class_name:proc_name|*CONSTRUCTOR) for Java methods or for RPG procedures that will be called by Java
FROMFILE(file_name)	Names a file with input data for a pre-runtime array or table.
IMPORT{(external_name)}	Indicates that storage for the data item is allocated in another ILE module with the EXPORT keyword. This module can use the same storage. (For information about ILE, see Chapter 13; for information about using EXPORT and IMPORT to share data items, see Chapter 15.)

continued ...

FIGURE 4.2 *CONTINUED*

Keyword	Description
INZ{(constant)|*EXTDFT|*USER|*JOB| *SYS|*NULL|*LIKEDS)	Initializes the data item.
LIKE(name)	(1) Specifies that the data item's attributes (length, type) are based on another variable. (2) Specifies that an object's class is the same as that of another object.
LIKEDS(name)	Specifies that a data structure, return value, or parameter has the same subfields as another data structure.
NOOPT	Specifies that no optimization be performed for this data item.
OCCURS(numeric_const)	Specifies the number of occurrences of a multiple-occurrence data structure.
OPDESC	Passes operational descriptors with parameters defined within a prototype.
OPTIONS	Specifies one or more parameter-passing options: *NOPASS Parameter need not be passed. *OMIT *OMIT is allowed for parameter. *STRING Parameter may be a pointer or a character expression. *RIGHTADJ Character, graphic, or UCS-2 parameter is right-adjusted. *VARSIZE Parameter may be shorter than defined length.
OVERLAY(name{:pos}|*NEXT)	Specifies that a data structure subfield overlays the storage of another subfield.
PACKEVEN	Zeroes out the high-order digit when a packed field has an even number of digits.
PERRCD(numeric_const)	Specifies the number of elements per record for an array or table.
PREFIX(prefix_string{:number})	Specifies a string to be prefixed (added or replaced) to subfield names of an externally described data structure.
PROCPTR	Defines an item as a procedure pointer.
QUALIFIED	Specifies that the subfields in a named data structure must be qualified by the data structure name (i.e., they must be referred to using the format *structure.field*).
STATIC	(1) Defines a local variable within static storage, holding its value across procedure calls (for more information, see Chapter 14). (2) Specifies a Java method as a static method. If not specified, the method is assumed to be an instance method.
TIMFMT(format{separator})	Specifies a default time format and separator (see Chapter 2 for values).
TOFILE(file_name)	Specifies a file to which an array or table is to be written.
VALUE	Specifies that a parameter will be passed by value instead of by reference (for more information, see Chapter 14).
VARYING	Indicates a varying-length character or graphic field.

Defining Standalone (Work) Fields

Most RPG programs define work fields "on the fly," using the result field of the calculation specifications. If you need a work field at a specific line location, you simply specify the result field's length and decimal positions at that line and — bingo! — you've defined the data. Although this method of defining data is very convenient when you first write a program, it is susceptible to conflicting definitions and is nearly impossible to maintain. On subsequent visits to the program, you must search through the entire source to find the definitions; if you want to make a change, you must ensure you haven't missed an instance of the field.

RPG III's DEFN (Field Definition) opcode encourages you to define work fields in one place by grouping DEFN statements together, but the opcode has limitations. And the idea of mixing data definitions with calculations seems messy at best and error-prone at worst. RPG IV offers the "definitive" means of defining, in one section of the program, work fields that are consistent with all other definitions; now it's up to you to get into the habit of using it exclusively.

To define a standalone field in the D-spec, you name the field, specify an S in column 24, and define the data type and length in the specification:

```
*.. 1 ...+... 2 ...+... 3 ...+... 4 ...+... 5 ...+... 6 ...+... 7 ...+... 8
DName++++++++++ETDsFrom+++To/L+++IDc.Keywords+++++++++++++++++++++++++++++++
D Pack155        S              15P 5
D Char10         S              10A
```

The first example here defines a field called Pack155 — a packed-decimal work field 15 digits long, with five decimal places. Notice that instead of specifying a from/to location for the field, you can simply indicate the field length in positions 33–39. In the second example above, Char10 is a 10-character alphanumeric field. These examples mimic the same functionality and ease of coding that the C-spec definition previously offered, but with the advantage of separating the data-definition function into its own section of the program.

☑ **Indent data item names to enhance readability.**

Notice that the examples above indent the name of the definition so that there is a space between the D in column 6 and the name — you can "float" definition names within the allotted space like this to aid readability.

☑ **Use the LIKE keyword to define identical data items.**

The D-spec also can duplicate the function provided by the *LIKE DEFN opcode: to define a field's characteristics relative to an already defined field. The LIKE keyword names the field to use as the basis for the field you are defining:

```
*.. 1 ...+... 2 ...+... 3 ...+... 4 ...+... 5 ...+... 6 ...+... 7 ...+... 8
DName++++++++++ETDsFrom+++To/L+++IDc.Keywords+++++++++++++++++++++++++++++++
D MorePack        S                      LIKE(Pack155)
D MoreChar        S                +5     LIKE(Char10)
D MoreZone        S                      LIKE(Zone092)
```

The first example here defines a field called MorePack, which has the same attributes as the field called Pack155. Next, we define field MoreChar to have the same data type as Char10, but with a length five bytes longer than Char10's (indicated by the +5 in positions 33–39). By the way, unlike RPG III's LIKE *DEFN (or RPG IV's equivalent *LIKE DEFINE), the LIKE keyword produces exactly the same data attributes as the original field. In the third example, if Zone092 is a zoned (signed) decimal field, MoreZone will also be zoned. (*LIKE DEFN, on the other hand, would result in a packed field with the same number of digits and decimals.)

You can instruct RPG to initialize fields to specific values by using the INZ definition keyword. The keyword value specifies the value to which the field should be initialized. The following examples illustrate some field definitions with initialization specified.

```
*.. 1 ...+... 2 ...+... 3 ...+... 4 ...+... 5 ...+... 6 ...+... 7 ...+... 8
DName++++++++++ETDsFrom+++To/L+++IDc.Keywords+++++++++++++++++++++++++++++++
D Pack155        S             15P 5 INZ
D Char10         S             10A   INZ('Original')
```

In the first example, field Pack155 will be initialized to 0. Because we didn't specify a value, the system will use the zero default for numeric fields. In the second example, the initial value for field Char10 will be "Original " (with two trailing blanks). Had we not specified a value, the field would have been initialized to blanks.

☑ Use INZ(*USER) to get the user name.

Keyword INZ accepts some special values to help with field initialization. You can specify figurative constants (e.g., *BLANKS, *ZEROS, *ON, *OFF) for most fields. Dates (in native date formats) can be initialized to *SYS or *JOB, while times and timestamps can be initialized to *JOB. Specifying INZ(*USER) initializes a character field (at least 10 characters long) to the current user profile name.

Defining Named Constants

Specifying a C in column 24 of a D-spec lets you define a named constant to the RPG IV program. The following examples name two constants, UpperCase and LowerCase:

```
*.. 1 ...+... 2 ...+... 3 ...+... 4 ...+... 5 ...+... 6 ...+... 7 ...+... 8
DName++++++++++ETDsFrom+++To/L+++IDc.Keywords+++++++++++++++++++++++++++++++
D UpperCase      C                   CONST('ABCDEFGHIJKLMNOPQRSTUVWXYZ')
D LowerCase      C                   'abcdefghijklmnopqrstuvwxyz'
```

The value of UpperCase is the uppercase alphabet; the value of LowerCase is the lowercase alphabet. Notice that the CONST keyword is optional.

If the constant value is too long to fit on a single D-spec line, you can continue it (up to 1,024 characters) to subsequent lines:

```
*.. 1 ...+... 2 ...+... 3 ...+... 4 ...+... 5 ...+... 6 ...+... 7 ...+... 8
DName++++++++++ETDsFrom+++To/L+++IDc.Keywords+++++++++++++++++++++++++++++++
D Gettysburg     C                   'Four score and seven years ago our -
D                                     fathers brought forth, upon this -
D                                     continent, a new nation...'
```

You can use either the + or the – continuation character. The + will continue with the next nonblank character in the keyword section of the subsequent line; the – will continue with the content beginning in column 44.

Numeric named constants take on the characteristics and precision of the number you specify for their value. The following examples define a few numeric constants.

```
*.. 1 ...+... 2 ...+... 3 ...+... 4 ...+... 5 ...+... 6 ...+... 7 ...+... 8
DName++++++++++ETDsFrom+++To/L+++IDc.Keywords++++++++++++++++++++++++++++++++
D Pi              C                   3.14159
D MilesToKm       C                   1.609
D KmToMiles       C                   .62
```

You can also define numeric constants with hexadecimal values. The following example shows the hexadecimal values for the function keys that a user may press to exit a display screen. Using these named constants in conjunction with the file information data structure lets your program easily identify which key the user pressed.

```
*.. 1 ...+... 2 ...+... 3 ...+... 4 ...+... 5 ...+... 6 ...+... 7 ...+... 8
DName++++++++++ETDsFrom+++To/L+++IDc.Keywords++++++++++++++++++++++++++++++++
D F01             C                   X'31'
D F02             C                   X'32'
D F03             C                   X'33'
D F04             C                   X'34'
D F05             C                   X'35'
D F06             C                   X'36'
D F07             C                   X'37'
D F08             C                   X'38'
D F09             C                   X'39'
D F10             C                   X'3A'
D F11             C                   X'3B'
D F12             C                   X'3C'
D F13             C                   X'B1'
D F14             C                   X'B2'
D F15             C                   X'B3'
D F16             C                   X'B4'
D F17             C                   X'B5'
D F18             C                   X'B6'
D F19             C                   X'B7'
D F20             C                   X'B8'
D F21             C                   X'B9'
D F22             C                   X'BA'
D F23             C                   X'BB'
D F24             C                   X'BC'
D Enter           C                   X'F1'
D Help            C                   X'F3'
D PageUp          C                   X'F4'
D PageDn          C                   X'F5'
D Print           C                   X'F6'
```

Appendix C shows some additional coding for named constants that you may find useful in identifying program or file errors that can occur during the execution of a program.

Defining Data Structures

The D-spec excels at defining complex data structures. The rules for defining a data structure and its subfields are similar to those for work fields and named constants. To define a data structure, you name it and specify DS in columns 24–25. Then you follow the definition with subfield definitions; these contain blanks in columns 24–25. The following example defines a simple data structure with subfields:

```
*.. 1 ...+... 2 ...+... 3 ...+... 4 ...+... 5 ...+... 6 ...+... 7 ...+... 8
DName++++++++++ETDsFrom+++To/L+++IDc.Keywords+++++++++++++++++++++++++++++++
D NameDta          DS
D   Name                    1     35
D   Address                36     70
D   City                   71     91
D   State                  92     93
D   ZipCode                94    103
D   Phone                 104    113
```

In this example, the subfields are indented to make the structure easier to understand at a glance.

> ☑ **Use length notation for consistency when coding data structure subfields.**

Instead of (or in addition to) specifying absolute from and to positions for subfields, you can simply use a length notation to show the lengths of the subfields (this is similar to the length notation allowed by DDS). Here is the same data structure defined in this manner:

```
*.. 1 ...+... 2 ...+... 3 ...+... 4 ...+... 5 ...+... 6 ...+... 7 ...+... 8
DName++++++++++ETDsFrom+++To/L+++IDc.Keywords+++++++++++++++++++++++++++++++
D NameDta          DS
D   Name                         35
D   Address                      35
D   City                         21
D   State                         2
D   ZipCode                      10
D   Phone                        10
```

This method of defining data structures makes it easy to see the lengths of subfields within a data structure. It will also make future changes easier and safer, because it eliminates the need to change every location in the data structure if the length of a single subfield changes. You also can mix from/to with length notation. Unless it's important for you to know the exact positions of subfields, you'll probably want to use length notation to define subfields.

When you specify from/to locations for numeric data structure subfields, code the number of *bytes* the data item occupies in the data structure. When you use length notation, specify the number of *digits* in the number. Be sure to use a consistent notation technique to eliminate confusion.

Learn the D-Spec Quickly

Describing data to your program is as important as describing actions on that data. With its new D-spec, RPG IV provides a vastly improved method of describing data. RPG IV guts the I-spec, leaving it only to describe input from program-described files and to rename fields from externally described files. The D-spec also signals the death of the E-spec, which is not used in RPG IV. The D-spec assumes all responsibility for defining data structures, arrays, work fields, and named constants. Although syntactically the D-spec is not that much of a departure from the rest of RPG IV, its ability to describe data concisely will improve the quality of your programs, and you should plan to use it extensively.

Rather than using contrived columnar positions (à la the I-spec and its columnar support of named constants or initial values), much of the D-spec's functionality comes from its use of keywords to annotate the data being described. Most of the keywords are fairly self-explanatory and represent direct mappings from the old I-spec or E-spec functionality they replace. You'll learn these keywords quickly.

Dedicate some time early in your learning curve to studying the ins and outs of the D-spec. Use all its capabilities, and avoid defining variables the old-fashioned ways. Using the D-specs will make your programs clearer and easier to maintain.

What about data structure subfields that overlap other subfields or are a subset of other subfields? Again, the D-spec handles this requirement quite nicely. Here's one way to pick out the five-digit zip code and a few other subfields from our sample data structure:

```
*.. 1 ...+... 2 ...+... 3 ...+... 4 ...+... 5 ...+... 6 ...+... 7 ...+... 8
DName++++++++++ETDsFrom+++To/L+++IDc.Keywords++++++++++++++++++++++++++++++++
D NameDta          DS
D   Name                      1     35
D   Address                  36     70
D   City                     71     91
D   State                    92     93
D   ZipCode                  94    103
D     Zip5                   94     98
D     ZipPlus               100    103
D   Phone                   104    113
D     AreaCode              104    106
D     Prefix                107    109
D     Extension             110    113
```

As you can see, coding overlapping fields with D-specs is nearly the same as coding them with RPG III I-specs. In the example above, Zip5 is defined as the first five positions (94–98) of ZipCode (94–103). AreaCode, Prefix, and Extension are similarly defined.

☑ **OVERLAY simplifies the coding of overlapping fields in a data structure.**

You also can use the OVERLAY keyword to gain the readability benefits of length notation for subfields. OVERLAY tells RPG to reuse the storage occupied by a portion of another subfield. The following example duplicates the function of the previous example but is clearer:

```
*.. 1 ...:+... 2 ...+... 3 ...+... 4 ...+... 5 ...+... 6 ...+... 7 ...+... 8
Name++++++++++ETDsFrom+++To/L+++IDc.Keywords+++++++++++++++++++++++++++++++
D NameDta          DS
D   Name                        35
D   Address                     35
D   City                        21
D   State                        2
D   ZipCode                     10
D     Zip5                       5     OVERLAY(ZipCode)
D     ZipPlus                    4     OVERLAY(ZipCode:7)
D   Phone                       10
D     AreaCode                   3     OVERLAY(Phone)
D     Prefix                     3     OVERLAY(Phone:4)
D     Extension                  4     OVERLAY(Phone:7)
```

In this example, Zip5 consists of the first five characters in ZipCode, and ZipPlus consists of the last four. We specified the length in the length field, and because we didn't specify a starting position with the initial OVERLAY keyword, RPG defaults to the first position of ZipCode. Similarly, AreaCode is the first three characters of the Phone field. The field named Prefix is the same as the fourth through sixth characters of Phone; the OVERLAY keyword specifies that the overlay begin at the fourth position, while the field length defines a three-character field. Similarly, Extension occupies the final four characters of Phone.

As of V4R4, RPG IV also lets you specify *NEXT instead of a specific overlay position, thus improving the maintainability of the code. The following example shows yet another way to code the previous data structure:

```
*.. 1 ...+... 2 ...+... 3 ...+... 4 ...+... 5 ...+... 6 ...+... 7 ...+... 8
DName++++++++++ETDsFrom+++To/L+++IDc.Keywords+++++++++++++++++++++++++++++++
D NameDta          DS
D   Name                        35
D   Address                     35
D   City                        21
D   State                        2
D   ZipCode                     10
D     Zip5                       5     OVERLAY(ZipCode)
D     ZipPlus                    4     OVERLAY(ZipCode:7)
D   Phone                       10
D     AreaCode                   3     OVERLAY(Phone)
D     Prefix                     3     OVERLAY(Phone:*NEXT)
D     Extension                  4     OVERLAY(Phone:*NEXT)
```

Notice that you could not use *NEXT for ZipPlus, because the sixth position of ZipCode is skipped by the overlays.

To initialize a data structure and/or its subfields, you use the INZ keyword. Just as in RPG III, initialization works "top down." If you combine data structure initialization with subfield initialization, the data structure is initialized first and then the subfields.

☑ The QUALIFIED and LIKEDS keywords enhance data structure coding.

At V5R1, several keywords add the ability to easily identify specific data structure subfields by *qualifying* the name — that is, by coding both the data structure name and the subfield name, separated by a period (e.g., Structure.Field). With this ability, you can include multiple copies of the same data structure, and you can reuse variable names in the same program. Once you code the QUALIFIED keyword in the data structure's definition, you must thereafter refer to subfields in that data structure by their qualified names. In the following data structures, you would refer to the subfield names as Customer.Name, Vendor.Name, Customer.Address, Vendor.Address, and so on:

```
*.. 1 ...+... 2 ...+... 3 ...+... 4 ...+... 5 ...+... 6 ...+... 7 ...+... 8
DName++++++++++ETDsFrom+++To/L+++IDc.Keywords+++++++++++++++++++++++++++++++++
D Customer         DS                       QUALIFIED
D   Name                          35
D   Address                       35
D   City                          21
D   State                          2
D   ZipCode                       10
D   Phone                         10

D Vendor           DS                       QUALIFIED
D   Name                          35
D   Address                       35
D   City                          21
D   State                          2
D   ZipCode                       10
D   Phone                         10
```

Along the same lines, the LIKEDS keyword lets one data structure inherit the subfield structure from another data structure, *without* requiring you to code the subfields explicitly:

```
*.. 1 ...+... 2 ...+... 3 ...+... 4 ...+... 5 ...+... 6 ...+... 7 ...+... 8
DName++++++++++ETDsFrom+++To/L+++IDc.Keywords+++++++++++++++++++++++++++++++++
D NameDta          DS                       QUALIFIED
D   Name                          35
D   Address                       35
D   City                          21
D   State                          2
D   ZipCode                       10
D   Phone                         10

D Customer         DS                       LIKEDS(NameDta) QUALIFIED

D Vendor           DS                       LIKEDS(NameDta) QUALIFIED
```

As with a qualified data structure, you must refer to the subfields by their qualified names.

Incidentally, you can specify LIKEDS for prototyped parameters or return values when you want to pass a data structure's subfields between procedures. An enhancement to the

INZ keyword lets you specify INZ(*LIKEDS) to initialize a child data structure the same way as its parent data structure.

☑ A multiple-occurrence data structure can now have 32,767 occurrences.

The D-spec handles multiple-occurrence data structures with the OCCURS keyword, which tells the program how many occurrences (up to 32,767) of the data structure to define. In the following example, we define two occurrences of our NameDta data structure:

```
*.. 1 ...+... 2 ...+... 3 ...+... 4 ...+... 5 ...+... 6 ...+... 7 ...+... 8
DName++++++++++ETDsFrom+++To/L+++IDc.Keywords+++++++++++++++++++++++++++++++
D NameDta         DS                     OCCURS(2)
D   Name                         35
D   Address                      35
D   City                         21
D   State                         2
D   ZipCode                      10
D   Phone                        10
```

Defining Special Data Structures

There are no special requirements for coding a file information feedback data structure. You can still use the optional special values (in the From field) instead of subfield locations for predefined information fields, just as you did with RPG III I-specs. Remember to specify the INFDS keyword on the F-spec for any file that will use an information data structure. The following is an example:

```
*.. 1 ...+... 2 ...+... 3 ...+... 4 ...+... 5 ...+... 6 ...+... 7 ...+... 8
FFilename++IPEASFRlen+LKlen+AIDevice+.Keywords+++++++++++++++++++++++++++++++
DName++++++++++ETDsFrom+++To/L+++IDc.Keywords+++++++++++++++++++++++++++++++
FMaintCust CF   E            WORKSTN INFDS(DSDisplay)
D   DSDisplay      DS
D   FileName       *FILE
D   FileOpen             9       9
D   FileEof             10      10
D   MsgID               46      52
D   ScrSize        *SIZE
D   KeyPress           369     369
D   CursorLoc          370     371B 0
```

You define the program status data structure (commonly called the PSDS) the same way you define other data structures, except you add an S in position 23 of the data structure heading. Again, you can use special values instead of from/to locations if you like. Here's an example of a program status data structure:

```
*.. 1 ...+... 2 ...+... 3 ...+... 4 ...+... 5 ...+... 6 ...+... 7 ...+... 8
DName++++++++++ETDsFrom+++To/L+++IDc.Keywords+++++++++++++++++++++++++++++++
D   ProgStatus     SDS
D   ProgName       *PROC
D   ErrMsgID            40      46
D   ErrMsg              91     169
D   JobName            244     253
D   UserID             254     263
D   JobNumber          264     269
```

Data-area data structures require a U in column 23. Just as in RPG III, the RPG IV program will read/lock the data area named in the data structure at the beginning of the program, and it will update/unlock the data area at the end of the program. Also, just as in RPG III, if you don't specifically name the data-area data structure, the program will use the local data area (*LDA). Here is an example:

```
*.. 1 ...+... 2 ...+... 3 ...+... 4 ...+... 5 ...+... 6 ...+... 7 ...+... 8
DName++++++++++ETDsFrom+++To/L+++IDc.Keywords++++++++++++++++++++++++++++++++
D Company         UDS
D   CpyName                           35
D   CpyAddr                           35
D   CpyCity                           21
D   CpyState                           2
D   CpyZipCode                        10
```

The data area must be a character data type. And the data area and data-area data structure must have the same name unless you use the *DTAARA DEFINE opcode or, better, the new DTAARA keyword to rename it. In the following example, data area COMPANY is read into the CpyDta data structure in the RPG IV program.

```
*.. 1 ...+... 2 ...+... 3 ...+... 4 ...+... 5 ...+... 6 ...+... 7 ...+... 8
DName++++++++++ETDsFrom+++To/L+++IDc.Keywords++++++++++++++++++++++++++++++++
D CpyDta          UDS                      DTAARA(COMPANY)
D   CpyName                           35
D   CpyAddr                           35
D   CpyCity                           21
D   CpyState                           2
D   CpyZipCode                        10
```

Mapping Indicator Data Structures

You can define a data structure to contain the state of indicators passed to and from DDS-defined workstation and/or printer files. If you build a workstation file or a printer file specifying the INDARA keyword in its DDS, data-management routines will pass a 99-byte array in which each element will contain the state of the corresponding numeric indicator (array element 1 is *IN01, element 2 is *IN02, and so on).

To map this array to a data structure in your RPG IV program, you must name the data structure using the INDDS keyword in the workstation/printer file's F-spec. Then you can refer to named subfields within the data structure instead of to numbered indicators. This support documents the use of indicators and makes the program much more readable and maintainable than was previously allowed. The example on the next page shows you how to map a data structure to indicators; notice there is no special coding to define the data structure itself.

```
*.. 1 ...+... 2 ...+... 3 ...+... 4 ...+... 5 ...+... 6 ...+... 7 ...+... 8
FFilename++IPEASFRLen+LKLen+AIDevice+.Keywords+++++++++++++++++++++++++++++++
DName++++++++++ETDsFrom+++To/L+++IDc.Keywords+++++++++++++++++++++++++++++++++
FMaintCust CF   E           WORKSTN INDDS(DSIndAra)
D DSIndAra          DS
D  Help                     1        1N
D  Exit                     3        3N
D  Refresh                  5        5N
D  Cancel                  12       12N
D  HiIntensity             50       50N
D  SflClr                  90       90N
D  SflDsp                  91       91N
D  SflDspCtl               92       92N
D  SflEnd                  93       93N
```

Defining Externally Described Data Structures

Up to now, we have discussed program-described data structures. Data structures, including data-area data structures and indicator-mapping data structures, also can be externally described. If you code an E in column 22 of the data structure definition, the system will retrieve the subfield definitions from an externally described file at compile time. You code the name of the file that contains the subfield definitions either in columns 7–21 or as a value for the new EXTNAME keyword:

```
*.. 1 ...+... 2 ...+... 3 ...+... 4 ...+... 5 ...+... 6 ...+... 7 ...+... 8
DName++++++++++ETDsFrom+++To/L+++IDc.Keywords+++++++++++++++++++++++++++++++++
D NameDta        E DS
```

or

```
D NameStruct     E DS                    EXTNAME(NAMEDTA)
```

You can rename subfields in an externally described data structure by listing the subfields (be sure to key an E in column 22 for each one) and including the EXTFLD keyword, which names the externally described field:

```
*.. 1 ...+... 2 ...+... 3 ...+... 4 ...+... 5 ...+... 6 ...+... 7 ...+... 8
DName++++++++++ETDsFrom+++To/L+++IDc.Keywords+++++++++++++++++++++++++++++++++
D NameStruct     E DS                    EXTNAME(NAMDTA)
D   CustName      E                      EXTFLD(NAME)
D   CustAddr      E                      EXTFLD(ADDR)
D   CustCity      E                      EXTFLD(CITY)
D   CustState     E                      EXTFLD(STATE)
D   CustZip       E                      EXTFLD(ZIP)
```

If you want to globally rename the fields in the data structure, the PREFIX keyword also works:

```
*.. 1 ...+... 2 ...+... 3 ...+... 4 ...+... 5 ...+... 6 ...+... 7 ...+... 8
DName++++++++++ETDsFrom+++To/L+++IDc.Keywords+++++++++++++++++++++++++++++++++
D NameStruct     E DS                    EXTNAME(NAMDTA)
D                                        PREFIX(Cust)
```

If you explicitly rename any externally described field (using the EXTFLD keyword) in *addition* to using the PREFIX keyword, the prefix will *not* be applied to that field. If the external file doesn't include all the subfields in the data structure, you can add program-described subfields after you make any necessary externally described subfield entries.

Specifying INZ(*EXTDFT) for an externally described data structure or its externally described subfields lets you initialize the data structure or subfields to the external default specified in the DDS for the structure. You can override the external value by coding the INZ keyword with or without a value; in this case, the RPG default values will be used.

Defining Arrays and Tables

Arrays and tables are mainstays of RPG programs. They are collections of data fields of the same attributes (length, type, and so on), usually containing the same type of information (sales data, for instance). In RPG, there is little difference between an array and a table, except for the way you refer to them in your program. An array name by itself refers to all elements in the array, whereas a table name always refers to the single element found in the last LOOKUP operation. You can refer to a single element of an array by specifying its position; you cannot refer to specific positions for table data. Otherwise, RPG supports tables and arrays almost identically. To distinguish between the two, a table name always starts with TAB (an array name never does). With that in mind, the following discussion about arrays also applies to tables.

Runtime arrays, which load the array data when the program is run, are easily defined in RPG IV by coding a standalone field that includes the new DIM (Dimension) keyword. DIM specifies the number of elements in the array. This definition takes the place of the defunct E-spec. The following example shows the comparable RPG III and RPG IV code:

RPG III

```
*.. 1 ...+... 2 ...+... 3 ...+... 4 ...+... 5 ...+... 6 ...+... 7 ...
E....FromfileTofile++Name++N/rN/tbLenPDSArrnamLenPDSComments++++++++*
E                   SALES     4 9 2
```

RPG IV

```
*.. 1 ...+... 2 ...+... 3 ...+... 4 ...+... 5 ...+... 6 ...+... 7 ...+... 8
DName++++++++++ETDsFrom+++To/L+++IDc.Keywords++++++++++++++++++++++++++++++++
D Sales         S              9 2 DIM(4)
```

These examples define a runtime array of four nine-digit numbers (two decimal places). In your program calculations, you can refer to the entire array by specifying its name (Sales), or you can refer to individual elements of the array by including the array index to specify the element — Sales(4), for example. Notice that RPG IV falls in line with many other languages by changing the notation for array indexes; that is, it includes them in parentheses instead of using a comma separator.

You can initialize a runtime array using the INZ keyword, you can provide values for the array data in the program's calculations, or you can load the data from a file. By naming the array or its elements in the I-specs, you load the data from a file.

The following example illustrates one method:

```
*.. 1 ...+... 2 ...+... 3 ...+... 4 ...+... 5 ...+... 6 ...+... 7 ...+... 8
DName++++++++++ETDsFrom+++To/L+++IDc.Keywords++++++++++++++++++++++++++++++
IRcdname+++....Ri.........................................................
I.............Ext-field+..................Field+++++++++L1M1..PLMnZr......
D Sales        S            9 2 DIM(4)
I QtrSales     01
I              SalesQtr1                Sales(1)
I              SalesQtr2                Sales(2)
I              SalesQtr3                Sales(3)
I              SalesQtr4                Sales(4)
```

While runtime arrays load the array data when the program is run, compile-time arrays provide the array data in the program source — the array data becomes part of the compiled program. Just as with RPG III, you include the source data for the array at the end of the program source, following a **CTDATA statement. To define the compile-time array in the D-specs, you would simply include the CTDATA (Compile-time data) keyword, as in the following example:

```
* ..+... 1 ...+... 2 ...+... 3 ...+... 4 ...+... 5 ...+... 6 ...+... 7 ...+... 8
  DName++++++++++ETDsFrom+++To/L+++IDc.Keywords++++++++++++++++++++++++++++++
  D Days        S            2 0 DIM(12)
  D                              CTDATA
  D                              PERRCD(12)
```

and include at the end of the source:

```
* ..+... 1 ...+... 2 ...+... 3 ...+... 4 ...+... 5 ...+... 6 ...+... 7 ...+... 8
**CTDATA Days
312831303130313130313031
```

This example loads (at compile time) an array that contains the maximum number of days in each month of the year. The optional PERRCD keyword tells the compiler how many array elements are in each record of the compile-time data at the end of the source; if you omit PERRCD, the compiler defaults to one element per record. (Of course, in this example, you'd have to use a C-spec to change the 28 in Days(2) to 29 for leap years.)

In RPG III, you would have coded the same array as follows:

```
* ..+... 1 ...+... 2 ...+... 3 ...+... 4 ...+... 5 ...+... 6 ...+... 7 ...
  E....FromfileTofile++Name++N/rN/tbLenPDSArrnamLenPDSComments++++++++*
  E                DAYS   12  12  2 0
```

and included at the end of the source:

```
* ..+... 1 ...+... 2 ...+... 3 ...+... 4 ...+... 5 ...+... 6 ...+... 7 ...
**
312831303130313130313031
```

Notice that the **CTDATA statement in the RPG IV version is new. With RPG III, you must be careful to provide the compile-time data in the same order in which you define arrays in the E-specs. With RPG IV, you can provide the array data in any order if you name the array using the **CTDATA statement. RPG IV still supports the ** statement, but the **CTDATA statement gives you more flexibility and is less error-prone.

Pre-runtime arrays are similar to runtime arrays in that they load their data when the program is run; unlike runtime arrays, however, the array data is in a file that is loaded *before* any I-specs, C-specs, or O-specs are processed. To define these arrays, you must name on the D-spec the file that contains the array data. Here's a comparison of the RPG III and RPG IV code for a pre-runtime array:

RPG III

```
*.. 1 ...+... 2 ...+... 3 ...+... 4 ...+... 5 ...+... 6 ...+... 7 ...
E....FromfileTofile++Name++N/rN/tbLenPDSArrnamLenPDSComments++++++++*
E    SALESDTA        SALES   1 100  9P2
```

RPG IV

```
*.. 1 ...+... 2 ...+... 3 ...+... 4 ...+... 5 ...+... 6 ...+... 7 ...+... 8
DName++++++++++ETDsFrom+++To/L+++IDc.Keywords+++++++++++++++++++++++++++++++
D Sales           S              9  2 DIM(100)
D                                      FROMFILE(SalesDta)
D                                      PERRCD(1)
D                                      EXTFMT(P)
```

In this example, the SalesDta file contains the information to be loaded into the Sales array before the program begins its processing. The FROMFILE keyword names the file. The EXTFMT (External format) keyword tells the compiler that the data in the file is packed decimal.

We could have also included a TOFILE keyword in this example to name the file to which the array would be written when the program ends (with LR on). You must also include an F-spec for the TOFILE. If the F-spec is the same as the FROMFILE, the file must be a combined file (C in column 17 of the F-spec); otherwise, it should be an output (O) file.

The data for pre-runtime arrays (and sometimes for compile-time arrays) typically exists in an alternating format; that is, the file record might contain the data for two alternating arrays in a single record — perhaps salesperson number, then sales amount, for example. RPG IV handles alternating arrays with the D-spec ALT keyword. Here's an example:

```
*.. 1 ...+... 2 ...+... 3 ...+... 4 ...+... 5 ...+... 6 ...+... 7 ...+... 8
DName++++++++++ETDsFrom+++To/L+++IDc.Keywords++++++++++++++++++++++++++++++++
D Slsprs          S              3  0 DIM(100)
D                                      FROMFILE(SalesDta)
D                                      ASCEND
D Sales           S              9  2 DIM(100)
D                                      ALT(Slsprs)
D                                      EXTFMT(P)
```

In this example, each record in the SalesDta file includes first the salesperson number and then the sales amount. When the program loads the arrays, it loads the appropriate data from each record into the two arrays. ASCEND indicates that the Slsprs data will be in ascending order.

Coding Long Field Names

RPG IV supports names up to 4,096 characters long, with some restrictions. In fixed-column statements, names can be as long as will fit in the entry (usually 14 characters). In D-specs, free-form calculations, and those C-specs that allow the extended Factor 2, names can be longer.

To declare a long name, use the D-spec, as the following examples show:

```
*.. 1 ...+... 2 ...+... 3 ...+... 4 ...+... 5 ...+... 6 ...+... 7 ...+... 8
DName++++++++++ETDsFrom+++To/L+++IDc.Keywords++++++++++++++++++++++++++++++
D MiddleInitial    S              1A
D MothersMaidenName...
D                  S             35A
D HoursWorked...
D YearToDate       S              5S 0
D TheReadersDigestCondensedVersionOf...
D DatabaseDesignAndProgrammingForDB2_400...
D ByPaulConte      S           4096A
```

In the first example, the variable MiddleInitial has a 13-character name. Next, MothersMaidenName is even longer and won't fit in the allotted 15 columns, so we use an ellipsis (…) to continue the rest of the D-spec to the next line. If the name alone is longer than a line, you can even include ellipses within the name, as in the next example, HoursWorkedYearToDate.

You can use the longer names nearly anywhere you can use a shorter name. The following example uses a longer name in the keyword portion of a D-spec:

```
*.. 1 ...+... 2 ...+... 3 ...+... 4 ...+... 5 ...+... 6 ...+... 7 ...+... 8
DName++++++++++ETDsFrom+++To/L+++IDc.Keywords++++++++++++++++++++++++++++++
D HrsWrkYTD        S                    LIKE(HoursWorkedYearToDate)
```

or

```
D HrsWrkYTD        S                    LIKE(HoursWorked...
D                                       YearToDate)
```

In the program's calculations, you can use long names wherever they fit, using ellipses if necessary, such as in the following examples:

```
*.. 1 ...+... 2 ...+... 3 ...+... 4 ...+... 5 ...+... 6 ...+... 7 ...+... 8
CL0N01Factor1+++++++Opcode(E)+Extended-factor2++++++++++++++++++++++++++++++
 /FREE

   IF HoursWorkedYearToDate > 2000;
   Eligible401K = *ON;
   ENDIF;

 /END-FREE
```

or

```
C                   IF           HoursWorkedYearToDate > 2000
C                   EVAL         Password = MothersMaidenName
```

or

```
C                   EVAL         Password = MothersMaiden...
C                                Name
```

For those fixed-form specifications that still remain, you can still use somewhat longer names, but you'll have to restrict yourself to names that will fit. There is no alias function that would assign a short name as the equivalent of a long name.

Chapter 5

Input Specification Changes

In an effort to purify RPG's input specification (I-spec), RPG IV purges the I-spec of the extra roles it has played over the years. The D-spec has taken over the miscellaneous data-definition functions (e.g., of data structures, named constants) that the I-spec had taken on over time. In RPG IV, the I-spec's sole purpose is to describe input file data.

Like RPG III, RPG IV supports the use of both externally described files and program-described files. When the RPG IV compiler retrieves the external description of a file, it also retrieves the record formats and field layouts without requiring you to specify them in the program. Therefore, the I-spec is optional with externally described files. It is used primarily to add RPG functions, such as control-level indicators, to the external definition of a file. Within a program, you also can use I-specs to rename fields in an externally described file.

Although using externally described files is widespread among RPG programmers, RPG IV still supports the use of program-described files, for which a programmer must lay out the record format using I-specs.

☑ I-specs support longer names but have few other layout changes.

Except for the expansion of some columns to accommodate larger file, record, and field names, you'll find that the I-spec has changed little in RPG IV. The only other notable change is the addition of support for date/time/timestamp and integer data types. Figures 5.1A and 5.1B illustrate the specifications for both externally described and program-described file input.

FIGURE 5.1A
Input Specification Layout: Externally Described Files

```
*.. 1 ...+... 2 ...+... 3 ...+... 4 ...+... 5 ...+... 6 ...+... 7 ...+... 8
IRcdname+++....Ri.................................................................
I.............Ext-field+.................Field++++++++L1M1..PlMnZr......
```

Record Identifier Specifications	
Columns	Description
1–5	Sequence number
6	I
7–16	Record name
17–20	(Blank)
21–22	Record identifying indicator: Blank, 01–99, L1–L9, LR, H1–H9, U1–U8, RT
23–80	(Blank)
81–100	Comments

continued ...

FIGURE 5.1A *CONTINUED*

Field Description Specifications

Columns	Description
1–5	Sequence number
6	I
7–20	(Blank)
21–30	External field name to be renamed
31–48	(Blank)
49–62	Field name in program
63–64	Control level: Blank, L1–L9
65–66	Matching fields: Blank, M1–M9
67–68	(Blank)
69–74	Field indicators (plus/minus/zero): Blank, 01–99, H1–H9, U1–U8, RT
75–80	(Blank)
81–100	Comments

FIGURE 5.1B

Input Specification Layout: Program-Described Files

```
*.. 1 ...+... 2 ...+... 3 ...+... 4 ...+... 5 ...+... 6 ...+... 7 ...+... 8
IFilename++SqNORiPos1+NCCPos2+NCCPos3+NCC.................................
I.........And..RiPos1+NCCPos2+NCCPos3+NCC.................................
I......................Fmt+SPFrom+To+++DcField++++++++L1M1FrPLMnZr......
```

Record Identifier Specifications

Columns	Description
1–5	Sequence number
6	I
7–16	File name
16–18	Logical relationship: AND, OR (used only for multiline record identifier specifications)
17–20	Sequence checking options
21–22	Record identifying indicator: Blank, 01–99, L1–L9, LR, H1–H9, U1–U8, RT, **
23–46	Record identification codes
7–80	(Blank)
81–100	Comments

continued ...

Figure 5.1B *Continued*

Field Description Specifications	
Columns	**Description**
1–5	Sequence number
6	I
7–30	(Blank)
31–34	External format for a date or time field (see Chapter 2 for valid entries), *VAR for variable-length fields
35	Separator character for a date or time field (see Chapter 2 for valid entries)
36	Data type: (Blank) Zoned decimal or character A Character B Binary C Unicode D Date F Float numeric G Graphic I Signed intege L Zoned decimal with preceding (left) sign N Indicator P Packed decimal R Zoned decimal with following (right) sign S Zoned decimal T Time U Unsigned integer Z Timestamp
37–41	Field location: From position (1–32766)
42–46	Field location: To position (1–32766)
47–48	Decimal positions: Blank, 0–30
49–62	Field name in program
63–64	Control level: Blank, L1–L9
65–66	Matching fields: Blank, M1–M9
67–68	Field record relation: Blank, 01–99, L1–L9, MR, U1–U8, H1–H9, RT
69–74	Field indicators (plus/minus/zero): Blank, 01–99, H1–H9, U1–U8, RT
75–80	(Blank)
81–100	Comments

New Data Types

RPG IV now directly supports date (D), time (T), and timestamp (Z) data types, as well as signed integers (I), unsigned integers (U), indicators (N), and Unicode characters (C). To support these new data types in program-described files, specify the data type in column 36. To further describe date, time, and timestamp fields, use two new areas that have been added to the I-spec field definition: the date/time format (columns 31–34) and the date/time separator (column 35). The values of the format and the separator in the I-spec are consistent with the values in the control specification (for information about these values, see Chapter 2). The following specifications show examples of defining the various date-related data types:

```
*.. 1 ...+... 2 ...+... 3 ...+... 4 ...+... 5 ...+... 6 ...+... 7 ...+... 8
IFilename++SqNORiPos1+NCCPos2+NCCPos3+NCC.............................
I....................Fmt+SPFrom+To+++DcField++++++++L1M1FrPLMnZr......
ICustHist  NS 01
I                         *MDY/D   1   8 TransDate
I                         *HMS:T   9  16 TransTime
I                              Z  17  42 TransTmStp
```

You also can define date, time, and timestamp data on the new D-spec. For more details about the new data types and the D-spec itself, see Chapter 4.

Field Renaming: New Perspectives

Renaming fields for use within an RPG program is a technique familiar to most RPG programmers, and RPG IV doesn't change the technique much. Here are comparable RPG III and RPG IV specifications:

RPG III

```
*.. 1 ...+... 2 ...+... 3 ...+... 4 ...+... 5 ...+... 6 ...+... 7 ...+... 8
IRcdname+....Ri.......................................................
I............Ext-field+......................Field+L1M1..PLMnZr..........
ICUSTREC    01
I           COMPANYNBR                       CPYNBR
I           CUSTNUMBER                        CUSNBR
I           CUSTNAME                          CUSNAM
```

RPG IV

```
*.. 1 ...+... 2 ...+... 3 ...+... 4 ...+... 5 ...+... 6 ...+... 7 ...+... 8
IRcdname+++....Ri.....................................................
I............Ext-field+................Field++++++++L1M1..PLMnZr......
ICustomerR    01
I           CompanyNbr                       CpyNbr
I           CustNumber                        CusNbr
I           CustName                          CusNam
```

Before RPG IV, if your database contained field names that exceeded six characters, you had to use the RPG III I-spec to rename the external field for use within the RPG program (as is done in the preceding example). Now that RPG IV supports long field names, you may find that renaming fields in the I-specs is no longer necessary. The result will be simplified RPG programs.

✓ Consider using the F-spec PREFIX keyword to rename fields.

You also should remember that the PREFIX keyword on the F-spec can now globally rename fields in externally described files. The following comparable RPG III and RPG IV code adds the prefix CU to the fields in a hypothetical customer file:

RPG III I-specs

```
*.. 1 ...+... 2 ...+... 3 ...+... 4 ...+... 5 ...+... 6 ...+... 7 ...+... 8
IRcdname+....Ri.................................................................
I.............Ext-field+....................Field+L1M1..PlMnZr..........
ICUSTREC      Ø1
I             CSNO                          CUCSNO
I             NAME                          CUNAME
I             ADDR                          CUADDR
I             CITY                          CUCITY
I             STAT                          CUSTAT
I             ZIP                           CUZIP
```

RPG IV F-spec

```
*.. 1 ...+... 2 ...+... 3 ...+... 4 ...+... 5 ...+... 6 ...+... 7 ...+... 8
FFilename++IPEASFRLen+LKLen+AIDevice+.Keywords++++++++++++++++++++++++++++
FCustomers UF   E         K DISK      PREFIX(CU)
```

As well as appending the field name to a PREFIX, you can overlay the first few characters of the field name, using the overlay syntax for the PREFIX keyword, as described in Chapter 3.

Chapter 6

Calculation Specification Changes

The heart and soul of most RPG programs lies in the calculation specifications (C-specs). Historically, this area has also been the most cramped division of the syntax. With RPG IV, "calc specs" have undergone dramatic revisions in an attempt to overcome their limitations. At Version 5, RPG IV allows virtually free-form coding for most operations, with few or no columnar restrictions between positions 8 and 80. This free-form specification lets you exploit longer field names, free-form expressions, enhanced file and error processing, improved string handling, indentation, enhanced readability, and improved coexistence with other modern languages.

Even in versions prior to Version 5, RPG IV makes some inroads into the free-form world. Factor 1, Factor 2, and the result field are increased to 14 columns, primarily to accommodate longer field names. With some operations, you can even extend Factor 2 to a relatively spacious 45 columns, within which you can code free-form expressions. Opcodes (with optional extenders) can now occupy 10 columns on the specification (double the RPG III size).

New opcodes support free-form assignment (covered in Chapter 7). The language now also sports date and time operations (covered in Chapter 9) and new data types, including pointers (covered in Chapter 10).

A new language feature, the *built-in function*, lends to the functionality and readability of RPG IV programs. Chapter 8 covers built-in functions, or BIFs, in detail; you can think of them as free-form operation codes that can easily be embedded into free-form expressions. IBM supplies about 70 BIFs that you can code in free-form expressions in the same manner that you code opcodes in fixed-format specification. Using RPG IV's support for sub-procedures (covered in Chapter 14), you can even code your own user-defined functions and include them in your programs as easily as IBM's built-in functions.

Beginning with Version 5, the free-form specification effectively replaces the traditional C-specs. The layout of the free-form specification is

```
*.. 1 ...+... 2 ...+... 3 ...+... 4 ...+... 5 ...+... 6 ...+... 7 ...+... 8
 /FREE
    OpCode(ext)  Factor 1  Factor 2  Result;  // Comment
 /END-FREE
```

Here's a code example:

```
*.. 1 ...+... 2 ...+... 3 ...+... 4 ...+... 5 ...+... 6 ...+... 7 ...+... 8
 /FREE
    Setll CustNbr Customers;
    Read Customers;
    Chain(n) CustNbr Customers; // Chain to Customers file using CustNbr
 /END-FREE
```

Examine this free-form example to discern the following points:

- Free-form coding begins with a /FREE directive (in position 7) and ends with an /END-FREE directive (also in position 7). Between these directives, you code free-form statement lines.

- Free-form statements can begin anywhere in positions 8–80; positions 6–7 must be blank. Indenting is allowed.

- Free-form statements begin with an opcode (and extender, if any), followed by Factor 1, Factor 2, and the result field operands separated by blanks. Operands that are not required may be omitted.

- Free-form statements end with a semicolon (;).

- Comments begin with double slash characters (//) and can be placed anywhere on the line starting in position 7. A comment can be coded on a line of its own or can follow "inline" after a free-form statement.

- The portion of a line after the semicolon must be blank or contain an inline comment.

- Level indicators, conditioning indicators, and resulting indicators are not allowed; resulting indicators are replaced by built-in functions.

You can mix free-form expressions with traditional C-specs, but you should avoid that practice. Figure 6.1 describes the C-spec before Version 5.

FIGURE 6.1
Calculation Specification Layout

```
*.. 1 ...+... 2 ...+... 3 ...+... 4 ...+... 5 ...+... 6 ...+... 7 ...+... 8
CLØN01Factor1++++++Opcode(E)+Factor2++++++Result++++++++Len++D+HiLoEq....
CLØN01Factor1++++++Opcode(E)+Extended-factor2+++++++++++++++++++++++++++++
C..............................Extended-factor2-continuation++++++++++++++++
```

Columns	Description
1-5	Sequence number
6	C
7–8	Control level: Blank, L0, L1–L9, LR, SR, AN, OR
9–11	Indicators: Blank, 01–99, KA–KN, KP–KY, L1–L9, LR, MR, H1–H9, RT, U1–U8, OA–OG, OV
12–25	Factor 1
26–35	Operation code and extender
36–49 or 36–80	Factor 2, or extended Factor 2
50–63	Result field
64–68	Result field length
69–70	Result field decimal positions
71–76	Resulting indicators (high/low/equal): Blank, 01–99, KA–KN, KP–KY, H1–H9, L1–L9, LR, RT, U1–U8, OA–OG, OV
77–80	(Blank)
81–100	Comments

Maintaining a Legacy

Modern RPG programming discourages the use of the predefined numbered indicators 01–99. By using built-in functions and the INDDS keyword, you can completely avoid their use. RPG lets you refer to the numbered indicators, if you must, using the *INxx notation, where xx represents the numbered indicator. The preferred alternative is to use named indicators (see Chapter 10 for more information).

Conditioning indicators and resulting indicators, vestigial remnants of earlier RPG syntaxes, are no longer used in well-written RPG IV programs, and the Version 5 free-form specification does not support them. In earlier releases, calculation specifications limit conditional indicators to one per specification line. Instead of using conditioning indicators, you can code an IF statement — for example, IF *IN99. Instead of using resulting indicators, you can code built-in functions.

The Version 5 free-form specification also drops support for control level indicators (which are usually limited to programs that use the RPG cycle). If you must use level indicators, code an /END-FREE directive to revert to the fixed-form C-spec. Then, after you code a line with the level indicator in positions 7–8, you can again code a /FREE directive and resume free-form specifications.

New Opcodes

While most of its new function comes from built-in functions, RPG IV adds a few operation codes to the RPG suite — primarily to support the Integrated Language Environment (ILE), date/time arithmetic, and enhanced error-handling features. These opcodes are covered elsewhere in this book, but here is a brief description of the additions.

The ADDDUR (Add Duration) and SUBDUR (Subtract Duration) operations have been added to support date arithmetic. They add or subtract durations (e.g., days, months) to or from date, time, or timestamp variables or determine the difference between two dates, times, or timestamps. EXTRCT (Extract Date/Time/Timestamp) extracts a segment (e.g., the month portion) from a date, time, or timestamp field. TEST tests a field to see whether it contains a valid date, time, or timestamp value. At Version 5, new built-in functions render several of these operations obsolete. For more information about these date-related operations and functions, see Chapter 9.

The EVAL (Evaluate Expression) and EVALR (Evaluate Expression, Right-Adjust) operations support free-form expressions. EVAL evaluates a free-format assignment statement in Factor 2; EVALR performs the same function for character expressions and right-adjusts the result. Chapter 7 covers free-form expressions in detail.

CALLP (Call a Prototyped Procedure or Program) calls a bound ILE procedure and also provides enhancements to dynamic program calls that your program might make. CALLB (Call a Bound Procedure) also calls an ILE bound procedure, but without some of the advantages of CALLP. To find out more about ILE and calling procedures, see Chapters 13 and 14.

MONITOR (Begin a Monitor Group), ENDMON (End a Monitor Group), and ON-ERROR work together to handle errors that might occur in a block of code. These operations are further described later in this chapter.

LEAVESR (Leave a Subroutine) exits a subroutine, passing control to the ENDSR (End of Subroutine) operation. ELSEIF combines the ELSE and IF operations into a single opcode. These operations are further described later in this chapter.

Last, ALLOC (Allocate Storage), DEALLOC (Deallocate Storage), and REALLOC (Reallocate Storage with New Length) are seldom-used operations that let your RPG program manipulate storage dynamically at runtime. Version 5 renders ALLOC and REALLOC obsolete, replacing them with the %ALLOC and %REALLOC functions. These operations are not discussed in this book but are documented in Appendix A.

Renamed/Deleted Opcodes

Taking advantage of the wider space it allows for opcodes, RPG IV has renamed the opcodes listed in Figure 6.2. It's important to remember that RPG IV doesn't recognize the corresponding RPG III opcodes, and they will cause compiler errors if you try to use them.

FIGURE 6.2
Renamed Operation Codes

RPG III opcode	RPG IV opcode	Description
BITOF	BITOFF	Set bits off
CHEKR	CHECKR	Check reverse
COMIT	COMMIT	Commit
DEFN	DEFINE	Field definition
DELET	DELETE	Delete a record
EXCPT	EXCEPT	Calculation time output
LOKUP	LOOKUP	Look up a table or array element
OCCUR	OCCUR	Set/get occurrence of a data structure
REDPE	READPE	Read prior equal key
RETRN	RETURN	Return to caller
SELEC	SELECT	Begin a select group
SETOF	SETOFF	Set indicator off
UNLCK	UNLOCK	Unlock a data area or release a record
UPDAT	UPDATE	Update an existing record
WH*xx*	WHEN*xx*	When true, then select

Using the Extended Factor 2

One of the most welcome changes to RPG IV in early releases was its implementation of an extended Factor 2, which let certain opcodes make use of free-format specifications in a 45-column-wide Factor 2 (columns 36–80). Version 5's free-form specification carries the concept even further, allowing column-free coding anywhere in columns 8–80. In pre–Version 5 releases, the following opcodes use the extended Factor 2:

- CALLP (Call a Prototyped Procedure or Program)
- DOU (Do Until)
- DOW (Do While)
- ELSEIF (Else If)
- EVAL (Evaluate Expression)
- EVALR (Evaluate Expression, Right-Adjust)
- FOR (For)
- IF (If)
- WHEN (When True, Then Select)

The DOU, DOW, FOR, IF, and WHEN opcodes have analogs in familiar opcodes: DOU*xx*, DOW*xx*, DO, IF*xx*, and WHEN*xx* (WH*xx*). EVAL and EVALR, as noted above, are RPG IV assignment opcodes, covered in detail in Chapter 7. CALLP uses a free-format syntax to call a prototyped procedure or program (for details, see Chapter 14), and ELSEIF combines the ELSE and IF operations into a single operation.

☑ **Free-form expressions enhance the readability of DO loops and other conditional code.**

It's easy to understand the new free-format operations if you think of them as being evolutions of the older operation codes — but without using Factor 1. The entire expression is now contained in Factor 2. For example, to code a DO loop, you simply move the old Factor 1 over to Factor 2 and include a comparison operator:

RPG III

```
*.. 1 ...+... 2 ...+... 3 ...+... 4 ...+... 5 ...+... 6 ...+... 7 ..
CLØNØ1NØ2NØ3Factor1+++OpcdeFactor2+++ResultLenDHHiLoEqComments++++++
C           KEYPRS      DOUEQFØ3KEY
 ...
C                       ENDDO
```

RPG IV

```
*.. 1 ...+... 2 ...+... 3 ...+... 4 ...+... 5 ...+... 6 ...+... 7 ...+... 8
CLØNØ1Factor1+++++++Opcode(E)+Extended-factor2+++++++++++++++++++++++++++++++
C                   DOU       KeyPressed = FØ3Key
 ...
C                   ENDDO
```

or, at Version 5:

```
/FREE
   DOU KeyPressed = FØ3Key;
     ...
   ENDDO;
/END-FREE
```

These examples all process the calculations in the DO loop until the value of the KeyPressed field is equal to the value of F03Key. Notice that the RPG IV versions of the DO loop are much more readable than the RPG III version because the entire logical expression is together rather than being separated by the opcode. Within the expression, you can adjust spacing and indentation to further enhance comprehension.

The FOR operation (available at V4R4) is a free-format implementation of RPG III's fixed-format DO operation. It begins a block of operations and uses a counter to control the number of times to do the operations. Just as with the DO operation, you can code a counter starting value, increment value, and limit, but you do so within a free-form expression:

RPG III

```
*.. 1 ...+... 2 ...+... 3 ...+... 4 ...+... 5 ...+... 6 ...+... 7 ..
CLØNØ1NØ2NØ3Factor1+++OpcdeFactor2+++ResultLenDHHiLoEqComments++++++
C              1         DO    15        INDEX
...
C                        ENDDO
C              2         DO    100       INDEX
...
C                        ENDDO2
C            100         DO    2         INDEX
...
C                        ENDDO-2
```

RPG IV

```
*.. 1 ...+... 2 ...+... 3 ...+... 4 ...+... 5 ...+... 6 ...+... 7 ...+... 8
CLØNØ1Factor1++++++Opcode(E)+Extended-factor2+++++++++++++++++++++++++++++++
C                        FOR        Index = 1 to 15
...
C                        ENDFOR
C                        FOR        Index = 2 to 100 by 2
...
C                        ENDFOR
C                        FOR        Index = 100 downto 2 by 2
...
C                        ENDFOR
```

or, at Version 5:

```
/FREE
   FOR Index = 1 to 15;
   ...
   ENDFOR;

   FOR Index = 2 to 100 by 2;
   ...
   ENDFOR;

   FOR Index = 100 downto 2 by 2;
   ...
   ENDFOR;
/END-FREE
```

You also can create complex expressions in the extended Factor 2. For example, the following code might be in a program to calculate pension plan eligibility:

RPG III

```
*.. 1 ...+... 2 ...+... 3 ...+... 4 ...+... 5 ...+... 6 ...+... 7 ..
CLØNØ1NØ2NØ3Factor1+++OpcdeFactor2+++ResultLenDHHiLoEqComments+++++
C           MONWRK      IFGE 6
C           HRSWRK      ORGE 1000
 ...
C                       ENDIF
```

RPG IV

```
*.. 1 ...+... 2 ...+... 3 ...+... 4 ...+... 5 ...+... 6 ...+... 7 ...+... 8
CLØNØ1Factor1++++++Opcode(E)+Extended-factor2+++++++++++++++++++++++++++++
C                  IF        (MonthsWrk >= 6) OR (HoursWrk >= 1000)
 ...
C                  ENDIF
```

or, at Version 5:

```
/FREE
   IF (MonthsWrk >= 6) OR (HoursWrk >= 1000);
     ...
   ENDIF;
/END-FREE
```

RPG IV expressions follow familiar algebraic rules of operator precedence (multiplication before addition and so on), but you can use parentheses to change the order. Using parentheses within an expression even when they are not required makes your code more readable.

☑ Extended Factor 2 specifications can span multiple source lines.

Unlike RPG III, RPG IV does not require you to use several RPG IV calculation lines to specify complex expressions. You can, however, continue an expression on subsequent calculation lines if the expression is too long to fit within the 45 columns allotted to the extended Factor 2 or if the expression would be more readable on multiple lines. The only requirement for expression continuation lines is that columns 7–35 be blank. The preceding example could have been written to use continuation lines:

```
*.. 1 ...+... 2 ...+... 3 ...+... 4 ...+... 5 ...+... 6 ...+... 7 ...+... 8
CLØNØ1Factor1++++++Opcode(E)+Extended-factor2+++++++++++++++++++++++++++++
C                  IF        (MonthsWrk >= 6) OR
C                            (HoursWrk  >= 1000)
 ...
C                  ENDIF
```

or, at Version 5:

```
/FREE
   IF (MonthsWrk >= 6) OR
      (HoursWrk >= 1000);
     ...
   ENDIF;
/END-FREE
```

☑ Use + or − to continue a literal in an expression.

Notice that RPG IV requires the use of a continuation character (+ or −) to implement a continuation only if you are continuing a literal within the expression. For example, the plus signs in the following specification are part of the expression, not continuation characters:

```
*.. 1 ...+... 2 ...+... 3 ...+... 4 ...+... 5 ...+... 6 ...+... 7 ...+... 8
CLØNØ1Factor1+++++++Opcode(E)+Extended-factor2+++++++++++++++++++++++++++++++
C                   IF          TotalPay <> (RegHours * Rate)        +
C                                           (OvtHours * Rate * 1.5) +
C                                           (DblHours * Rate * 2)
...
C                   ENDIF
```

or, at Version 5:

```
/FREE
    IF TotalPay <> (RegHours * Rate) +
                   (OvtHours * Rate * 1.5) +
                   (DblHours * Rate * 2);
       ...
    ENDIF;
/END-FREE
```

When you must continue a literal in an expression, however, the + becomes the continuation character. For example, the following specifications use a + to indicate continuation.

```
*.. 1 ...+... 2 ...+... 3 ...+... 4 ...+... 5 ...+... 6 ...+... 7 ...+... 8
CLØNØ1Factor1+++++++Opcode(E)+Extended-factor2+++++++++++++++++++++++++++++++
C                   IF          Gettysburg = 'Four score and seven years +
C                                            ago'
...
C                   ENDIF
```

When you use + to indicate literal continuation, the literal continues with the first nonblank character in the next extended Factor 2. You also can use a hyphen (−) to indicate continuation; in this case, the literal continues with the character in column 36 of the next C-spec:

```
*.. 1 ...+... 2 ...+... 3 ...+... 4 ...+... 5 ...+... 6 ...+... 7 ...+... 8
CLØNØ1Factor1+++++++Opcode(E)+Extended-factor2+++++++++++++++++++++++++++++++
C                   IF          Gettysburg = 'Four score and seven years −
C                                            ago'
...
C                   ENDIF
```

You've seen that the + can be used as part of a numeric expression or as a way to continue a literal to the next calculation line. A third use of the + in RPG IV is as a concatenation operator for character expressions. We'll talk more about this topic when we discuss free-form expressions in Chapter 7.

The new (at Version 5) ELSEIF operation code combines the existing ELSE and IF operations to simplify the process of checking for multiple conditions. Although you'll probably continue to use the SELECT/WHEN/OTHER construction for this purpose, the following code illustrates the ELSEIF alternative. Notice that the entire IF block, including all the ELSEIF conditions, requires but a single ENDIF:

```
*.. 1 ...+... 2 ...+... 3 ...+... 4 ...+... 5 ...+... 6 ...+... 7 ...+... 8
CLØNØ1Factor1++++++Opcode(E)+Extended-factor2++++++++++++++++++++++++++++++
C                   SELECT
C                   WHEN       Code = '1'
C                   EVAL       Action = 'Add'
C                   WHEN       Code = '2'
C                   EVAL       Action = 'Change'
C                   WHEN       Code = '3'
C                   EVAL       Action = 'Copy'
C                   WHEN       Code = '4'
C                   EVAL       Action = 'Delete'
C                   OTHER
C                   EVAL       Action = 'Display'
C                   ENDSL

C                   IF         Code = '1'
C                   EVAL       Action = 'Add'
C                   ELSEIF     Code = '2'
C                   EVAL       Action = 'Change'
C                   ELSEIF     Code = '3'
C                   EVAL       Action = 'Copy'
C                   ELSEIF     Code = '4'
C                   EVAL       Action = 'Delete'
C                   ELSE
C                   EVAL       Action = 'Display'
C                   ENDIF
```

or, at Version 5:

```
/FREE
   SELECT;
   WHEN Code = '1';
     Action = 'Add';
   WHEN Code = '2';
     Action = 'Change';
   WHEN Code = '3';
     Action = 'Copy';
   WHEN Code = '4';
     Action = 'Delete';
   OTHER;
     Action = 'Display';
   ENDSL;

   IF Code = '1';
     Action = 'Add';
   ELSEIF Code = '2';
     Action = 'Change';
   ELSEIF Code = '3';
     Action = 'Copy';
   ELSEIF Code = '4';
     Action = 'Delete';
   ELSE;
     Action = 'Display';
   ENDIF;
/END-FREE
```

Using the Operation Extender

Some RPG IV operations support an operation extender, which changes or enhances the operation. For example, the ADD, SUB, MULT, and DIV opcodes support rounding through the half-adjust extender (H). In RPG III, these extenders were usually specified in column 53 of the C-spec. In RPG IV syntax, you specify operation extenders with operation codes and enclose them in parentheses. In the following example, the half-adjust extender designates that the result of the multiplication operation should be rounded.

```
*.. 1 ...+... 2 ...+... 3 ...+... 4 ...+... 5 ...+... 6 ...+... 7 ...+... 8
CLØNØ1Factor1+++++++Opcode(E)+Factor2+++++++Result++++++++Len++D+HiLoEq....
C        TotTaxable    MULT(H)   TaxRate       TaxAmount
```

The half-adjust, padding (P), and no-lock (N) extenders have direct correlations with RPG III's column 53.

Some new extenders, such as M and R — discussed in Chapter 7 — add new function. M and R specify the rules to use in determining the precision for free-form expressions.

Many opcodes also support an E error-handling extender that you can use instead of coding a resulting indicator in the Error (Lo) position. Any opcode that allows the error resulting indicator supports the E extender alternative; the CALLP opcode (discussed in Chapter 14) also allows the E extender. You can specify either the E extender or the resulting indicator, but not both. This extender is usually used with the %ERROR built-in function, which is discussed in Chapter 8. Here's a brief example of its use:

```
*.. 1 ...+... 2 ...+... 3 ...+... 4 ...+... 5 ...+... 6 ...+... 7 ...+... 8
CLØNØ1Factor1+++++++Opcode(E)+Extended-factor2+++++++++++++++++++++++++++++
C                      READ(EN)   Customers
C                      IF         %ERROR(Customers)
  ...
C                      ENDIF
```

or, at Version 5:

```
/FREE
   READ(EN) Customers;
     IF %ERROR(Customers);
       ...
     ENDIF;
/END-FREE
```

Note that you can code more than one extender with an opcode. This example uses both the E and the N extender. This code will read the Customers file, without locking the record. If an error occurs, the code associated with the %ERROR function will handle the error. See Chapter 8 for more details.

Figure 6.3 lists the valid extenders.

FIGURE 6.3
Operation Code Extenders

Extender	Description
Blank	No operation extension supplied.
A	DUMP operation is always performed.
D	CALLP bound call passes operational descriptors.
D	TEST validates date field.
E	Error handling.
H	Half-adjust (round) result of numeric operation.
M	Default (maximum digits) precision rules.
N	Update record is read but not locked.
N	DEALLOC, if successful, sets pointer to *NULL.
P	Pad the result field with blanks.
R	Result decimal positions precision rules.
T	TEST validates time field.
Z	TEST validates timestamp field.

Error Block Watch in Force

Three Version 5 opcodes — MONITOR, ENDMON, and ON-ERROR — give you the ability to target specific error handling for a Monitor block of code within your program. This new support is similar to Java's try/catch blocks; it lets you specify a code block that you want to try to process. If an error occurs anywhere within that block, you can "catch" the error and specify the code that you want to run in response to the error. The following code (and the Version 5 alternative on the next page) illustrates the process.

```
*.. 1 ...+... 2 ...+... 3 ...+... 4 ...+... 5 ...+... 6 ...+... 7 ...+... 8
CL0N01Factor1+++++++Opcode(E)+Extended-factor2++++++++++++++++++++++++++++++
C                   MONITOR
C                   DOU       %EOF(TimeRecord)
C                   READ      TimeRecord
C                   IF        %EOF(TimeRecord)
C                   LEAVE
C                   ELSE
C                   EVAL      TotalPay = (RegHours * Rate)        +
C                                       (OvtHours * Rate * 1.5) +
C                                       (DblHours * Rate * 2)
C                   UPDATE    TimeRecord
C                   ENDIF
C                   ENDDO
C                   ON-ERROR  1218
C     'Locked'      DSPLY
C                   LEAVE
C                   ON-ERROR  1011:1211:*FILE
C     'File error'  DSPLY
C                   LEAVE
C                   ON-ERROR  *PROGRAM
C     'Pgm error'   DSPLY
C                   LEAVE
C                   ENDMON
```

or, at Version 5:

```
/FREE
   MONITOR;
     DOU %EOF(TimeRecord);
       READ TimeRecord;
       IF %EOF(TimeRecord);
         LEAVE;
       ELSE;
         TotalPay = (RegHours * Rate) +
                    (OvtHours * Rate * 1.5) +
                    (DblHours * Rate * 2);
         UPDATE TimeRecord;
       ENDIF;
     ENDDO;
     ON-ERROR 1218;                                  // Record locked
         Dsply 'TimeRecord record locked.';
         Leave;
     ON-ERROR 1011:1211:*FILE;                       // File error
         Dsply 'Unexpected file error occurred.';
         Leave;
     ON-ERROR *PROGRAM;                              // Non-file error
         Dsply 'Unexpected program error occurred.';
         Leave;
   ENDMON;
/END-FREE
```

A Monitor block starts with a MONITOR opcode; the program then processes subsequent lines in the block, up to the first ON-ERROR opcode. If all the code in the Monitor block is processed without error, control passes to the first line following an ENDMON opcode. If, however, one of the lines in the block causes an error, control is passed to the appropriate ON-ERROR group.

The program/file status code determines which ON-ERROR group gains control. This is the same status code that the %STATUS BIF provides. You can specify any status code from 00100 to 09999 or *PROGRAM, *FILE, or *ALL. You can use *PROGRAM for generic program errors, *FILE for generic file errors, or *ALL for all generic errors. Only one ON-ERROR group is processed — the first one that covers the error status. It's a good idea to place generic ON-ERROR groups after specific groups to ensure you've covered all possible errors. Once the ON-ERROR group is processed, control passes to the statement following the ENDMON operation.

You can specify Monitor blocks anywhere in your program, including within IF, DO, and SELECT groups — even nested within other Monitor blocks or ON-ERROR groups. Monitor blocks can also encompass IF, DO, and SELECT groups.

The Free-form (R)evolution

As you can see from the previous examples, the Version 5 free-form specification is a logical evolution of the two previous fixed-form versions of the calculation specifications. For the remainder of the examples in this book, we will use only the free-form specification wherever possible. Some operation codes aren't supported in the free-form specification. Figure 6.4 lists the opcodes that free-form syntax does not support.

FIGURE 6.4
Operation Codes Not Supported by Free-form Syntax

Opcode	Alternative
ADD	Use + operator.
ADDDUR	Use + operator with duration function.
ALLOC	Use %ALLOC function.
AND*xx*	Use AND operator.
BITOFF	
BITON	
CAB*xx*	Use IF/LEAVE/ITER.
CALL	Use CALLP.
CALLB	Use CALLP.
CAS*xx*	Use SELECT/WHEN/OTHER.
CAT	Use + operator.
CHECK	Use %CHECK function.
CHECKR	Use %CHECKR function.
COMP	Use the =, <, >, <=, >=, or <> operator.
DEFINE	Use definition specification.
DIV	Use / operator or %DIV function.
DO	Use FOR.
DOU*xx*	Use DOU.
DOW*xx*	Use DOW.
EXTRCT	Use %SUBDT function.
GOTO	Use LEAVE/ITER.
IF*xx*	Use IF.
KFLD	
KLIST	
LOOKUP	Use %LOOKUP/%TLOOKUP function.
MHHZO	
MHLZO	
MLHZO	
MLLZO	
MOVE	Use EVALR and/or various functions.
MOVEA	
MOVEL	Use EVAL and/or various functions.
MULT	Use * operator.
MVR	Use %REM function.
OCCUR	Use %OCCUR function.
OR*xx*	Use OR operator.
PARM	Use PR/PI definitions.
PLIST	Use PR/PI definitions.
REALLOC	Use %REALLOC function.

continued ...

FIGURE 6.4 *CONTINUED*

Opcode	Alternative
SCAN	Use %SCAN function.
SETOFF	Use *INxx = *OFF.
SETON	Use *INxx = *ON.
SHTDN	Use %SHTDN function.
SQRT	Use %SQRT function.
SUB	Use – operator.
SUBDUR	Use %DIFF function or – operator with duration function.
SUBST	Use %SUBST function.
TAG	
TESTB	
TESTN	
TESTZ	
TIME	Use %DATE/%TIME/%TIMESTAMP function.
WHENxx	Use WHEN.
XFOOT	Use %XFOOT function.
XLATE	Use %XLATE function.
Z-ADD	
Z-SUB	

A few of the opcodes on this large list may surprise you, because they include some of the most frequently used ones and even some that have been introduced only recently; most of the opcodes on the list, however, have equivalents in built-in functions or in normal algebraic operators.

With few exceptions, you should consider the opcodes listed in Figure 6.4 to be obsolete. For most of these opcodes, Figure 6.4 and Appendix A suggest an alternative function or operator.

Specifying Array Elements

In RPG, you refer to an entire array by using the name of the array. To refer to a specific element of any array, you must include the index along with the array name. RPG IV changes the syntax for referencing individual array elements: Instead of using a comma delimiter (as in RPG III), you enclose the index in parentheses. This syntax is consistent with most other languages. The index must be a numeric field or a constant.

The following examples compare some RPG III and RPG IV specifications for arrays (the %LOOKUP and %EQUAL BIFs are discussed in Chapter 8):

RPG III

```
*.. 1 ...+... 2 ...+... 3 ...+... 4 ...+... 5 ...+... 6 ...+... 7 ..
CLØN01N02N03Factor1+++OpcdeFactor2+++ResultLenDHHiLoEqComments++++++
C           CURMON    LOKUPMONTHS,X                      99

C                     MOVELMSG,17    DSPMSG     P

C                     MOVE *ON       *IN,X
```

RPG IV

```
*.. 1 ...+... 2 ...+... 3 ...+... 4 ...+... 5 ...+... 6 ...+... 7 ...+... 8
 /FREE
    X = %LOOKUP(CurrentMonth:Months:X);
      IF %EQUAL;                        // --------------------------------
        *IN99 = *ON;                    //
      ELSE;                             // Optional code to set indicator 99
        *IN99 = *OFF;                   //
      ENDIF;                            // --------------------------------

    DisplayMsg = Message(17);

    *IN(X) = *ON;
 /END-FREE
```

Chapter 7

Free-form Expressions

With the DOU, DOW, FOR, IF, and WHEN operations (discussed in Chapter 6), RPG introduces the world of free-form logical expressions for the first time in its 40-year life. The new EVAL operation code also makes use of the extended Factor 2 to let you code free-form, complex expressions — numeric, character, relational, or logical. Now, instead of having to step through a complex calculation using multiple opcodes over many source lines, you can code a single expression to assign a value to a result.

Version 5 carries the concept even further, expanding the area in which you can code free-form expressions to nearly the entire line and even making the EVAL operation optional in many instances. With this evolution, RPG IV calculation specifications become virtually 100 percent free-form.

Using EVAL to Assign Numeric Values

When you use EVAL, the expression (in the extended Factor 2, before Version 5) takes the form

```
result = expression
```

The program will evaluate the expression and place the result into the result field. The result must be a variable (e.g., a field, an array, an array element, or a data structure subfield); it cannot be a constant. Let's start with an easy example:

RPG IV

```
*.. 1 ...+... 2 ...+... 3 ...+... 4 ...+... 5 ...+... 6 ...+... 7 ...+... 8
 /FREE
    EVAL TotalPay = RegularPay + OvertimPay;
 /END-FREE
```

This example, which adds RegularPay and OvertimPay together to get TotalPay, is equivalent to the following RPG III code:

RPG III

```
*...1....+....2....+....3....+....4....+....5....+....6....+....7...
CLØN01N02N03Factor1+++OpcdeFactor2+++ResultLenDHHiLoEqComments+++++
C           REGPAY    ADD  OVTPAY    TOTPAY
```

Notice how much easier it is to read the more natural RPG IV version of the code.

To round (half-adjust) the result of an EVAL expression, you use the H operation extender, as in the following code:

```
*.. 1 ...+... 2 ...+... 3 ...+... 4 ...+... 5 ...+... 6 ...+... 7 ...+... 8
 /FREE
    EVAL(H) TaxAmount = TotTaxable * TaxRate;
 /END-FREE
```

The program will round the result to the precision defined by the result field. In the preceding example, if TaxAmount is defined as nine digits with two decimal places, rounding will occur at the last decimal place.

☑ EVAL is optional at Version 5.

In Version 5's free-form specification, specifying EVAL is optional unless you need to code an operation code extender, such as H. Instead of specifying EVAL in the first example above, we could have left it off; the second example would require its use:

```
*.. 1 ...+... 2 ...+... 3 ...+... 4 ...+... 5 ...+... 6 ...+... 7 ...+... 8
 /FREE
     TotalPay = RegularPay + OvertimPay;           // EVAL not required
     EVAL(H) TaxAmount = TotTaxable * TaxRate;      // EVAL required
 /END-FREE
```

Notice how naturally the first expression reads. The compiler will assume you want to use EVAL for assignment expressions. For the remainder of the examples in this book, we will code the EVAL operation only when necessary. In releases earlier than Version 5, of course, EVAL's use is required for assignment expressions.

☑ Use ** for powers.

RPG IV supports all the arithmetic operators you'd expect (+, −, *, /), plus a new one: ** for exponentiation (powers). If Albert Einstein had been an RPG programmer, he might have written

```
*.. 1 ...+... 2 ...+... 3 ...+... 4 ...+... 5 ...+... 6 ...+... 7 ...+... 8
 /FREE
     E = m * c**2;
 /END-FREE
```

Make Friends Quickly with Free-form Expressions

If D-specs don't represent the biggest change in RPG IV, then the free-form expressions surely do. EVAL sets out to endow RPG IV with free-form expressions, resulting in cleaner, more direct code and far fewer intermediate variables. The fewer intermediate variables required, the less chance that an intermediate variable will trash a pending value somewhere else.

Free-form pays dividends in another way as well. You can use it to eliminate some of RPG's vestigial "column cram." Version 5's free-form specification — and in earlier releases, EVAL's elongated Factor 2 — lets you alleviate crowded-column syndrome by using full-length field names where they might not fit into RPG IV's standard 14-column factors. For example, the array reference MonthSales(Counter) would never fit into any of the standard areas, but it adjusts quite nicely to free-form. Using expressions is clearly the superior alternative to cramming contrived, shorter field names into the specification columns.

You should put learning the EVAL opcode and the free-form specification near the top of your short list, use the new specification whenever possible, and establish clear standards on how to "punctuate" it (see Chapter 15 for suggestions).

EVAL expressions can be as complex as necessary, and they can span more than one source line. The following example illustrates a multiple-line complex expression:

```
*.. 1 ...+... 2 ...+... 3 ...+... 4 ...+... 5 ...+... 6 ...+... 7 ...+... 8
 /FREE
    TotalPay = (RegHours * Rate)        +
               (OvtHours * Rate * 1.5) +
               (DblHours * Rate * 2);
 /END-FREE
```

In this example, the EVAL expression is continued onto two subsequent source lines. But the + characters at the end of each line aren't continuation characters; they are arithmetic addition operators. (Also note that a single semicolon delimiter serves the entire expression, regardless of how many lines it occupies.)

☑ **Multiple-line arithmetic expressions do not require a continuation character.**

Arithmetic expressions do not require a continuation character. You simply continue the expression in the extended Factor 2 of the next line, leaving the rest of the specification empty (except for the C in column 6). In pre–Version 5 RPG, you can split a numeric literal across two lines, as the following code demonstrates, but the technique is ugly and generally unnecessary; Version 5 prohibits it.

```
*.. 1 ...+... 2 ...+... 3 ...+... 4 ...+... 5 ...+... 6 ...+... 7 ...+... 8
CLØN01Factor1++++++Opcode(E)+Extended-factor2+++++++++++++++++++++++++++++
C                  EVAL      Liters = Bushels * 35.
C                            238
```

This example multiplies the number of bushels by 35.238 to get the number of liters. Obviously, the expression is better written as

```
*.. 1 ...+... 2 ...+... 3 ...+... 4 ...+... 5 ...+... 6 ...+... 7 ...+... 8
 /FREE
    Liters = Bushels * 35.238;
 /END-FREE
```

EVAL follows a predictable order when it evaluates an expression with multiple operators:

1. Expressions within parentheses are evaluated first, followed by . . .

2. built-in functions (see Chapter 8)

3. + or − (when used as a numeric sign) and NOT

4. ** (exponentiation)

5. * or / (multiplication or division)

6. + or − (addition or subtraction)

7. = (equal), >= (greater than or equal to), > (greater than), <= (less than or equal to), < (less than), <> (not equal to)

8. AND (logical and)

9. OR (logical or)

When you code complex expressions, you should make generous use of parentheses to aid readability, even when the parentheses aren't needed to change the order of operator precedence.

Using EVAL with String Expressions

In addition to numeric expressions, EVAL supports character string expressions. Using EVAL is a particularly convenient way to concatenate strings. The following example constructs a print line from individual city, state, and zip code fields:

```
*.. 1 ...+... 2 ...+... 3 ...+... 4 ...+... 5 ...+... 6 ...+... 7 ...+... 8
 /FREE
     PrintLine = City  + ' ' + State + ' ' + ZipCode;
 /END-FREE
```

This code concatenates the fields, including a blank between them. Trailing blanks are not trimmed in this example; when we discuss built-in functions in Chapter 8, you'll see how to trim trailing blanks.

Just as you can with numeric expressions, you can combine string literals, named constants, and character fields in a string expression. For example:

```
*.. 1 ...+... 2 ...+... 3 ...+... 4 ...+... 5 ...+... 6 ...+... 7 ...+... 8
 /FREE
     PrintLine = 'Dear ' + Title + ' ' + LastName;
 /END-FREE
```

You must enclose string literals within apostrophes ('). Both sides of an assignment expression must have compatible data types; for example, you can't mix character and numeric variables, constants, or literals in the same expression.

☑ **Multiple-line literals require + or – for continuation.**

If you must continue a string literal from one line of an expression to the next, you need the + or – continuation character. The following examples, which use different continuation characters, yield identical results:

```
*.. 1 ...+... 2 ...+... 3 ...+... 4 ...+... 5 ...+... 6 ...+... 7 ...+... 8
CLØNØ1Factor1++++++Opcode(E)+Extended-factor2++++++++++++++++++++++++++++++++
C                       EVAL      Gettysburg = 'Four score and seven years +
C                                             ago our fathers...'

or

C                       EVAL      Gettysburg = 'Four score and seven years ago-
C                                             our fathers...'
```

Remember that when you use the + continuation character, the continuation starts with the first nonblank character in the next line's extended Factor 2; if you use the –, the continuation begins at column 36 of the continuation line.

Of course, the free-form specification makes it less likely that you'll need to continue literals:

```
*.. 1 ...+... 2 ...+... 3 ...+... 4 ...+... 5 ...+... 6 ...+... 7 ...+... 8
  /FREE
     Gettysburg = 'Four score and seven years ago our fathers...';
  /FREE
```

Remember also that you should usually use a named constant instead of a literal, unless the literal has an obvious meaning (see Chapter 15 for this and other style guidelines).

Using EVAL with Arrays

You can use EVAL to assign a value to an entire array or to a single element of an array. To assign a value to an entire array, you use either the array name without an index or an asterisk (*) instead of a specific array index. The following example assigns the value 2000 to all elements of the Years array:

```
*.. 1 ...+... 2 ...+... 3 ...+... 4 ...+... 5 ...+... 6 ...+... 7 ...+... 8
  /FREE
     Years(*) = 2000;
     Years = 2000;                                    //
  /END-FREE                                           // Equivalent code
```

The first alternative above is probably the better of the two because it explicitly documents the fact that Years is an array and not a single field.

An array reference can appear on either side of an EVAL equation — that is, either as the result or as part of the expression. To refer to a specific element of any array, include the index to name the element you want. For example, the following code increments the second element of the TransCount array by one:

```
*.. 1 ...+... 2 ...+... 3 ...+... 4 ...+... 5 ...+... 6 ...+... 7 ...+... 8
  /FREE
     TransCount(2) = TransCount(2) + 1;
  /END-FREE
```

The array index can also be a variable, as in the following example:

```
*.. 1 ...+... 2 ...+... 3 ...+... 4 ...+... 5 ...+... 6 ...+... 7 ...+... 8
  /FREE
     TransCount(Dept) = TransCount(Dept) + 1;
  /END-FREE
```

Using EVAL with Indicators

You can use any RPG data type in an expression, including indicators. RPG IV discourages the use of the predefined number indicators 01–99 but still supports them; good style would dictate using named indicators instead (as Chapter 9 describes). To use a numbered indicator in an expression, you use the familiar *IN*xx* notation.

The RPG IV relational expression below replaces the corresponding RPG III COMP operation:

RPG III

```
*...1....+....2....+....3....+....4....+....5....+....6....+....7...
CLØNØ1NØ2NØ3Factor1+++OpcdeFactor2+++ResultLenDHHiLoEqComments++++++
C           HRSWRK    COMP 40                99
```

RPG IV

```
*.. 1 ...+... 2 ...+... 3 ...+... 4 ...+... 5 ...+... 6 ...+... 7 ...+... 8
/FREE
   *IN99  = (HoursWrked > 40);
/END-FREE
```

Not only is the expression easier to read (it's hard to figure out which RPG III indicator position was used), but it's also about as self-documenting as numbered indicators could ever be.

You also can use indicators in logical expressions. For example, the following code turns *IN90 on or off to equal the condition of *IN91:

```
*.. 1 ...+... 2 ...+... 3 ...+... 4 ...+... 5 ...+... 6 ...+... 7 ...+... 8
/FREE
   *IN90 = *IN91;
/END-FREE
```

Multiple-operand logical expressions also are no problem for the EVAL opcode. Consider the following examples:

```
*.. 1 ...+... 2 ...+... 3 ...+... 4 ...+... 5 ...+... 6 ...+... 7 ...+... 8
/FREE
   *IN90 = *IN91 AND *IN92;
   *IN90 = *IN91 OR *IN92;
   *IN90 = *IN91 OR (UMONTH > 2);
/END-FREE
```

The first example sets on *IN90 if both *IN91 and *IN92 are also on; otherwise, *IN90 is set off. The second example sets on *IN90 if either *IN91 or *IN92 is on. In the third example, we combine a logical and a relational expression to set on *IN90 if *IN91 is already on or if the month is past February. Notice that, unlike CL, RPG IV logical operators (AND, OR) are not preceded by an asterisk.

The result of a logical expression (either 1 or 0) is compatible with a character data type. This means that you can use character fields as well as indicators as results for a logical expression. It is not always wise to mix data types, however.

When you code an EVAL expression, be careful to make the purpose of the expression clear and simple. For example, the following code snippet is proof of what happens in RPG IV when "bad code happens to good programs":

```
*.. 1 ...+... 2 ...+... 3 ...+... 4 ...+... 5 ...+... 6 ...+... 7 ...+... 8
CLØNØ1Factor1++++++Opcode(E)+Extended-factor2+++++++++++++++++++++++++++++++++
CLØNØ1Factor1++++++Opcode(E)+Factor2++++++Result+++++++Len++D+HiLoEq....
C                  EVAL      Result = (Hours > 1000) + (Age >= 22) + *IN99
C                  MOVEA     Result      *IN(90)
```

This example (which might determine pension plan eligibility) concatenates three logical expressions into a single character field. If Result is a three-byte character field, indicators 90, 91, and 92 will all be affected by the EVAL and MOVEA opcodes, whose purposes are effectively hidden by poor coding.

Fortunately, RPG IV is diligently shedding its dependence on traditional numbered indicators. Using such features as indicator data structures (Chapter 4) and built-in functions (Chapter 8), you can effectively eliminate all indicator usage from your RPG IV programs.

Using EVAL to Avoid Work Fields

Traditionally, many RPG calculations require intermediate "work" fields to temporarily hold the result of one calculation so that the result can "feed" a subsequent calculation. For example, a simple matter of calculating total pay can require several intermediate work fields:

RPG III

```
*...1....+....2....+....3....+....4....+....5....+....6....+....7...
CLØN01N02N03Factor1+++OpcdeFactor2+++ResultLenDHHiLoEqComments++++++
C          REGHRS    MULT RATE      REGPAY 92
C          OVTHRS    MULT RATE      OVTPAY 92
C                    MULT 1.5       OVTPAY
C          DBLHRS    MULT RATE      DBLPAY 92
C                    MULT 2         DBLPAY
C          REGPAY    ADD  OVTPAY    TOTPAY
C                    ADD  DBLPAY    TOTPAY
```

With RPG IV, you can reduce this calculation to a single expression:

RPG IV

```
*.. 1 ...+... 2 ...+... 3 ...+... 4 ...+... 5 ...+... 6 ...+... 7 ...+... 8
/FREE
    TotalPay  = (RegularHours * Rate)        +
                (OvertimeHours * Rate * 1.5) +
                (DoubleHours * Rate * 2);
/END-FREE
```

Not only does this expression eliminate three work fields (REGPAY, OVTPAY, and DBLPAY), but it's also much clearer than the comparable RPG III code. If you use the H half-adjust extender with this expression, be aware that the half-adjust occurs only once, when the final assignment is made to the result field:

```
*.. 1 ...+... 2 ...+... 3 ...+... 4 ...+... 5 ...+... 6 ...+... 7 ...+... 8
/FREE
    EVAL(H) TotalPay  = (RegularHours * Rate)        +
                        (OvertimeHours * Rate * 1.5) +
                        (DoubleHours * Rate * 2);
/END-FREE
```

In Chapter 8, we'll use the %DECH built-in function to perform intermediate rounding.

By eliminating work fields, you also minimize the potential of two identically named fields "crashing," either during the compile or, worse, at runtime. How many times have you thrown a WORK1 field into a program only to realize that two months earlier you had already included WORK1 for a different purpose or with a different length or data type? If you conscientiously use EVAL to reduce the number of work fields in your program, you'll also reduce the possibility of this error; plus, without errant work field names and definitions, your program will be easier to read.

Using EVAL to Avoid "Column Cram"

Longer names — wow! At first glance, increased field name limits seem to open up all kinds of possibilities for eliminating those cryptic six-character field names you've been saddled with in RPG. YDSLQ1 suddenly becomes YTDSlsQtr1; CTSTZP is much more comprehensible as CityStateZip. Sure, you still have to abbreviate once in a while (quite often, in fact), but those extra characters let you make your code much more readable and maintainable. However, RPG's naming limitations can suddenly seem cramped again when you bump into some of the same limits you've always endured with RPG's fixed-column layout.

Free-form expression can help ease the pain, especially with those (now obsolete) operations, such as CAT and SUBST, that can overload Factor 1 or Factor 2, or both, with more than one field name. EVAL is also handy when you've taken advantage of expanded naming limits for both an array name and an index name. The following RPG IV alternatives do the same thing, but the EVAL alternative is more intelligible:

```
*.. 1 ...+... 2 ...+... 3 ...+... 4 ...+... 5 ...+... 6 ...+... 7 ...+... 8
CLØNØ1Factor1+++++++Opcode(E)+Extended-factor2+++++++++++++++++++++++++++++++
CLØNØ1Factor1+++++++Opcode(E)+Factor2+++++++Result++++++++Len++D+HiLoEq....
C     SlsPrsNam(Slp)CAT(P)    '/':Ø           NameBrnch(Slp)
C                   CAT(P)    BrchOff(Slp):ØNameBrnch(Slp)
```

or

```
/FREE
   NameBranch(SlsPersNbr) = %TRIM(SlsPrsName(SlsPersNbr)) + '/' +
                            %TRIM(BranchOffice(SlsPersNbr));
/END-FREE
```

This code creates (in an array element) a string that consists of a salesperson's name and branch office, separated by a slash (/) — for example, Lomax/Philadelphia. The names and branches are stored in arrays indexed by the salesperson's number. The %TRIM built-in function trims leading and trailing blanks (more about this function in Chapter 8). Even though this code may seem contrived, it points out that conventional methods and opcodes may force you to forego the advantages of longer names; expressions, however, may restore the ability to use longer names when other opcodes won't allow them.

Numeric Overflow with EVAL Expressions

EVAL is very flexible when it evaluates an expression. It will make note of any necessary intermediate results, maintaining full precision without your having to define field lengths or decimal places. The equation's result field, however, must be long enough to hold the result. Unlike the other RPG opcodes, EVAL will cause a runtime error if the result field is too small. EVAL allows truncation at the right end of a number (i.e., it will truncate extra decimal places), but it will not truncate left-end digits.

The RPG IV arithmetic opcodes (e.g., ADD, SUB, MULT, DIV) normally allow numeric overflow without a runtime error, truncating the left-end digits just as they always have. The ILE RPG/400 compiler, however, now lets you force numeric overflow to generate a runtime error. To cause the arithmetic opcodes to halt a program when they encounter a numeric overflow, you specify parameter TRUNCNBR(*NO) when you use the CRTRPGMOD (Create RPG Module) or CRTBNDRPG (Create Bound RPG Program) command.

> ☑ **You can specify which precision rules you want to use with EVAL.**

Improving EVAL's Precision

Free-form expressions lend a great deal of free-format flexibility to RPG, letting you code familiar expressions in the extended Factor 2. However, EVAL may provide imprecise results, especially with very complex expressions. This imprecision comes about because of the rules that EVAL uses to determine the precision of temporary intermediate results.

For example, the following code would result in an incorrect answer:

```
*.. 1 ...+... 2 ...+... 3 ...+... 4 ...+... 5 ...+... 6 ...+... 7 ...+... 8
DName++++++++++ETDsFrom+++To/L+++IDc.Keywords++++++++++++++++++++++++++++++++
D A               S             15  2 INZ(4)
D B               S             15  2 INZ(5)
D C               S             15  2 INZ(3)
D D               S             15  2

 /FREE
    EVAL(H) D = A*B/C;
 /END-FREE
```

While your $2.95 pocket calculator will give you the correct answer of 6.67 to the above expression, your considerably more expensive AS/400 would answer with 6.66. The latter's imprecision, seemingly insignificant by itself, could mushroom into serious errors in many financial applications. For an explanation of how this error occurs, see "EVAL Imprecision: The Details" (page 75).

RPG IV addresses this problem by letting you choose the precision rules that you want to use with expressions — by using two new H-spec keywords and/or two new operation extenders.

The H-spec keyword EXPROPTS(*MAXDIGITS) ensures that a maximum value can be computed without causing numeric overflow; this is the default precision method that RPG has used since its inception. The EXPROPTS(*RESDECPOS) keyword, on the other hand, ensures that no decimal positions are lost in the assignment. In the above example, EXPROPTS(*RESDECPOS) would yield the correct answer, 6.67. The "result decimal positions" rule is closer to the way Cobol works than to the old "maximum digits" method.

In addition to specifying the precision rule you want to use throughout a program, you can code the rule to apply to a specific expression by using one of two operation extenders: M to use the maximum digits rules for precision or R to use the result decimal positions rule. The following examples show how to get both the "wrong" and "right" answers to the example above:

```
*.. 1 ...+... 2 ...+... 3 ...+... 4 ...+... 5 ...+... 6 ...+... 7 ...+... 8
 /FREE
    EVAL(MH) D = A*B/C;
    EVAL(RH) D = A*B/C;
 /END-FREE
```

Notice in this example that there are two operation extender codes within the parentheses following each EVAL.

Which method should you use to improve EVAL's precision? In general, you'll want to use the result decimal positions rule for precision throughout your program. To ensure correct results, always include the EXPROPTS(*RESDECPOS) entry in your program's H-specs; then specify EVAL(M), with the extender, only when you must use the maximum digits rule. EVAL operations that you specify without the R extender will then default to using the result decimal positions rule.

```
*.. 1 ...+... 2 ...+... 3 ...+... 4 ...+... 5 ...+... 6 ...+... 7 ...+... 8
H EXPROPTS(*RESDECPOS)

 /FREE
    EVAL(H) D = A*B/C;
 /END-FREE
```

Free-form's EVAL Twin: EVALR

When using the EVAL opcode with character expressions, EVAL is the free-form equivalent to coding MOVEL(P); that is, the result is always left-adjusted, with trailing positions padded with blanks. The EVALR opcode, available starting with V4R4, performs the same functions for character expressions but right-adjusts the result and pads any preceding positions with blanks. EVALR's use is usually limited to character expressions and is never valid for numeric expressions. Chapter 8 contains an example of using EVALR with the %TRIMR built-in function.

EVAL Imprecision: The Details

Sometimes the default precision rules used by RPG free-form expressions can produce unexpected results. For example, the following expression will result in an incorrect answer of 0, even though a quick look will tell you the correct answer is .01:

```
 *... 1 ...+... 2 ...+... 3 ...+... 4 ...+... 5 ...+... 6 ...+... 7 ...+... 8
DName++++++++++ETDsFrom+++To/L+++IDc.Keywords++++++++++++++++++++++++++++++++
D A               S              5  2 INZ('.01')
D B               S              7  4 INZ(1)
D C               S             15  5 INZ(1)
D D               S             13  0 INZ(1)
D Result          S             11  4
 /FREE
   EVAL(H)   Result = A*B*C*D;
 /END-FREE
```

How can this happen? It might help to break down the expression into its individual components and then calculate each intermediate result just as EVAL would. By default, EVAL uses the "maximum digits" rule — the "M" precision rule — which minimizes the chances that numeric overflow will occur. When EVAL encounters an intermediate result that might cause overflow (for example, more than 30 digits total), it truncates the decimal positions (to the right of the decimal point) to compensate. The expression is evaluated as follows:

Expression component	Multiplication result
A=000.01	
B=001.0000	000.010000
C=0000000001.00000	000000000.010000000000
D=0000000000001.	0.000000000000000000000000000000
Result	0000000.0000

Notice that in the third temporary result, EVAL must truncate all but one decimal position following the decimal point to maximize the number of digits to the left of the decimal point, thus ensuring against numeric overflow. Unfortunately, the critical second decimal position falls out of the result.

The alternative "result decimal positions" rule ensures that any intermediate value can never be reduced to fewer decimal positions (to the right of the decimal point) than the result. Under this method, the expression is evaluated as follows:

Expression component	Multiplication result
A=000.01	
B=001.0000	000.010000
C=0000000001.00000	0000000000.01000000000
D=0000000000001.	00000000000.0100
Result	0000.0100

In this case, the "R" precision rule gives the correct result, but numeric overflow is more likely to occur.

Chapter 8

RPG Built-in Functions

Built-in functions (affectionately referred to as BIFs) represent an entirely new concept for RPG, but they have been features of other AS/400 languages, including CL, for a long time. You can think of BIFs as operation codes that return a value without requiring that the value be placed in a result field — free-format operation codes. Until now, RPG handled some of these functions with opcodes (e.g., SUBST), shoe-horning all the arguments into Factor 1 and/or Factor 2 and using a colon (:) separator between the arguments. In other cases, the language didn't support the function at all, requiring you instead to devise your own coding schemes to get the job done. With RPG IV, you can make use of easily coded, efficient, built-in functions to do some of the things that previously required programming "tricks."

Originally, IBM introduced BIFs to RPG with only a few basic operations, but it quickly added dozens more, and you can expect this particular area of the language to be greatly expanded in future releases. Figure 8.1 lists the built-in functions and describes their purposes.

FIGURE 8.1
Built-in Functions

Built-in function	Return value
%ABS	Absolute value of expression
%ADDR	Address of variable
%ALLOC	Pointer to dynamically allocated storage
%CHAR	Value converted to character data
%CHECK, %CHECKR	First/last position in string that does not contain specified character(s)
%DATE	Value converted to date
%DAYS	Value converted to days duration
%DEC, %DECH	Value converted to packed numeric data
%DECPOS	Number of decimal digits
%DIFF	Difference between dates, times, or timestamps
%DIV	Integer quotient from division operation
%EDITC, %EDITW	Edited value of expression
%EDITFLT	External display representation of floating-point number
%ELEM	Number of elements or occurrences
%EOF	End-of-file condition
%EQUAL	SETLL or LOOKUP equal condition

continued ...

FIGURE 8.1 *CONTINUED*

Built-in function	Return value
%ERROR	Error condition
%FLOAT	Value converted to floating-point numeric data
%FOUND	Record-found condition
%GRAPH	Value converted to graphic data
%HOURS	Value converted to hours durations
%INT, %INTH	Value converted to integer numeric format
%LEN	Length in digits or characters
%LOOKUP*xx*, %TLOOKUP*xx*	Array/table index result of element look-up
%MINUTES	Value converted to minutes duration
%MONTHS	Value converted to months duration
%MSECONDS	Value converted to microseconds duration
%NULLIND	Null-indicator condition
%OCCUR	Current occurrence of multiple-occurrence data structure
%OPEN	File-open condition
%PADDR	Address of procedure
%PARMS	Number of parameters passed to procedure
%REALLOC	Pointer to reallocated storage
%REM	Remainder from division operation
%REPLACE	Result of string replacement
%SCAN	Position of search argument in string
%SECONDS	Value converted to seconds duration
%SHTDN	System shutdown request indicator
%SIZE	Size in bytes of variable or literal
%SQRT	Square root of expression
%STATUS	File or program status code
%STR	Characters in null-terminated string
%SUBDT	Portion of date, time, or timestamp
%SUBST	Substring
%THIS	Object referring to class for native method call
%TIME	Value converted to time
%TIMESTAMP	Value converted to timestamp
%TRIM, %TRIML, %TRIMR	String with blanks trimmed
%UCS2	UCS-2 value of an expression
%UNS, %UNSH	Value converted to unsigned integer numeric format
%XFOOT	Sum of array elements
%XLATE	Translated string
%YEARS	Value converted to years duration

Notice that each BIF begins with a percent sign (%). When you code a BIF, you supply arguments to the function in the following format, separating each argument with a colon:

`%function(argument:argument)`

A function's arguments can be variables, constants, expressions, and sometimes even other BIFs. Although you'll usually use BIFs in a program's calculations, they are also supported in D-specs, using compile-time values.

Learn to Use BIFs

Built-in functions (BIFs) are another interesting and potentially powerful feature of RPG IV. BIFs work similarly to the % functions in CL. Get in the habit of writing "indicator-free" code using BIFs to enhance the readability and maintainability of your RPG IV programs. You use them to calculate a value, and you can use their return values in expressions.

The %SUBST BIF, for example, essentially takes the place of the SUBST (Substring) opcode (although SUBST remains in legacy RPG IV) and gives you another good way to beat RPG IV's crowded columns. There isn't a %CAT BIF to concatenate two strings, but that function is accomplished simply by using the + character and the EVAL opcode in RPG IV.

Some built-in functions, such as %EOF, %FOUND, and %EQUAL, serve to eliminate the need for resulting indicators with file operations, such as READ and CHAIN. The %ERROR and %STATUS BIFs enable you to code robust error-handling routines without resorting to resulting indicators.

Several BIFs let you perform date functions in free-form expressions. %DATE, %TIME, and %TIMESTAMP retrieve current values or convert expressions or variables to date, time, or timestamp data types. %YEARS, %MONTHS, and %DAYS, among others, convert a value to a duration, so that you can add and subtract dates using simple expressions. %DIFF determines the difference between two dates, and %SUBDT extracts a portion (substring) of a date. These functions essentially replace the ADDDUR, SUBDUR, and EXTRCT fixed-form operations that earlier RPG IV releases used to do the same things. Chapter 9 covers these BIFs in detail.

You can put on the back burner for a while functions such as %ADDR and %PADDR, which return the address of a variable and the address of a procedure (generally a called program), respectively. Unless you use application programming interfaces (APIs), the need to understand pointers isn't critical for most RPG applications. The same goes for the %PARMS function, which you will need only when you get proficient with RPG subprocedures and service programs. You'll find the other functions, though, quite useful, especially when you're manipulating strings and working with arrays.

For CL programmers, the concept of a routine returning a value that can be used in an expression is old hat, but for RPG, the concept is foreign. Once you understand it, you'll quickly begin to appreciate the potential of BIFs. In no time, you'll be longing for more functions; indeed, you'll find that this area is one that IBM will greatly enhance in the future. Fortunately, you don't have to wait for IBM to catch up to your requirements; you can learn to build your own user-defined functions using RPG's support for subprocedures, which we'll discuss in Chapter 14.

String Manipulation Using BIFs

Some of the built-in functions make it easier for you to examine and manipulate character strings in your programs. Among these functions are %TRIM*x*, %SUBST, %SCAN, and %REPLACE.

> ☑ **Use BIFs with character expressions.**

Stripping Blanks with the Trim BIFs

The %TRIM*x* functions return a string that has been stripped of any leading and/or trailing blanks. There are three %TRIM*x* BIFs:

- %TRIM strips both leading and trailing blanks.
- %TRIML strips leading (left) blanks only.
- %TRIMR strips trailing (right) blanks only.

The %TRIM*x* functions reduce the amount of code required to combine fields while eliminating leading and trailing blanks. Previously, RPG III required a convoluted series of SCAN, CHECK, CHEKR, and CAT statements to accomplish what you can do in a single, comprehensible EVAL statement using one or more of the %TRIM*x* BIFs.

The only argument for any of the %TRIM*x* functions is the string that is to be trimmed; this argument can be a variable, a literal, or a constant. The following example constructs a formatted print line from individual city, state, and zip code fields:

```
*.. 1 ...+... 2 ...+... 3 ...+... 4 ...+... 5 ...+... 6 ...+... 7 ...+... 8
 /FREE
    PrintLine = %TRIM(City)    + ' ' + %TRIM(State)    + ' ' +
                %TRIM(ZipCode);
 /END-FREE
```

This code removes all leading and trailing blanks from each of the fields and then concatenates the fields, including a blank between them.

Here's an example that uses RPG IV's EVALR opcode and the %TRIMR function to trim trailing blanks from a character field, right-adjust the field, and move the field's value into a numeric field. (Recall that EVALR right-adjusts a character expression's value, padding with blanks on the left.)

```
*.. 1 ...+... 2 ...+... 3 ...+... 4 ...+... 5 ...+... 6 ...+... 7 ...+... 8
DName++++++++++ETDsFrom+++To/L+++IDc.Keywords++++++++++++++++++++++++++++++++++
CLØN01Factor1+++++++Opcode(E)+Factor2++++++Result++++++++Len++D+HiLoEq....
CLØN01Factor1+++++++Opcode(E)+Extended-factor2+++++++++++++++++++++++++++++++++
D CharFld        S              5A   INZ('123 ')
D NumFld         S              5S 0

C                   EVALR     CharFld = %TRIMR(CharFld)
C                   MOVE(P)   CharFld         NumFld
```

After the EVALR operation, the value of CharFld will be ' 123' (two leading blanks). After the MOVE(P), NumFld will contain 123.

Using the %SUBST Function

The %SUBST function extracts a portion of a string, expanding on the functionality offered by the SUBST opcode. You must specify the string and the starting position of the substring; the substring length is optional. Take a look at the following examples.

```
*.. 1 ...+... 2 ...+... 3 ...+... 4 ...+... 5 ...+... 6 ...+... 7 ...+... 8
DName++++++++++ETDsFrom+++To/L+++IDc.Keywords+++++++++++++++++++++++++++++++
DUpperCase          C                      'ABCDEFGHIJKLMNOPQRSTUVWXYZ'

 /FREE
    Start  = %SUBST(UpperCase:1:3);
    Middle = %SUBST(UpperCase:12:5);
    End    = %SUBST(UpperCase:24);
 /END-FREE
```

In the first example, the value of the Start variable will be 'ABC' — the first three characters in UpperCase. Next, Middle will contain 'LMNOP' — the five characters starting at position 12. Finally, End will contain 'XYZ' — the last three characters; because we didn't specify a length in this example, the substring will extend to the end of the source string. The EVAL opcode will ensure that the result fields are right-padded with blanks if necessary; if the target field is too small to contain the entire substring, EVAL will truncate the substring.

%SUBST arguments can also be expressions, as the following example shows:

```
*.. 1 ...+... 2 ...+... 3 ...+... 4 ...+... 5 ...+... 6 ...+... 7 ...+... 8
CL0N01Factor1+++++++Opcode(E)+Factor2+++++++Result++++++++Len++D+HiLoEq....
CL0N01Factor1+++++++Opcode(E)+Extended-factor2++++++++++++++++++++++++++++++
C       '/'          SCAN     LastFirst     SlashPosit
C                    EVAL     First = %SUBST(LastFirst:SlashPosit+1)
C                    EVAL     Last  = %SUBST(LastFirst:1:SlashPosit-1)
```

This code extracts a person's first and last names from a string that contains the last name and first name separated by a slash. For example, if the value of LastFirst is 'SMITH/JOHN', the code would extract 'SMITH' as the value for Last and 'JOHN' as the value for First. If you use an expression as a BIF argument, your program must ensure that the expression will return a valid argument; otherwise, the program may abort with a runtime error.

In addition to using %SUBST to extract a substring value, you can use it as the result of an assignment (i.e., to change the contents of a portion of a string). Consider the following example:

```
*.. 1 ...+... 2 ...+... 3 ...+... 4 ...+... 5 ...+... 6 ...+... 7 ...+... 8
DName++++++++++ETDsFrom+++To/L+++IDc.Keywords+++++++++++++++++++++++++++++++
D Swine            S            21     INZ('PigPigPigPigPigPigPig')

 /FREE
    %SUBST(Swine:10:6) = 'Pearls';
 /END-FREE
```

This RPG example of "casting pearls among the swine" changes the value of Swine to 'PigPigPigPearlsPigPig' by specifying the %SUBST function on the left side of the EVAL expression.

More practically, you can insert the value of a variable into a string using the %SUBST BIF, as the following example shows.

```
*.. 1 ...+... 2 ...+... 3 ...+... 4 ...+... 5 ...+... 6 ...+... 7 ...+... 8
DName++++++++++ETDsFrom+++To/L+++IDc.Keywords++++++++++++++++++++++++++++++++
D BarGraph        S            100     INZ(*ALLX'20')
D Percent         S              3 0

D Ruler           C                     '*...+... 1 ...+... 2 ...+... 3 -
D                                       ...+... 4 ...+... 5 ...+... 6 -
D                                       ...+... 7 ...+... 8 ...+... 9 -
D                                       ...+... 0'

 /FREE
   IF Percent > 0;
      %SUBST(BarGraph:1:Percent) = Ruler;
   ENDIF;
 /END-FREE
```

In this example, BarGraph is initially filled with hexadecimal '20' characters, which an AS/400 display would interpret as the end of a field. The EVAL statement changes the value of BarGraph so that a ruler line will appear in the first part of the field, extending for the number of characters indicated by the Percent variable. You could use this code to display a progress bar in a program.

Performing a String %SCAN

The %SCAN function searches a string for a search argument and then returns an integer that represents the first position in the string that contains the search argument. To use %SCAN, you'll code two or three arguments:

```
%SCAN(search-argument:string{:starting-position})
```

If you don't code a starting position, the search starts at the first position in the string:

```
*.. 1 ...+... 2 ...+... 3 ...+... 4 ...+... 5 ...+... 6 ...+... 7 ...+... 8
 /FREE
    SlashPosit = %SCAN('/':LastFirst);          //
    SlashPosit = %SCAN('/':LastFirst:1);        // Equivalent code
 /END-FREE
```

As you can see, the %SCAN function performs much the same work as the SCAN opcode, but within a free-form expression. In this example, if LastFirst contained a value of 'SMITH/JOHN', SlashPosit would have a value of 6, indicating that the '/' character is in the sixth position of the string. If %SCAN found no instance of the '/' character, it would return a 0.

In our earlier example of the %SUBST function, we could have embedded the %SCAN function to eliminate the need for a standalone variable for the second %SUBST argument:

```
*.. 1 ...+... 2 ...+... 3 ...+... 4 ...+... 5 ...+... 6 ...+... 7 ...+... 8
 /FREE
    First = %SUBST(LastFirst:(%SCAN('/':LastFirst)+1));
    Last = %SUBST(LastFirst:1:(%SCAN('/':LastFirst)-1));
 /END-FREE
```

If you've used the SCAN opcode in the past, you may know that SCAN can return an array that contains every occurrence of the search argument in the string, not just the first occurrence. The %SCAN function cannot do this; it's limited to returning just the next occurrence. You'll need to loop through multiple %SCANs, starting at a new position every time, to find every occurrence. The following example shows one approach you might take; it also uses the %SIZE function, which we discuss a little later in this chapter.

```
*.. 1 ...+... 2 ...+... 3 ...+... 4 ...+... 5 ...+... 6 ...+... 7 ...+... 8
 /FREE
    SlashPos = 0;

    DOU SlashPos = 0 OR SlashPos = %SIZE(LastFirst);
       SlashPos = %SCAN('/':LastFirst:SlashPos+1);
       ...
    ENDDO;
 /END-FREE
```

Using the %REPLACE Function

The %REPLACE function substitutes a specified number of characters in a string with replacement characters. %REPLACE accepts from two to four arguments:

%REPLACE(*replacement*:*string*{:*starting-position*{:*length-to-replace*}})

If you don't specify a starting position, %REPLACE begins at the first position in the string. If you don't specify a number of characters to replace, %REPLACE assumes you want the same number of characters as the replacement string contains. Here's a familiar example, adapted from the %SUBST section earlier:

```
*.. 1 ...+... 2 ...+... 3 ...+... 4 ...+... 5 ...+... 6 ...+... 7 ...+... 8
DName++++++++++ETDsFrom+++To/L+++IDc.Keywords+++++++++++++++++++++++++++++++++
D Swine           S             21    INZ('PigPigPigPigPigPigPig')

 /FREE
    Swine = %REPLACE('Pearls':Swine:10:6);
 /END-FREE
```

As you can see, %REPLACE and %SUBST are closely related. The new value of Swine is 'PigPigPigPearlsPigPig' — just as in the earlier example.

%REPLACE does not require that the fourth argument (the number of characters to replace) match the number of characters in the first argument (the replacement string). In fact, you can specify 0 as the number of characters to replace; in this case, %REPLACE *inserts* the replacement string into the source string, "spreading out" the source string to make room:

```
*.. 1 ...+... 2 ...+... 3 ...+... 4 ...+... 5 ...+... 6 ...+... 7 ...+... 8
DName++++++++++ETDsFrom+++To/L+++IDc.Keywords+++++++++++++++++++++++++++++++++
D Full            S             30    INZ('John Adams')
D                                     VARYING
D Middle          S             10    INZ('Quincy')
D                                     VARYING

 /FREE
    Full = %REPLACE(' '+Middle : Full : %SCAN(' ':Full) : 0);
 /END-FREE
```

In this example, an entire %SCAN function is coded as a single third argument to the %REPLACE function; RPG IV would first search the Full field for a blank, which it would use as the replacement point for the %REPLACE function. It would then insert ' Quincy' (with a leading blank) just before that replacement point and then continue with ' Adams' (again with a leading blank) as the rest of the string. The end result would be 'John Quincy Adams' as the ending value for Full. In this example, we needed to use variable-length fields (coded with the VARYING keyword) because some of the %REPLACE arguments are variable-length expressions (for more information about such expressions, see "Using Variable-Length Fields" on page 96).

☑ **Build self-documenting code using BIFs.**

Functions for Program Self-Examination

Several built-in functions let your program examine its own structure and make adjustments as necessary if that structure changes. You can use these functions to make subsequent maintenance of the program less error-prone, to make your program "self-modifying," or to better document relationships between data items in the program. Among these functions are %SIZE, %LEN, and %ELEM.

%SIZE-ing Up a Field

The %SIZE BIF offers RPG an entirely new function. %SIZE returns the number of bytes occupied by a field, literal, array, data structure, or named constant. You can use %SIZE in D-specs wherever you can use a numeric constant; you can also include %SIZE in an extended Factor 2 expression. You may find %SIZE useful in writing "self-modifying" code. For example, the following code forces the ArrCust array to always have the same number of elements as the number of bytes in the CustName field in a database file. If you change the size of CustName in the file, you could recompile the code with no further modification.

```
*.. 1 ...+... 2 ...+... 3 ...+... 4 ...+... 5 ...+... 6 ...+... 7 ...+... 8
DName++++++++++ETDsFrom+++To/L+++IDc.Keywords++++++++++++++++++++++++++++++++
D ArrCust          S              1      DIM(%SIZE(CustName))

 /FREE
    FOR Index = 1 TO %SIZE(CustName);
       ...
    ENDFOR;
 /END-FREE
```

In addition to making the source easier to maintain, coding the FOR statement in this manner tends to document the reason for the loop (i.e., to process each element of the array).

If you use the name of an array, table, or multiple-occurrence data structure as the argument for the %SIZE function, RPG will return the size of one element or occurrence. To retrieve the size of the entire array, table, or multiple-occurrence data structure, you must include a second argument, *ALL, as in the following example:

```
*.. 1 ...+... 2 ...+... 3 ...+... 4 ...+... 5 ...+... 6 ...+... 7 ...+... 8
DName++++++++++ETDsFrom+++To/L+++IDc.Keywords+++++++++++++++++++++++++++++++
D Regions         S             10    DIM(7)

 /FREE
    SizeOfRegions = %SIZE(Regions);                      // SizeOfRegions = 10
    SizeOfRegions = %SIZE(Regions:*ALL);                 // SizeOfRegions = 70
 /END-FREE
```

The first expression here would result in a value of 10 for the SizeOfRegions variable because each element of the Regions array is 10 bytes long. The second expression, on the other hand, would give SizeOfRegions a value of 70 — the size of the entire array.

Remember that %SIZE returns a number of *bytes*. When you use it to determine the size of a packed or binary field, it will not return the number of digits in the field. Consider the following example:

```
*.. 1 ...+... 2 ...+... 3 ...+... 4 ...+... 5 ...+... 6 ...+... 7 ...+... 8
DName++++++++++ETDsFrom+++To/L+++IDc.Keywords+++++++++++++++++++++++++++++++
D Pack5           S              5P 0
D Binary9         S              9B 0

 /FREE
    SizeOf = %SIZE(Pack5);                               // SizeOf = 3
    SizeOf = %SIZE(Binary9);                             // SizeOf = 4
 /END-FREE
```

The first EVAL statement would return a value of 3 to SizeOf, because a five-digit packed field occupies only three bytes. Similarly, the second EVAL statement would return a value of four bytes.

Using the %LEN Function

Because %SIZE returns the number of bytes occupied by a field, you might be tempted to use it to determine the length of the value of a character field. You'd be disappointed. But there is a function that will return the number of digits or characters in a variable expression: %LEN. The %LEN function gets or sets the number of characters in the value of a character expression, as the following example shows:

```
*.. 1 ...+... 2 ...+... 3 ...+... 4 ...+... 5 ...+... 6 ...+... 7 ...+... 8
DName++++++++++ETDsFrom+++To/L+++IDc.Keywords+++++++++++++++++++++++++++++++
D CustName        S             35    INZ('John Doe')

 /FREE
    SizeOfCustName = %SIZE(CustName);                    // SizeOfCustName = 35
    LenOfCustName = %LEN(%TRIM(CustName));               // LenOfCustName = 8
 /END-FREE
```

The first expression would return a value of 35 to SizeOfCustName because CustName occupies 35 bytes, regardless of its value. The second expression, however, would result in LenOfCustName having a value of 8, the number of bytes occupied by the 'John Doe' trimmed value of CustName. Notice that you can embed a function within another function when the function argument is itself an expression.

The expression within the %LEN function can be complex, as the following example shows:

```
*.. 1 ...+... 2 ...+... 3 ...+... 4 ...+... 5 ...+... 6 ...+... 7 ...+... 8
 /FREE
    IF %LEN(%TRIM(City) + ' ' + %TRIM(State) + ' ' + %TRIM(ZipCode)) <= 35;
    ...
    ENDIF;
 /END-FREE
```

When used with numeric expressions, %LEN returns a value representing the precision of the expression, not the number of significant digits.

Using the %ELEM Function

The %ELEM BIF returns either the number of elements in an array or table or the number of occurrences in a multiple-occurrence data structure. You can use this function to improve the maintainability of your code. Let's take a look at this use of BIFs in a sample block of D-specs:

```
*.. 1 ...+... 2 ...+... 3 ...+... 4 ...+... 5 ...+... 6 ...+... 7 ...+... 8
DName++++++++++ETDsFrom+++To/L+++IDc.Keywords+++++++++++++++++++++++++++++++
D WeeklySls       DS            9  2 DIM(53)
D WeeklyComm      DS              LIKE(WeeklySls)
D                                 DIM(%ELEM(WeeklySls))
 /FREE
    FOR Index = 1 TO %ELEM(WeeklySls);
    ...
    ENDFOR;
 /END-FREE
```

In this example, the WeeklySls array contains sales figures by week; it has 53 elements, corresponding to the maximum number of weeks in a year. The WeeklyComm array, which holds commissions by week, is defined as being LIKE the WeeklySls array. Note that the LIKE keyword applies only to the data attributes of the referenced field; it does not apply to the DIM keyword for the referenced field. By using the %ELEM function within the DIM keyword for array WeeklyComm, however, you can ensure that WeeklyComm also has the same number of elements as WeeklySls. If for some reason you needed to change the number of elements in WeeklySls, the number of elements in WeeklyComm would automatically be adjusted when you recompiled the program, as would the number of times the FOR loop is executed. Remember that you can include BIFs in a program's D-specs, as long as the BIFs can be resolved at compile time.

Let's look at another example of using BIFs to improve program maintainability:

```
*.. 1 ...+... 2 ...+... 3 ...+... 4 ...+... 5 ...+... 6 ...+... 7 ...+... 8
DName++++++++++ETDsFrom+++To/L+++IDc.Keywords+++++++++++++++++++++++++++++++++
D CustDS          DS
D  WorkName                            LIKE(CustName)
D  NameArray                1          OVERLAY(WorkName)
D                                      DIM(%SIZE(WorkName))
D  ArrayLimit               3  0       INZ(%ELEM(NameArray))
```

In this example, we create a data structure to hold a work field and then describe the work field as an array of single-byte elements. The number of elements in the array is placed into the ArrayLimit variable. Should the size of the base field, CustName, ever change, recompiling the program would adjust all the sizes and values of the dependent variables.

☑ **Get rid of indicators. Use functions instead.**

Using Functions to Eliminate Indicators

You've already seen how you can use the INDDS indicator data structure to eliminate numbered indicators when communicating conditions to DDS display and printer files. Now you'll discover how to virtually eliminate resulting indicators from your program by using built-in functions. The BIFs we'll discuss in this section are %EOF, %FOUND, and %EQUAL.

Checking for End-of-File Using %EOF

Traditionally, RPG's READ*x* opcodes have required you to code a resulting indicator that sets itself on when the READ*x* operation encounters an end-of-file (or beginning-of-file) condition. That resulting indicator is no longer required, because the %EOF function takes its place. Consider the following comparison between RPG III and RPG IV.

RPG III

```
*...1....+....2....+....3....+....4....+....5....+....6....+....7...
CLØN01N02N03Factor1+++OpcdeFactor2+++ResultLenDHHiLoEqComments++++++
C                     READ CUSTMAST                99
C           *IN99     IFEQ *ON
...
C                     ENDIF
```

RPG IV

```
*.. 1 ...+... 2 ...+... 3 ...+... 4 ...+... 5 ...+... 6 ...+... 7 ...+... 8
/FREE
  READ CustMast;
    IF %EOF(CustMast);
    ...
    ENDIF;
  READ CustMast;
    IF  %EOF;                    // Equivalent code...file name is optional
    ...
    ENDIF;
/END-FREE
```

The %EOF function returns a true condition if the most recent READ*x* operation (or WRITE to a subfile) resulted in the end-of-file condition. The file name is optional; if you omit it, %EOF refers to the most recent file operation for any file.

Notice how much easier it is to read the RPG IV version than the RPG III version of this code. The %EOF notation documents the precise condition you're coding for, without any ambiguous numeric indicators. The RPG IV code is also less error-prone because the resulting indicator isn't isolated at the extreme right side of the specification.

Be aware that the Source Entry Utility (SEU) syntax checker no longer checks to ensure that the EOF resulting indicator is coded, because the indicator is no longer required.

Eureka! The %FOUND Function

Have you ever had the nagging feeling that the CHAIN opcode works backwards — because the resulting indicator turns *on* if the operation *fails*? Well, the %FOUND function sets things right again, returning a true condition if the CHAIN operation finds a record. %FOUND is the opposite condition of the NR (no record found) resulting indicator. %FOUND works with the CHECK, CHECKR, DELETE, LOOKUP, SCAN, SETGT, and SETLL opcodes, as well as with CHAIN. Here's how you use it:

```
*.. 1 ...+... 2 ...+... 3 ...+... 4 ...+... 5 ...+... 6 ...+... 7 ...+... 8
 /FREE
    CHAIN CustNbr CustMast;
    IF %FOUND(CustMast);
     ...
    ENDIF;
 /END-FREE
```

As with %EOF, the file name is optional if you want to refer to the most recent operation, but it's probably a good idea to explicitly code the file name.

If you truly can't get used to having CHAIN work in this positive manner, you can make it work the old way by using NOT in the expression:

```
*.. 1 ...+... 2 ...+... 3 ...+... 4 ...+... 5 ...+... 6 ...+... 7 ...+... 8
 /FREE
    CHAIN CustNbr CustMast;
    IF NOT %FOUND(CustMast);
     ...
    ENDIF;
 /END-FREE
```

When you use the traditional LOOKUP operation with the %FOUND function, you still need to use resulting indicators, to tell the program which type of LOOKUP it is to do (Hi, Lo, and/or Eq). If any of the LOOKUP conditions is successful, the %FOUND function returns a true condition:

```
*.. 1 ...+... 2 ...+... 3 ...+... 4 ...+... 5 ...+... 6 ...+... 7 ...+... 8
CLØNØ1Factor1+++++++Opcode(E)+Factor2+++++++Result+++++++Len++D+HiLoEq....
CLØNØ1Factor1+++++++Opcode(E)+Extended-factor2+++++++++++++++++++++++++++++
C        Search     LOOKUP     Names                              80  70
C                   IF         %FOUND
 ...
C                   ENDIF
```

In this example, the %FOUND function will be true if LOOKUP finds an array element greater than or equal to the Search field. Indicators 70 and 80 will also be set to match the LOOKUP result.

All Things %EQUAL

In addition to the %FOUND function, LOOKUP and SETLL can benefit from the %EQUAL function, which returns a true condition if the most recent LOOKUP or SETLL returned an exact match. The coding is the same as for the %FOUND condition:

```
*.. 1 ...+... 2 ...+... 3 ...+... 4 ...+... 5 ...+... 6 ...+... 7 ...+... 8
CLØNØ1Factor1+++++++Opcode(E)+Factor2+++++++Result++++++++Len++D+HiLoEq....
C        Search        LOOKUP    Names                              80 70
C                      SELECT
C                      WHEN      %EQUAL
  ...
C                      WHEN      %FOUND
  ...
C                      OTHER
  ...
C                      ENDIF
```

In this example, %EQUAL is true (and *IN70 is on) when the LOOKUP opcode finds an array element exactly equal to the Search field; %FOUND is true as well. If %FOUND is true but %EQUAL is not (i.e., if *IN80 is on but *IN70 is off), then an element greater than Search was found. If both conditions (and thus both indicators) are false, LOOKUP did not find an array element that satisfied the LOOKUP condition.

Using %LOOKUPxx Instead of LOOKUP

At Version 5, the %LOOKUP*xx* and %TLOOKUP*xx* functions effectively replace the LOOKUP operation code. %LOOKUP*xx* works with arrays; %TLOOKUP*xx* works with tables. %LOOKUP*xx* returns the index number of an array element that matches the search argument you specify; if a matching element is not found, %LOOKUP*xx* returns zero (0). The *xx* portion of the %LOOKUP function can be one of the following values:

Value	Action
(Blank)	Find an exact match (equal lookup).
LT	Find the element nearest to but less than the search argument.
LE	Find an exact match or the element nearest to but less than the search argument.
GE	Find an exact match or the element nearest to but greater than the search argument.
GT	Find the element nearest to but greater than the search argument.

The %LOOKUP function takes the following form:

```
%LOOKUP(search-argument:array{:starting-position{:number-of-elements}})
```

The first two arguments are the search argument and the array to be searched. The third (optional) argument can specify a starting position for the lookup, while the fourth (also optional) argument can limit the lookup to a specific number of elements. Here are some examples of %LOOKUP in action:

```
*.. 1 ...+... 2 ...+... 3 ...+... 4 ...+... 5 ...+... 6 ...+... 7 ...+... 8
  /FREE
    Index = %LOOKUP(Search:Names);
      IF Index > 0;                 // Equal lookup was successful
      ...
      ENDIF;

    Index = %LOOKUPGE(Search:Names);
      IF Index > 0;                 // Lookup found element >= search argument
      ...
      ENDIF;

    Index = %LOOKUP(Search:Names:2);
      IF Index > 0;                 // Equal lookup, starting at second
      ...                           // element, was successful
      ENDIF;
  /END-FREE
```

✓ **%LOOKUP*xx* and %TLOOKUP*xx* do not affect %FOUND or %EQUAL.**

Unlike the LOOKUP opcode, %LOOKUP*xx* does *not* set the value of %FOUND or %EQUAL (nor does %TLOOKUP*xx*, described next).

The %TLOOKUP*xx* function performs search operations on tables; it searches a table for an element that matches the search argument you specify. If the search is successful, %TLOOKUP*xx* returns an *ON condition and sets the current table element to the one that satisfies the search; if the %TLOOKUP*xx* search is not successful, the BIF returns *OFF. The *xx* in %TLOOKUP*xx* uses the same search conditions as %LOOKUP*xx*. This is the format for the %TLOOKUP*xx* function:

```
%TLOOKUP(search-argument:table{:alternate-table})
```

The third (optional) argument to %TLOOKUP*xx* lets you set the current element of a second table to its element that corresponds to the same element in the primary table. Here are some examples:

```
*.. 1 ...+... 2 ...+... 3 ...+... 4 ...+... 5 ...+... 6 ...+... 7 ...+... 8
  /FREE
    IF = %TLOOKUP(StateProv:TabState);
      State = TabState;             // StateProv was found in TabState
    ELSE;
      ...                           // StateProv is not in table
    ENDIF;

    IF = %TLOOKUP(StateProv:TabState:TabName);
      State = TabState;             // StateProv was found in TabState
      StName = TabName;             // %TLOOKUP also set TabName
    ELSE;
      ...                           // StateProv is not in table
    ENDIF;
  /END-FREE
```

☑ **Use BIFs to improve error checking.**

Error Handling with Built-in Functions

Three built-in functions give you a great deal of flexibility in coding error conditions that your program might encounter. These functions are %ERROR, %STATUS, and %OPEN.

%ERROR Checking

The %ERROR function replaces the ER resulting indicator position. %ERROR returns a true condition if the last opcode coded with an E error-handling extender ended in error. %ERROR is always related to the last E extender, and it is usually used in conjunction with the %STATUS function, discussed next.

What's Your %STATUS?

The %STATUS function gives you access to the internal codes that the system sets whenever the file status or program status changes, usually when an error occurs. These status codes are listed in Appendix B. You can code an optional file name to get the status code for a specific file. The following example uses %STATUS to check for status code 01218 (Unable to allocate record):

```
*.. 1 ...+... 2 ...+... 3 ...+... 4 ...+... 5 ...+... 6 ...+... 7 ...+... 8
 /FREE
    READ(E) CustMast;
    SELECT;
      WHEN %EOF;                              // End of file
        ...
      WHEN %ERROR AND %STATUS = 01218;        // Unable to allocate record
        Msg = 'Record locked';
      WHEN %ERROR;                            // Another error
        Msg = 'File error occurred';
      OTHER;
        ...
    ENDSL;
 /END-FREE
```

The %STATUS function doesn't require you to code a file information feedback data structure (INFDS), a file exception subroutine (INFSR), or a program exception subroutine (*PSSR). Nor does it require you to use the E extender, although %STATUS most often appears in connection with %ERROR, which does require the extender. The status codes are available to you whether or not you include any of these traditional error-handling techniques.

This File Is %OPEN for Business

If you explicitly control the open and close of files in your program, by specifying the USROPN F-spec keyword, you'll want to be able to check the open status of a file. The %OPEN BIF tells you whether the file is open (true) or closed (false). The function also tells you the current status of files opened implicitly by the program when it loaded.

You must specify the name of a file as the only argument to the function:

```
*.. 1 ...+... 2 ...+... 3 ...+... 4 ...+... 5 ...+... 6 ...+... 7 ...+... 8
 /FREE
    IF NOT %OPEN(CustMast);
      OPEN CustMast;
    ENDIF;
    READ(E) CustMast;
 /END-FREE
```

Data-Conversion Functions

RPG IV offers several BIFs that deal with data conversion. These functions are useful when it's important that your data be represented in a specific data type; for example, you might need to specifically force the result of an expression to be packed decimal, or you might need to half-adjust an intermediate portion of an expression, in addition to or instead of half-adjusting the entire expression itself. The functions we'll discuss to accomplish these requirements are %DEC*x*, %INT*x*, %UNS*x*, and %CHAR.

Other conversion BIFs relate to conversion of dates, times, and timestamps: %DATE, %TIME, %TIMESTAMP, %YEARS, %MONTHS, %DAYS, %HOURS, %MINUTES, %SECONDS, and %MSECONDS. We'll discuss these, and other date-related BIFs, in Chapter 9.

Converting to Packed Decimal with %DECx

The %DEC and %DECH functions convert the value of a numeric expression (in the first argument) to packed-decimal format, with the number of digits and decimal places you specify (in the second and third arguments). %DEC performs no rounding, while %DECH half-adjusts the result. The syntax is

```
%DECx(expression{:digits:decimals})
```

The %DECH function is particularly useful when you need to half-adjust a portion of an expression or each intermediate result in an expression. Consider the following examples:

```
*.. 1 ...+... 2 ...+... 3 ...+... 4 ...+... 5 ...+... 6 ...+... 7 ...+... 8
 /FREE
    EVAL(H) TotalPay = (RegHours * Rate)        +
                       (OvtHours * Rate * 1.5) +
                       (DblHours * Rate * 2);

    TotalPay = %DECH((RegHours*Rate):15:2)       +
               %DECH((OvtHours*Rate*1.5):15:2) +
               %DECH((DblHours*Rate*2):15:2);
 /END-FREE
```

In the first example, each intermediate result maintains its full precision, without rounding. Only when the full value of the expression is finally assigned to TotalPay will the result be rounded. In the second example, each intermediate expression in the larger complex expression is individually rounded and represented with a specific precision. When the full expression is assigned to TotalPay, no rounding is necessary. In the typical payroll calculation, the second method is more common.

Using %INTx and %UNSx

The %INT, %INTH, %UNS, and %UNSH functions convert the value of a numeric expression to integer or unsigned integer format, with or without half-adjusting. These functions truncate any decimal digits in the expression's value. They accept only a single argument — the expression itself:

```
*.. 1 ...+... 2 ...+... 3 ...+... 4 ...+... 5 ...+... 6 ...+... 7 ...+... 8
 /FREE
    Area = %UNSH(3.14159 * Radius**2);
 /END-FREE
```

A common use for these functions is to enable a decimal or floating-point value to be used as an array index. You can include the function without any intermediate result fields, as the following example shows.

```
*.. 1 ...+... 2 ...+... 3 ...+... 4 ...+... 5 ...+... 6 ...+... 7 ...+... 8
 /FREE
    LetterGrade = Arr(%INTH(TotRating/Responses));
 /END-FREE
```

This code would perform a calculation, half-adjusting the result and representing it as an integer. That integer would then be used as the index to an Arr element, whose value would be assigned to LetterGrade.

Using the %CHAR Function

The %CHAR BIF converts an expression's value to a character representation. This function lets you incorporate numeric, date, time, and timestamp values within character strings in your program:

```
*.. 1 ...+... 2 ...+... 3 ...+... 4 ...+... 5 ...+... 6 ...+... 7 ...+... 8
DName+++++++++++ETDsFrom+++To/L+++IDc.Keywords++++++++++++++++++++++++++++++++
D Msg             S             80     VARYING
D JobDate         S              D     INZ(*SYS) DATFMT(*USA)
D JobTime         S              T     INZ(*SYS) TIMFMT(*USA)

 /FREE
    Msg = 'Job started at ' + %TRIM(%CHAR(JobTime)) + ' on ' +
          %TRIM(%CHAR(JobDate)) + '.';
 /END-FREE
```

In this example, we are building a message string along the lines of "Job started at 5:08 PM on 2/20/2002." We use the %CHAR function to convert JobTime and JobDate to character representations and then use the %TRIM function to trim the blanks from the result. Because the expression could have a variable-length result, Msg must be a variable-length field.

For numeric fields and expressions, you can also use the %EDITC and %EDITW functions, discussed next, to convert to character representation.

Editing Expressions with Built-in Functions

The %EDITC BIF edits a numeric expression to achieve the same results as RPG's output edit code (or the DDS EDTCDE keyword). For example, the following expression would return to a 15-character field the string '*****6,543.21CR' (using RPG's A edit code):

```
*.. 1 ...+... 2 ...+... 3 ...+... 4 ...+... 5 ...+... 6 ...+... 7 ...+... 8
/FREE
   CreditAmt = %EDITC(0-6543.21:'A':*ASTFILL);
/END-FREE
```

The optional *ASTFILL indicates asterisk (*) fill. You could also omit the option, specify *CURSYM to float a local currency symbol in the result, or specify a currency symbol, as in the following example:

```
*.. 1 ...+... 2 ...+... 3 ...+... 4 ...+... 5 ...+... 6 ...+... 7 ...+... 8
/FREE
   PrintPay = %EDITC(NetPay:'1':'$');
/END-FREE
```

To complement the %EDITC BIF, the %EDITW function uses edit words to return the edited value of a numeric expression. This BIF performs the same function as RPG's output edit word or the DDS EDTWRD keyword. For example, you could edit a Social Security number or a telephone number. The edit word must be a constant (usually a named constant, described in definition specifications):

```
*.. 1 ...+... 2 ...+... 3 ...+... 4 ...+... 5 ...+... 6 ...+... 7 ...+... 8
DName++++++++++ETDsFrom+++To/L+++IDc.Keywords+++++++++++++++++++++++++++++++++
D EditSocSec      C                   '0   -   -   '
D EditPhone       C                   '0(   )&   -   '
```

```
/FREE
   PrintSSN=%EDITW(SocSecNbr:EditSocSec);
   PrtPhone=%EDITW(Telephone:EditPhone);
/END-FREE
```

If most of your output is to O-specs or a DDS-described device, such as a display file or a printer file, you may not have much need for these two functions. If you're dealing with client/server or Internet output, EDI applications, or other hardware platforms that don't know about edit codes and edit words, these functions let you edit expressions "on the fly" for those other platforms. You can also use them to format message strings:

```
*.. 1 ...+... 2 ...+... 3 ...+... 4 ...+... 5 ...+... 6 ...+... 7 ...+... 8
/FREE
   MsgLine = 'Today is ' + %TRIM(%EDITC(*DATE:'Y'));
   Progress = %EDITC(CurrRec:Z) + ' of ' +
              %EDITC(TotRec:Z) + 'records processed.';
/END-FREE
```

Pointing Toward %ADDR and %PADDR

The %ADDR and %PADDR BIFs are two of the vehicles that bring pointer support to RPG IV. Pointers are variables that contain the *address* of other variables (or procedures) in a program, instead of the contents of the other variables. We'll discuss pointers in more detail in Chapter 10, but for now here's a quick discussion of these two BIFs.

%ADDR puts the address of an item (a variable, an array element, or an expression) into a pointer. The result is a variable (of a new data type called *basing pointer*) with the address of the specified variable.

```
*.. 1 ...+... 2 ...+... 3 ...+... 4 ...+... 5 ...+... 6 ...+... 7 ...+... 8
DName++++++++++ETDsFrom+++To/L+++IDc.Keywords++++++++++++++++++++++++++++++
D DaysOfWeek      DS              9    DIM(7)
D   DayPtr        S                *   INZ(%ADDR(DaysOfWeek))
```

In the example above, variable DayPtr is a pointer to the address of the DaysOfWeek array. Notice that we define DayPtr with data type *, which indicates it's a pointer. The %ADDR function used with the INZ keyword serves to initialize the pointer with the address of the DaysOfWeek array.

We could change the value of the address in the pointer by assigning a new value to it in the calculations, as in the following example:

```
*.. 1 ...+... 2 ...+... 3 ...+... 4 ...+... 5 ...+... 6 ...+... 7 ...+... 8
 /FREE
      DayPtr = %ADDR(DaysOfWeek(4));
 /END-FREE
```

Here, we include the %ADDR BIF in an EVAL expression to assign the value of DayPtr to match the address of the fourth element of the DaysOfWeek array.

%PADDR returns the address of a procedure (program) entry point. The variable that receives the address must be a procedure pointer data type. You can use procedure pointers with the new CALLP (Call a Prototyped Procedure or Program) operation (and the earlier CALLB, or Call a Bound Procedure, operation) to execute a called procedure (or program) without explicitly naming it in the call.

We'll talk more about procedure pointers in Chapter 10 and more about the CALLB opcode in Chapter 13. For now, let's just look at a fixed-form example that defines a procedure pointer and uses the pointer — with static binding — to call a procedure:

```
*.. 1 ...+... 2 ...+... 3 ...+... 4 ...+... 5 ...+... 6 ...+... 7 ...+... 8
DName++++++++++ETDsFrom+++To/L+++IDc.Keywords++++++++++++++++++++++++++++++
CL0N01Factor1+++++++Opcode(E)+Factor2++++++Result++++++++Len++D+HiLoEq....
CL0N01Factor1+++++++Opcode(E)+Extended-factor2++++++++++++++++++++++++++++
D CustProc        S                *   PROCPTR
D                                      INZ(%PADDR('ADDCUST'))

C                     CALLB      CustProc
C                     EVAL       CustProc = %PADDR('DSPCUST')
C                     CALLB      CustProc
```

This example defines a procedure pointer (data type *) using the PROCPTR keyword. By using the %PADDR function with the INZ keyword, we initialize the pointer value to be the address of the ADDCUST procedure. Then in the C-specs, we can CALLB the ADDCUST procedure simply by referring to the pointer variable, CustProc. We can then use %PADDR to give CustProc the address of a new procedure to call and then perform another CALLB to execute the new DSPCUST procedure. Note that the procedure name is case-sensitive, so ADDCUST is not the same procedure as AddCust; this is consistent with requirements for C procedures.

Detecting Null Database Values

RPG IV adds support for null database fields, including support for nulls in date fields. Null database support is an especially useful alternative for the new date-related data types, which do not allow zero values. Using the %NULLIND BIF, you can test for a null value or set a field to a null value:

```
*.. 1 ...+... 2 ...+... 3 ...+... 4 ...+... 5 ...+... 6 ...+... 7 ...+... 8
H ALWNULL(*USRCTL)

 /FREE
    IF %NULLIND(ExpireDate);
      ...
    ENDIF;

    %NULLIND(ExpireDate) = *ON;
 /END-FREE
```

The %NULLIND function requires the database field in question to be null-capable; that is, it must have been coded in DDS using the ALWNULL keyword. In addition, the RPG program must include ALWNULL(*USRCTL) in the H-specs, or you must compile the program with the ALWNULL(*USRCTL) option of the CRTBNDRPG (Create Bound RPG Program) or CRTRPGMOD (Create RPG Module) command.

Using Variable-Length Fields

RPG IV lets you define and process variable-length character fields. String-handling operations, in particular, are considerably easier to read, and in some cases faster, when you use variable-length fields instead of traditional fixed-length fields. Variable-length fields have *two* lengths: a *declared length*, which is the maximum length they can occupy, and a *current length*, which can vary during processing and which generally reflects the length of the current value of the field. In storage, the RPG program will allocate the declared length *plus two bytes*, which the system internally uses to track the current length.

When you initialize a variable-length field or assign a value to it, the current length of the field is set to the length of the value. Consider the following examples:

```
*.. 1 ...+... 2 ...+... 3 ...+... 4 ...+... 5 ...+... 6 ...+... 7 ...+... 8
DName++++++++++ETDsFrom+++To/L+++IDc.Keywords+++++++++++++++++++++++++++++++
D Full            S             30    INZ('John Adams')
D                                     VARYING
D Middle          S             10    INZ('Quincy')
D                                     VARYING

 /FREE
    Full = 'John Kennedy';
    Middle = 'Fitzgerald';
 /END-FREE
```

In these examples, when the fields are initialized, Full's current length is 10 and Middle's current length is 6. When the expressions are processed, the fields get current lengths of 12 and 10, respectively. Incidentally, legacy operations, such as MOVE and MOVEL, do *not* affect the current length.

continued ...

Using Variable-Length Fields ... *Continued*

When you employ variable-length fields in string operations, you need not use the %TRIMx functions to strip them of blanks. The string operations will simply deal with the current lengths of the variable-length fields. In the following examples, notice how much easier it is to read the string operations that use variable-length fields; these operations perform faster as well.

```
*.. 1 ...+... 2 ...+... 3 ...+... 4 ...+... 5 ...+... 6 ...+... 7 ...+... 8
DName++++++++++ETDsFrom+++To/L+++IDc.Keywords++++++++++++++++++++++++++++++++
D CityFix         S             30       INZ('Billings')
D StateFix        S             10       INZ('Montana')

D CityVar         S             30       INZ('St. Louis')
D                                        VARYING
D StateVar        S             10       INZ('Missouri')
D                                        VARYING

/FREE
   String = %TRIM(CityFix) + ' ' + %TRIM(StateFix);  // Billings Montana
   String = CityVar + ' ' + StateVar;                // St. Louis Missouri
/END-FREE
```

%SIZE and %LEN

The %SIZE and %LEN built-in functions provide unique information for variable-length fields. The %SIZE function returns the declared size of a field *plus two bytes,* whereas the %LEN function returns the *current length* for a variable-length field:

```
*.. 1 ...+... 2 ...+... 3 ...+... 4 ...+... 5 ...+... 6 ...+... 7 ...+... 8
DName++++++++++ETDsFrom+++To/L+++IDc.Keywords++++++++++++++++++++++++++++++++
D Full            S             30       INZ('John Adams')
D                                        VARYING

/FREE
   X = %SIZE(Full);          // X=32
   X = %LEN(Full)';          // X=10
/END-FREE
```

You can also use the %LEN function on the left-hand side of an expression to change a field's current length and indirectly change its value:

```
*.. 1 ...+... 2 ...+... 3 ...+... 4 ...+... 5 ...+... 6 ...+... 7 ...+... 8
DName++++++++++ETDsFrom+++To/L+++IDc.Keywords++++++++++++++++++++++++++++++++
D Full            S             30       INZ('John Adams')
D                                        VARYING

/FREE
   %LEN(Full) = 4;           // Full = 'John'
   %LEN(Full) = 10;          // Full = 'JohnƄƄƄƄƄƄ'
/END-FREE
```

Notice that when we shorten the current length in this example, the value of the field is restricted to the value of the new length. When we subsequently increase the current length, the characters between the old length and the new length are set to blanks (shown as ƄƄƄƄƄƄ in the example).

Chapter 9

Using Date/Time Operations in RPG IV

Date and time data types are relatively new to OS/400 and are probably completely new to most RPG programmers because the language previously included only half-hearted support for date/time data types. RPG would convert these data types to character strings before processing them — *if* you specified CVTOPT(*DATETIME) on the CRTRPGPGM (Create RPG Program) command. RPG could do no date arithmetic, so most programmers were content with storing dates and times in numeric fields and then forcing the data through contrived routines to treat it as date or time data.

RPG IV, however, has competent support for date, time, and timestamp data types. It includes ways to define the data and use it in calculations. Now, for the first time in RPG, you can perform date arithmetic and comparisons with clarity and simplicity. In this chapter, we concentrate on date field support because most business programming uses dates more extensively than times or timestamps. Unless otherwise noted, however, the concepts also apply to fields with time and timestamp data types.

Defining Date and Time Data

Before you can perform calculations on date and time data types, you must know how to define the data. With RPG IV, you have three options: You can use date/time fields already defined in externally described database files, you can define date/time fields in the I-specs for program-described fields, or you can define date/time data in the D-specs for your program.

RPG IV groups three data types under the general heading of date fields: date, time, and timestamp. Date fields (data type D), of course, consist of a valid date, while time fields (data type T) store a time of day to seconds precision. Timestamp fields (data type Z) combine the date and time, storing a time value to 0.000001 second.

If your RPG IV program uses an externally described data file that contains date fields, no further definition in the program is necessary. Without any special notation for these fields, you can perform all the date calculations, manipulation, and testing we'll discuss in this chapter.

Program-described files also can contain specifications for date fields. The following example shows a program-described file with date, time, and timestamp fields:

```
*.. 1 ...+... 2 ...+... 3 ...+... 4 ...+... 5 ...+... 6 ...+... 7 ...+... 8
IFilename++SqNORiPos1+NCCPos2+NCCPos3+NCC.................................
I.....................Fmt+SPFrom+To+++DcField++++++++++L1M1FrPlMnZr......
ISalesTransNS 01
I                              D   1   10   TransDate
I                              T  11   18   TransTime
I                              Z  19   44   TransStamp
```

The data type column (36) defines TransDate, TransTime, and TransStamp as date (D), time (T), and timestamp (Z) fields, respectively.

In addition to defining date data types in files, you can define any variable with any of the date data types in D-specs. The following examples define standalone fields with date data types:

```
*.. 1 ...+... 2 ...+... 3 ...+... 4 ...+... 5 ...+... 6 ...+... 7 ...+... 8
DName++++++++++ETDsFrom+++To/L+++IDc.Keywords++++++++++++++++++++++++++++++++
D DateField       S            D
D TimeField       S            T
D StampField      S            Z
```

As with the I-spec, the D-spec uses the internal data type column (40) to indicate date, time, or timestamp data. When you describe a data variable with a D-spec, you need not indicate a from/to position or a length; the RPG compiler allocates the appropriate implied space.

Formatting Date and Time Data

When it comes to representing date/time fields internally in your RPG IV programs, you have a wide range of formatting choices. Each format has its own preset length and valid separator characters. The date and time formats require both leading and trailing zeros. Figure 9.1 lists the possible formats, separators, and internal lengths for data type D; Figure 9.2 shows information for data type T. When you indicate a length for a date/time field in RPG IV, it must correspond to the length shown in these tables.

FIGURE 9.1
Date Format Summary

Option	Description	Format	Valid separators	Example
*MDY	Month/day/year	mm/dd/yy	/ - , . & (blank)	12/31/97
*YMD	Year/month/day	yy/mm/dd	/ - , . & (blank)	97/12/31
*DMY	Day/month/year	dd/mm/yy	/ - , . & (blank)	31/12/97

continued ...

FIGURE 9.1 *CONTINUED*

Option	Description	Format	Valid separators	Example
*JUL	Julian	yy/ddd	/	97/365
			-	
			,	
			.	
			& (blank)	
*ISO	International Standards Organization	yyyy-mm-dd	-	1997-12-31
*USA	IBM USA standard	mm/dd/yyyy	/	12/31/1997
*EUR	IBM European standard	dd.mm.yyyy	.	31.12.1997
*JIS	Japanese industrial standard	yyyy-mm-dd	-	1997-12-31

FIGURE 9.2
Time Format Summary

Option	Description	Format	Valid separators	Example
*HMS	Hours:minutes:seconds	hh:mm:ss	:	19:30:00
			,	
			.	
			& (blank)	
*ISO	International Standards Organization	hh.mm.ss	.	19.30.00
*USA	IBM USA standard	hh:mm XM	:	07:30 PM
*EUR	IBM European standard	hh.mm.ss	.	19.30.00
*JIS	Japanese industrial standard	hh:mm:ss	:	19:30:00

Unlike D and T data types, timestamp fields (type Z) have only one internal format in RPG IV:

yyyy-mm-dd-hh.mm.ss.uuuuuu

The timestamp format is always 26 characters long. For example, the following is a valid timestamp value:

1997-12-31-19.30.00.135791

Leading zeros are required. If you don't specify a microseconds value in a timestamp, the system will pad to the right with zeros:

1997-12-31-19.30.00.000000

☑ Two-digit year formats support the years 1940–2039 only.

Notice in Figure 9.1 that four of the date formats (*MDY, *YMD, *DMY, and *JUL) represent the year as two digits instead of four. These formats support only dates between 1940 and 2039, inclusive. Year values from 40 to 99 will be treated as 1940–1999, while year values below 40 will be treated as 2000–2039. The system will always use these assumptions if it stores the dates externally.

☑ The default date/time format is *ISO.

RPG's default internal format for date/time variables is *ISO. You can specify a different default within a program by including the DATFMT and/or TIMFMT keyword in the control specifications (H-specs) for the program, as the following example shows:

```
*.. 1 ...+... 2 ...+... 3 ...+... 4 ...+... 5 ...+... 6 ...+... 7 ...+... 8
HKeywords+++++++++++++++++++++++++++++++++++++++++++++++++++++++++++++++++++
H DATFMT(*USA/)
H TIMFMT(*HMS:)
```

A related keyword, DATEDIT, specifies the format (*MDY, *YMD, or *DMY) of numeric fields used as dates, such as *DATE or UDATE. Note that these fields are not actually native dates but numbers that your program will edit as dates with the Y edit code. You must perform special calculations to process these fields as dates.

If you want to specify a date/time format at the field level, do it in the D-specs, as in the following examples:

```
*.. 1 ...+... 2 ...+... 3 ...+... 4 ...+... 5 ...+... 6 ...+... 7 ...+... 8
DName++++++++++ETDsFrom+++To/L+++IDc.Keywords++++++++++++++++++++++++++++++++
D DateField      S               D   DATFMT(*USA/)
D TimeField      S               T   TIMFMT(*HMS:)
```

If a date/time field is part of a program-described file, the hierarchy changes somewhat. For key fields, RPG looks first to the file's DATFMT or TIMFMT keyword if it is in the F-spec, then moves on to the H-spec, and then to *ISO format. For other date/time fields in files, RPG takes the following path to decide the format:

1. the field's I-spec entry in positions 31–35
2. the file's F-spec DATFMT/TIMFMT keyword
3. the H-spec's DATFMT/TIMFMT keyword
4. *ISO

The following sample code illustrates the use of keywords to format date/time fields in F-specs and I-specs:

```
*.. 1 ...+... 2 ...+... 3 ...+... 4 ...+... 5 ...+... 6 ...+... 7 ...+... 8
FFilename++IPEASFRLen+LKLen+AIDevice+.Keywords++++++++++++++++++++++++++++++++
IFilename++SqNORiPos1+NCCPos2+NCCPos3+NCC....................................
I.......................Fmt+SPFrom+To+++DcField++++++++++L1M1FrPLMnZr......
FSalesTransIPE F    132     4D DISK    DATFMT(*USA/)
ISalesTransNS 01
I                              *USA/D   1   10  TransDate
I                              *HMS:T  11   18  TransTime
I                                   Z  19   44  TransStamp
```

Initializing Date and Time Fields

You can set date and time fields to an initial value when a program begins, just as you can initialize other data types. Use the INZ D-spec keyword to initialize any data type, including date, time, and timestamp data types. You can specify INZ either with or without an initial value parameter. If you don't specify a value, the system will use the default date value January 1, 0001. The following code illustrates initialization for date-related fields.

```
*.. 1 ...+... 2 ...+... 3 ...+... 4 ...+... 5 ...+... 6 ...+... 7 ...+... 8
DName++++++++++ETDsFrom+++To/L+++IDc.Keywords+++++++++++++++++++++++++++++++
H DATFMT(*ISO)
D DateField1      S             D   INZ
D DateField2      S             D   DATFMT(*USA/)
D                               D   INZ
D DateField3      S             D   DATFMT(*USA/)
D                                   INZ(D'1997-12-31')
```

In these examples, DateField1 would begin the program with a value of January 1, 0001, and would be represented in the RPG program using the *ISO date format specified in the H-spec: 0001-01-01. The next field, DateField2, would also have a value of January 1, 0001, but would be represented in *USA format: 01/01/0001.

✓ **Initial date values must match the H-spec DATFMT format.**

The third field, DateField3, would begin life with a value of December 31, 1997, and would be represented in the RPG program in *USA format: 12/31/1997. Notice that even though the program is using *USA format to represent DateField3 in the third example, you must initialize the field using *ISO format; the constant value that you specify with the INZ keyword must match the DATFMT in the H-spec (or *ISO format, if you don't use an H-spec DATFMT keyword). If it is present, the H-spec DATFMT keyword dictates the format of all date literals in the RPG program.

How OS/400 Stores Date/Time Data

The OS/400 database stores date/time data types in a system-determined size and format external to the RPG IV program. Dates are always four bytes long; times are three bytes long; timestamps are 10 bytes long. Regardless of the format you use, UDB/400 will use these predetermined lengths when storing the data.

This architecture offers a couple of obvious advantages: The external data length conserves disk space, and you can perform date/time comparisons without worrying about the format. For example, you can accurately compare a date field in *MDY format with another field in *ISO format without performing any format conversion.

Interestingly, you cannot see the "raw" date data in its external format. The system will always convert the data to the format you specify before presenting it to a program. Even IBM-supplied commands, such as DSPFFD (Display File Field Description) and DSPPFM (Display Physical File Member), will seem to indicate that the data is stored formatted, occupying all the space the format demands. Because of this characteristic of the database, you must specify formatted lengths when using date/time fields in an RPG program.

Time fields follow the same rules as date fields when it comes to initial values. In the case of time fields, the default value is midnight (00:00). The following examples illustrate initialization of time fields.

```
*.. 1 ...+... 2 ...+... 3 ...+... 4 ...+... 5 ...+... 6 ...+... 7 ...+... 8
DName++++++++++ETDsFrom+++To/L+++IDc.Keywords++++++++++++++++++++++++++++++++
H TIMFMT(*ISO)
D TimeField1      S                      D   INZ
D TimeField2      S                      D   DATFMT(*HMS:)
D                                        D   INZ
D TimeField3      S                      D   DATFMT(*HMS:)
D                                        D   INZ(T'19.30.00')
```

Again, in the third example, the initial value must be in *ISO format — even though the field itself is in *HMS format — because the H-spec indicates *ISO format.

Timestamp fields have only one format, so there's no confusion about how to initialize them. The following examples initialize timestamp fields.

```
*.. 1 ...+... 2 ...+... 3 ...+... 4 ...+... 5 ...+... 6 ...+... 7 ...+... 8
DName++++++++++ETDsFrom+++To/L+++IDc.Keywords++++++++++++++++++++++++++++++++
D TimeStamp1      S                      D   INZ
D TimeStamp2      S                      D   INZ(Z'1997-12-31-19.30.00.000000')
```

The default initial value for timestamps is midnight, January 1, 0001:

0001-01-01-00.00.00.000000

With the D-spec INZ keyword, and with C-spec assignment expressions, you can move low values (*LOVAL) and high values (*HIVAL) to date and time fields, just as you can with other data types. Figure 9.3 lists the *LOVAL and *HIVAL values for each date format; Figure 9.4 shows the values for time fields.

FIGURE 9.3
Date Field *LOVAL and *HIVAL Values

Format	*LOVAL	*HIVAL
*MDY	01/01/40	12/31/39
*YMD	40/01/01	39/12/31
*DMY	01/01/40	31/12/39
*JUL	40/001	39/365
*ISO	0001-01-01	9999-12-31
*USA	01/01/0001	12/31/9999
*EUR	01.01.0001	31.12.9999
*JIS	0001-01-01	9999-12-31

FIGURE 9.4
Time Field *LOVAL and *HIVAL Values

Format	*LOVAL	*HIVAL
*HMS	00:00:00	24:00:00
*ISO	00.00.00	24.00.00
*USA	00:00 AM	12:00 AM
*EUR	00.00.00	24.00.00
*JIS	00:00:00	24:00:00

Notice that the date formats that use only two-digit years (*MDY, *YMD, *DMY, and *JUL) have entirely different *LOVAL and *HIVAL values than the other date formats. The *LOVAL for a timestamp field is the same as the default:

0001-01-01-00.00.00.000000

A timestamp's *HIVAL is

9999-12-31-24.00.00.000000

You can also code date, time, and timestamp fields with INZ(*SYS) to initialize them to the system date or time. You can initialize date fields to the job date as well, by coding INZ(*JOB).

Using Date Fields in Calculations

Once you've defined date and time fields, you can process them in your program's C-specs. You can perform many comparisons and assignments using the same opcodes and expressions you use with other data types. (Not all operations work with date data types, however; for example, you can't use ADD or SUB to add or subtract date data.) Two date/time constants or variables used in assignment or comparison operations need not be in the same format. You can compare, for example, a date in *MDY format with one in *ISO format.

In addition to supporting date data in many traditional operations, RPG IV features a dozen specialized date operations and built-in functions. The functions convert expressions to dates and *durations* so that you can use them in free-form expressions. A duration, or interval, is simply a means of expressing a value to represent an amount of time (e.g., years, months, days) that you want to incorporate into an expression. These new functions are

- %DATE (Convert value to date)
- %DAYS (Convert value to days duration)
- %DIFF (Calculate difference between two dates/times/timestamps)
- %HOURS (Convert value to hours duration)
- %MINUTES (Convert value to minutes duration)
- %MONTHS (Convert value to months duration)

- %MSECONDS (Convert value to microseconds duration)
- %SECONDS (Convert value to seconds duration)
- %SUBDT (Extract a portion of a date/time/timestamp)
- %TIME (Convert value to time)
- %TIMESTAMP (Convert value to timestamp)
- %YEARS (Convert value to years duration)

In addition to these functions, the new TEST operation code tests the value of a date, time, or timestamp to verify its validity.

Take Advantage of the New Date, Time, and Timestamp Data Types

RPG IV adds support for several new data types, perhaps the most important of which are date, time, and timestamp data types. These aren't new to OS/400; they are merely new to RPG, having been introduced with V2R1.1 and supported since by SQL. These data types, as well as the new operations provided for them, let you write more concise, correct code in less time.

The date data type can store any valid date from 01/01/0001 through 12/31/9999, the time data type can store any time to the second (i.e., *hh:mm:ss*), and the timestamp data type combines date, time, and microsecond values (useful for such applications as a client billing or tracing facility, in which precise timing is critical).

RPG IV's date support includes the ability to perform date and time arithmetic; thus, RPG IV can add values to and subtract them from date/time/timestamp data types using new date-related functions with free-form expressions. RPG finally lets you perform direct date and time arithmetic without kludgy data structures and mysterious MOVE and MULT opcodes.

You'll probably want to design new file layouts to take advantage of the date and time data types, but what about old files that use a numeric field as a date? Can you use RPG IV's date arithmetic with those fields? Certainly! The new date functions let you convert integer or character values into a date data-type variable and then perform arithmetic on the converted values.

Date Arithmetic in Free-form Expressions

You can include date, time, or timestamp data in a free-form expression to add or subtract a duration (interval) to or from a date or time or to calculate the interval between two dates, times, or timestamps. To add or subtract a duration, you must use a built-in function to specify which of several valid duration types you want to calculate:

- %YEARS
- %MONTHS
- %DAYS
- %HOURS

- %MINUTES
- %SECONDS
- %MSECONDS (microseconds)

Each of these functions converts a number (up to 15 digits) to the specified duration, so that you can simply use the + or – operator in a free-form expression to add or subtract dates, times, or timestamps. These functions can appear only on the right-hand side of an assignment expression; the left-hand side must be a date, time, or timestamp. The following examples illustrate some uses of date addition:

```
*.. 1 ...+... 2 ...+... 3 ...+... 4 ...+... 5 ...+... 6 ...+... 7 ...+... 8
/FREE
   MatureDate = NoteDate + %YEARS(TermYears);
   MatureDate = MatureDate + %MONTHS(TermMonths);
   MatureDate = MatureDate + %DAYS(TermDays);
/END-FREE
```

In this coding example, RPG IV calculates the maturity date of a loan, adding the years, months, and days that represent the loan's term. The expression's result (MatureDate in the example) must be of a type consistent with the duration type (e.g., you cannot add a microsecond to a date, or type D, field).

Let's look at a few more examples, including a couple of examples of subtraction.

```
*.. 1 ...+... 2 ...+... 3 ...+... 4 ...+... 5 ...+... 6 ...+... 7 ...+... 8
/FREE
   NoteDate = NoteDate + %DAYS(90);        // Add 90 days to NoteDate
   NoteDate = NoteDate + %DAYS(-90);       // Subtract 90 days from NoteDate
   NoteDate = NoteDate - %DAYS(90);        // Subtract 90 days from NoteDate
   SKingTitle = T'00.00.00' + %MINUTES(4);
   CloseTime = T'03.00.00'  - %MINUTES(15);
/END-FREE
```

The first example here, which adds 90 days to NoteDate, demonstrates that the interval can be a literal (it may also be a constant). If the interval is negative, RPG IV subtracts the interval rather than adds it; usually, however, you'll want to use the – operator to subtract dates, as the third example illustrates, so your code will be clearer. In the final two examples, we calculate four past midnight by adding four minutes to the time literal in the expression, and we calculate "quarter to three" by subtracting 15 minutes from yet another time literal.

Notice that we indicate the time literal by preceding it with a T; similarly, a date literal would be preceded by a D, and a timestamp literal by a Z. The H-spec DATFMT and TIMFMT keywords determine the format of date/time literals; if the keyword is omitted, RPG uses *ISO format.

Usually, the result of date arithmetic is self-evident, and RPG IV will always ensure that the result is a valid date, time, or timestamp. If the result is a timestamp field and the ADDDUR (Add Duration) operation causes the result to cross a midnight boundary, RPG IV will automatically adjust the date portion of the timestamp to ensure accuracy. If an addition using %MONTHS or %YEARS will result in an invalid date (e.g., February 30), RPG IV will use the end of the month instead; the effect may not be reversible. To understand how RPG IV will handle the end of the month, consider the following examples:

```
*.. 1 ...+... 2 ...+... 3 ...+... 4 ...+... 5 ...+... 6 ...+... 7 ...+... 8
/FREE
    XDate = D'2002-01-31' + %MONTHS(1);               // XDate = 2002-02-28
    XDate = D'2004-01-31' + %MONTHS(1);               // XDate = 2004-02-29
    XDate = D'2002-01-31' + %MONTHS(1) + %MONTHS(1);  // XDate = 2002-03-28
    XDate = D'2002-01-31' + %MONTHS(1) - %MONTHS(1);  // XDate = 2002-01-28
    XDate = D'2002-01-31' + %MONTHS(2);               // XDate = 2002-03-31
/END-FREE
```

What's the %DIFFerence?

The %DIFF function offers an additional twist: the ability to subtract two date/time/timestamp fields, constants, or literals to determine the interval between them. The following examples show how you do this.

```
*.. 1 ...+... 2 ...+... 3 ...+... 4 ...+... 5 ...+... 6 ...+... 7 ...+... 8
/FREE
    AgeInDays = %DIFF(Today:BirthDate:*DAYS);       // Calculate age in days

                     // Determine number of microseconds between two timestamps
    JobMSeconds = %DIFF(JobEnd:JobStart:*MSECONDS);

    XDiff = %DIFF(D'2003-12-30':D'2002-12-31':*YEARS);    // XDiff = 0
    XDiff = %DIFF(D'2003-12-30':D'2002-12-31':*MONTHS);   // XDiff = 11
    XDiff = %DIFF(D'2003-12-30':D'2002-12-31':*DAYS);     // XDiff = 364
/END-FREE
```

The %DIFF function returns a number (up to 15 digits). The result is rounded down and does not consider any remainder. The first two arguments in the %DIFF function are the two dates, times, or timestamps to be compared. The third argument is a duration code representing the duration to be returned. The duration code may be

- *YEARS (or *Y)
- *MONTHS (or *M)
- *DAYS (or *D)
- *HOURS (or *H)
- *MINUTES (or *MN)
- *SECONDS (or *S)
- *MSECONDS (or *MS) (microseconds)

The first two arguments need not be in the same format; indeed, they need not even be of the same data type. You can use %DIFF to calculate the interval between

- two dates (using *YEARS, *MONTHS, *DAYS)
- two times (using *HOURS, *MINUTES, *SECONDS)
- two timestamps
- a date and a timestamp (using *YEARS, *MONTHS, *DAYS)
- a time and a timestamp (using *HOURS, *MINUTES, *SECONDS)

Using the %SUBDT Function

RPG IV's %SUBDT function extracts a portion of a date/time/timestamp field and returns it to a free-form expression. For example, you could use this function to isolate the month in a date field, as in the first of the following examples:

```
*.. 1 ...+... 2 ...+... 3 ...+... 4 ...+... 5 ...+... 6 ...+... 7 ...+... 8
 /FREE
    NoteMonth = %SUBDT(NoteDate:*MONTHS);

    WitchingHour = %SUBDT(Midnight:*HOURS);

    MicroSecs = %SUBDT(TStamp:*MSECONDS);
 /END-FREE
```

The two arguments to the %SUBDT function specify the date/time/timestamp field and the duration code of the portion to extract. The function returns an unsigned number. You can use %SUBDT with any date/time format. If the date is in a format that supports only two-digit years (e.g., *MDY, *YMD), %SUBDT will return a four-digit year (1940–2039). If the date is in *JUL format, the *DAYS portion will always return the day of the month, not the day of the year.

Maintaining a Legacy: ADDDUR and SUBDUR

Before Version 5, RPG IV could not use date data within EVAL expressions. Instead, three new fixed-format operation codes performed date arithmetic (these opcodes worked with dates, times, and timestamps):

- ADDDUR (Add duration to a date)
- SUBDUR (Subtract a duration, or determine the difference between two dates)
- EXTRCT (Extract a portion of a date)

Version 5 effectively renders these new opcodes obsolete, replacing them with date BIFs. You'll probably encounter them, however, when maintaining older code.

ADDDUR (Add Duration)

The ADDDUR operation adds the duration specified in Factor 2 to a date or time; the result is a date, time, or timestamp. You must use a duration code to specify which duration type you want to calculate. The following examples illustrate some uses of the ADDDUR operation.

```
*.. 1 ...+... 2 ...+... 3 ...+... 4 ...+... 5 ...+... 6 ...+... 7 ...+... 8
CL0N01Factor1++++++Opcode(E)+Factor2++++++Result++++++++Len++D+HiLoEq....
C        NoteDate       ADDDUR    TermYears:*Y  MatureDate
C                       ADDDUR    TermMonths:*M MatureDate
C                       ADDDUR    TermDays:*D   MatureDate
 *                                              Add 90 days to NoteDate
C                       ADDDUR    90:*DAYS      NoteDate
 *                                              Subtract 90 days from NoteDate
C                       ADDDUR    -90:*D        NoteDate
 *                                              Calculate 4 minutes past midnight
C        T'00.00.00'    ADDDUR    4:*MN         SKingTitle
```

continued ...

Maintaining a Legacy: ADDDUR and SUBDUR ... *Continued*

When you use ADDDUR, Factor 2 of the C-spec must contain two parts: the interval to be added and the duration code. The duration cannot exceed 15 digits.

Note that Factor 1 is optional, just as it is with RPG's ADD opcode. If you use it, Factor 1 must be a date, time, or timestamp field, subfield, array, element, literal, or constant. The data type of any field, array, or element must match the data type of the result field. The result field must be of a type consistent with the duration type (e.g., you cannot add a microsecond to a date, or type D, field).

If the result field is a date or time field, RPG IV will ensure that the result is always a valid date or time. If the result is a timestamp field and ADDDUR causes the result to cross a midnight boundary, RPG IV will automatically adjust the date portion of the timestamp to ensure accuracy.

SUBDUR (Subtract Duration)

The SUBDUR operation complements ADDDUR, subtracting a duration from a date/time/timestamp field and resulting in another date/time/timestamp field, as in the following examples.

```
*.. 1 ...+... 2 ...+... 3 ...+... 4 ...+... 5 ...+... 6 ...+++++++Len++D+HiLoEq....
CLØNØ1Factor1+++++++Opcode(E)+Factor2++++++Result+++++++Len++D+HiLoEq....
 *                                                  Subtract 90 days from NoteDate
C                        SUBDUR      90:*D          NoteDate
 *                                                  Calculate "quarter to three"
C          T'Ø3.ØØ.ØØ'   SUBDUR      15:*MN         CloseTime
```

As with ADDDUR, SUBDUR will always result in a valid time without any further checking. Timestamp values require no data adjustments if the time portion crosses midnight.

The SUBDUR opcode has an alternate format that performs the same function as the %DIFF BIF, calculating the interval between two dates, times, or timestamps. The following examples illustrate how you do this.

```
*.. 1 ...+... 2 ...+... 3 ...+... 4 ...+... 5 ...+... 6 ...+... 7 ...+... 8
CLØNØ1Factor1+++++++Opcode(E)+Factor2++++++Result+++++++Len++D+HiLoEq....
 *                                                  Calculate age in days
C          Today        SUBDUR      BirthDate      AgeInDays:*D
 *                       Determine number of microseconds between two timestamps
C          JobEnd        SUBDUR      JobStart       JobSeconds:*MS
```

The result field is in two parts: a zero-decimal numeric field, array, or array element; and a duration code. If the value of Factor 1 is earlier than Factor 2, the result will be negative.

EXTRCT (Extract Date/Time/Timestamp)

The EXTRCT (Extract) operation extracts a portion of a date/time/timestamp field and moves it into the result field. For example:

```
*.. 1 ...+... 2 ...+... 3 ...+... 4 ...+... 5 ...+... 6 ...+... 7 ...+... 8
CLØNØ1Factor1+++++++Opcode(E)+Factor2++++++Result+++++++Len++D+HiLoEq....
C                        EXTRCT      NoteDate:*M    NoteMonth

C                        EXTRCT      Midnight:*H    WitchingHr

C                        EXTRCT      TStamp:*MS     MicroSecs
```

Factor 1 must be blank. Factor 2 contains both the date/time/timestamp field and the duration code, separated by a colon (:). The EXTRCT opcode uses the duration code to determine which portion of the field to extract.

continued ...

Maintaining a Legacy: ADDDUR and SUBDUR ... *Continued*

The result field is cleared before RPG assigns the value to it. The result field can be either a character variable or a numeric variable; RPG IV will left-adjust the data in a character field and right-adjust the data in a numeric field.

You can use EXTRCT with any date/time format. If you use a format that supports only two-digit years (e.g., *MDY or *YMD), EXTRCT will extract only a two-digit year into the result.

☑ **The TEST operation checks for valid date values.**

Using the TEST Operation

The new TEST operation tests the validity of date, time, and timestamp fields. This opcode ensures that the value of a date/time field is valid before you use it in your program. Consider the following example.

```
*.. 1 ...+... 2 ...+... 3 ...+... 4 ...+... 5 ...+... 6 ...+... 7 ...+... 8
/FREE
    TEST(E) QuitTime;
      IF %ERROR;
        ...
      ENDIF;
/END-FREE
```

In this example, QuitTime is a time data type field. The %ERROR function will be set on if TEST determines that QuitTime is not a valid time value. The field to be tested can be of the date (D), time (T), or timestamp (Z) data type.

Note that RPG's date/time operations will not generate an invalid date/time/timestamp value. There may be some cases, however, in which a program is able to corrupt a date/time/timestamp field. For example, if you include a date field as part of a data structure and then overlay a portion or the entire date field with another field, it would be possible to move invalid data into the date field. The following code shows how you could create invalid data.

```
*.. 1 ...+... 2 ...+... 3 ...+... 4 ...+... 5 ...+... 6 ...+... 7 ...+... 8
DName+++++++++++ETDsFrom+++To/L+++IDc.Functions+++++++++++++++++++++++++++++++
D                       DS
D  WorkDate                        D    DATFMT(*ISO)
D                                       INZ(D'1996-12-31')
D  NumYear                         4S 0 OVERLAY(WorkDate:1)
D  NumMonth                        2S 0 OVERLAY(WorkDate:6)
D  NumDay                          2S 0 OVERLAY(WorkDate:9)

/FREE
   NumMonth = 13;
   TEST(E) WorkDate;
     IF %ERROR;
       ...
     ENDIF;
/END-FREE
```

In this example, %ERROR would be set on because WorkDate contains an invalid month.

In addition to testing date/time fields, the TEST opcode can test *numeric or character fields* for valid date, time, or timestamp data. In these cases, you must use an operation extender with the opcode to tell RPG IV which test you want to perform. Take a look at the following examples.

```
*.. 1 ...+... 2 ...+... 3 ...+... 4 ...+... 5 ...+... 6 ...+... 7 ...+... 8
H DATFMT(*ISO)

/FREE
    CheckDate = 19971231;
    TEST(DE) CheckDate;
      IF %ERROR;
        ...
      ENDIF;

    CheckDate = 19971231;
    TEST(DE) *USA CheckDate;
      IF %ERROR;
        ...
      ENDIF;

    CheckDate = 12311997;
    TEST(DE) *USA CheckDate;
      IF %ERROR;
        ...
      ENDIF;

    QuitTime = 170000;
    TEST(TE) *HMS QuitTime;
      IF %ERROR;
        ...
      ENDIF;
/END-FREE
```

Notice the use of the operation extender in these examples: TEST(D) for dates, TEST(T) for times, and TEST(Z) for timestamps (not shown). Assume that CheckDate and QuitTime are numeric fields.

First, the value of CheckDate is tested to see whether it's a valid date. If you don't specify a format keyword indicating which date/time format to test, RPG will test for the format specified in the control specification DATFMT keyword; if there is no such keyword, the program will use *ISO format. Because CheckDate is a valid *ISO date value, %ERROR will be set off.

The second example is similar, except that the test will be for a *USA format date. Because the value is not in *USA format, %ERROR will be set on. The next example will find a valid *USA date, so %ERROR will be set off. Last, because QuitTime is a valid time in *HMS format, %ERROR will be set off.

☑ TEST supports additional date formats.

In addition to the valid date/time formats we've discussed, TEST supports the use of the *CYMD format, which stores dates in a *cyymmdd* format, in which *c* is a number that indicates the century:

- 0 = 1900s
- 1 = 2000s
- 2 = 2100s

. . .

- 9 = 2800s

In this format, the date December 31, 1999, would be represented by 0991231, and January 1, 2000, by 1000101. The IBM midrange uses this format widely to store dates in numeric or character fields. Dates processed in this format fit into different ranges than other formats that store dates with two-digit years; they can include dates between the years 1900 and 2899, inclusive. This format, along with *CMDY and *CDMY, is valid only with the TEST and MOVE (discussed elsewhere) operations.

TEST and MOVE also let you code *LONGJUL in Factor 1 to indicate a date value stored in *ccyymmdd* format. Yet another option, *JOBRUN, tells the TEST and MOVE operations to get the date format from the job's attributes.

The principle behind the TEST operation remains the same if it tests character fields. When it tests character fields, however, RPG also will check to see whether valid separator characters exist in the character value. The following examples illustrate the use of TEST with character fields (the tested fields are character fields with lengths matching their values).

```
*.. 1 ...+... 2 ...+... 3 ...+... 4 ...+... 5 ...+... 6 ...+... 7 ...+... 8
H DATFMT(*ISO)

/FREE
   CheckDate = '1997-12-31';
   TEST(DE) CheckDate;
     IF %ERROR;
       ...
     ENDIF;

   CheckDate = '12/31/1997';
   TEST(DE) *USA CheckDate;
     IF %ERROR;
       ...
     ENDIF;

   BirthDate = '048/08/12';
   TEST(DE) *CYMD/ BirthDate;
     IF %ERROR;
       ...
     ENDIF;
```

continued ...

continued ...

```
*.. 1 ...+... 2 ...+... 3 ...+... 4 ...+... 5 ...+... 6 ...+... 7 ...+... 8
    BirthDate = '055 04 23';
    TEST(DE) *CYMD& BirthDate;
      IF %ERROR;
        ...
      ENDIF;

    GradDate = '0660603';
    TEST(DE) *CYMD0 GradDate;
      IF %ERROR;
        ...
      ENDIF;
/END-FREE
```

To specify the absence of separator characters in a character field tested as a date, you must code a zero (0) immediately following the format, as shown in the last example above. To specify blank separators, use an ampersand (&).

Using Date Operations with Legacy Data

Because date/time/timestamp data types are relatively recent database enhancements, and because RPG has heretofore not supported them very well, you may find that many of the database files on your system contain dates in either character or numeric fields. You may also have separated the month, day, and year portions of dates into separate database fields. Even with this "legacy" data on your system, you can still take advantage of much of the new support for date/time data.

Four new functions support conversion between date-related data and numeric or character data:

- %CHAR (Convert to character representation)
- %DATE (Convert to date)
- %TIME (Convert to time)
- %TIMESTAMP (Convert to timestamp)

When an expression evaluates date, time, or timestamp data exclusively, you can use simple assignment expressions to "convert" date/time/timestamp fields from one format to another. In the following example, the expression moves an *MDY format date into an *ISO format date.

```
*.. 1 ...+... 2 ...+... 3 ...+... 4 ...+... 5 ...+... 6 ...+... 7 ...+... 8
DName++++++++++ETDsFrom+++To/L+++IDc.Functions++++++++++++++++++++++++++++++
CL0N01Factor1+++++++Opcode(E)+Factor2++++++Result+++++++Len++D+HiLoEq....
D MDYDate         S               D   DATFMT(*MDY)
D ISODate         S               D   DATFMT(*ISO)

 /FREE
    ISODate = MDYDate;
 /END-FREE
```

In one simple expression, this example converts the date format.

The %DATE, %TIME, and %TIMESTAMP functions convert numeric or character fields to dates, times, and timestamps. These functions take the form

```
%DATE(expression{:format})
%TIME(expression{:format})
%TIMESTAMP(expression{:*ISO|*ISO0})
```

The first argument to these functions is the value to convert. For %DATE and %TIME, it must be character, numeric, or timestamp data; for %TIMESTAMP, it must be character, numeric, or date data. If you omit this argument, the function will return current system data (system date, system time, or system timestamp). The second argument is the date/time format for numeric or character data; for %TIMESTAMP, if you specify this argument, you must specify *ISO or *ISO0. If the first parameter is a timestamp, *DATE, or UDATE, leave the second parameter blank.

The following example shows how you might use these functions to age an invoice record from a file that stores DueYMD as an eight-byte, packed-decimal field in *yyyymmdd* format.

```
*.. 1 ...+... 2 ...+... 3 ...+... 4 ...+... 5 ...+... 6 ...+... 7 ...+... 8
DName++++++++++ETDsFrom+++To/L+++IDc.Functions+++++++++++++++++++++++++++++
CLØNØ1Factor1+++++++Opcode(E)+Factor2++++++Result++++++++Len++D+HiLoEq....
D DueDate         S                   D
D Today           S                   D
D AgeDays         S                  5P Ø

 /FREE
    Today = %DATE();                            // Current system date
    DueDate = %DATE(DueYMD:*ISO);
    AgeDays = %DIFF(Today:DueDate:*DAYS);
 /END-FREE
```

To go in the other direction, you can also use built-in functions to convert dates to numeric or character fields:

```
*.. 1 ...+... 2 ...+... 3 ...+... 4 ...+... 5 ...+... 6 ...+... 7 ...+... 8
DName++++++++++ETDsFrom+++To/L+++IDc.Functions+++++++++++++++++++++++++++++
D ISODate         S                   D   DATFMT(*ISO)
D ISONum          S                  8P Ø
D ISOChar         S                 10A

 /FREE
    ISONum = %SUBDT(ISODate:*Y) * 10000 + %SUBDT(IsoDate:*M) * 100 +
             %SUBDT(IsoDate:*D);
    ISOChar = %CHAR(ISODate:*ISO);
 /END-FREE
```

Remember that the %CHAR function converts a date to character representation complete with separators (unless you specify no separators in the format, such as *ISO0). If the result field is numeric, use %SUBDT to convert the various parts of the date to numeric values, and construct the result field in an expression.

Using a data structure makes the conversion from date field to numeric field even easier, as the following example shows:

```
*.. 1 ...+... 2 ...+... 3 ...+... 4 ...+... 5 ...+... 6 ...+... 7 ...+... 8
DName++++++++++ETDsFrom+++To/L+++IDc.Functions++++++++++++++++++++++++++++++
D ISODate         S              D    DATFMT(*ISO)

D ISODS           DS
D ISONum                         8 0

 /FREE
     ISODS = %CHAR(ISODate:*ISO0);
 /END-FREE
```

Here, we define a data structure ISODS as the "target" for the %CHAR function; when we place the date into the data structure, the ISONum data structure subfield contains a numeric value that corresponds to the date value.

Let's take a look at a complete legacy example. In this case, we'll use a numeric, eight-digit arrival date (ArrDat) in *yyyymmdd* format and add a number of nights stayed (Nights) to it. We'll pass this calculation as an argument to the %CHAR function, placing the result in a data structure. The result will be a departure date (DepDat), also an eight-digit numeric field. We're assuming that fields ArrDat and Nights are defined in a file record format.

Using C to Convert Dates

In this chapter, we point out two techniques for using Version 5's free-form expressions to convert a date to a numeric field: using the %SUBDT function within a string expression and using the %CHAR function with a data structure. Perhaps, at a future release, IBM will see fit to support dates with the %INT function. Until then, there is a third alternative. You can incorporate the C language's atol (Convert string to long integer) function within your RPG program to convert a string representation of the date to a number. This approach requires a prototype definition and some other ILE features discussed in Chapter 14. Here's the necessary coding (for more information about the prototype definition, refer to Chapter 14):

```
*.. 1 ...+... 2 ...+... 3 ...+... 4 ...+... 5 ...+... 6 ...+... 7 ...+... 8
DName++++++++++ETDsFrom+++To/L+++IDc.Functions++++++++++++++++++++++++++++++
H BNDDIR('QC2LE')

D ATOL            pr            10I 0 EXTPROC('atol')
D                                *     VALUE OPTIONS(*STRING)

D ISODate         S              D    DATFMT(*ISO)
D ISONum          S              8 0

 /FREE
     ISONum = ATOL(%CHAR(ISODate:*ISO0));
 /END-FREE
```

```
*.. 1 ...+... 2 ...+... 3 ...+... 4 ...+... 5 ...+... 6 ...+... 7 ...+... 8
DName++++++++++ETDsFrom+++To/L+++IDc.Functions+++++++++++++++++++++++++++++++
D DepDatDS        DS
D   DepDat                        8 0

 /FREE
    DepDatDS = %CHAR(%DATE(ArrDat:*ISO) + %DAYS(Nights):*ISO0);
 /END-FREE
```

Using only a single line of code and a simple data structure — no complicated arrays, leap year calculations, or "30 days hath September" routines — the code above easily manipulates legacy data representing dates. Because our numeric data already was using a quasi-ISO format (*yyyymmdd*), we specified *ISO in the calculations.

If your database stores dates in separate month, day, and year fields, you should combine them into a single date before performing date calculations. The following example overlays a date field with existing numeric date components.

```
*.. 1 ...+... 2 ...+... 3 ...+... 4 ...+... 5 ...+... 6 ...+... 7 ...+... 8
DName++++++++++ETDsFrom+++To/L+++IDc.Functions+++++++++++++++++++++++++++++++
D                 DS
D   WorkDate              D   DATFMT(*ISO) INZ
D   NumYear              4S 0 OVERLAY(WorkDate:1)
D   NumMonth             2S 0 OVERLAY(WorkDate:6)
D   NumDay               2S 0 OVERLAY(WorkDate:9)
```

Notice that the overlay specifications leave room for date separators (at positions 5 and 8) in field WorkDate.

Maintaining a Legacy: MOVE Operations

At Version 5, you can include date calculations in free-form expressions. At earlier RPG IV releases, the MOVE, MOVEL (Move Left), and MOVEA (Move Array) fixed-format opcodes are "date aware"; that is, you can use MOVE or MOVEL to convert date/time/timestamp fields from one data type or format to another. MOVEA can move date/time fields into character-type fields, arrays, or array elements. The MOVE operation also provides a convenient way to change date formats, as the following example, which moves an *MDY format date into an *ISO format date, demonstrates.

```
*.. 1 ...+... 2 ...+... 3 ...+... 4 ...+... 5 ...+... 6 ...+... 7 ...+... 8
DName++++++++++ETDsFrom+++To/L+++IDc.Functions+++++++++++++++++++++++++++++++
CL0N01Factor1++++++Opcode(E)+Factor2++++++Result++++++++Len++D+HiLoEq....
D MDYDate         S              D   DATFMT(*MDY)
D ISODate         S              D   DATFMT(*ISO)

C                 MOVE      MDYDate       ISODate
```

In one simple MOVE operation, this example converts the date format.

continued ...

Maintaining a Legacy: MOVE Operations ... *Continued*

Similarly, to move date/time fields into character or numeric fields, you simply code the MOVE operation as you would for any other fields:

```
*.. 1 ...+... 2 ...+... 3 ...+... 4 ...+... 5 ...+... 6 ...+... 7 ...+... 8
DName+++++++++++ETDsFrom+++To/L+++IDc.Functions++++++++++++++++++++++++++++++
CLØNØ1Factor1+++++++Opcode(E)+Factor2++++++Result++++++++Len++D+HiLoEq....
D ISODate        S                    D    DATFMT(*ISO)
D ISONum         S                   8P Ø
D ISOChar        S                  1ØA

C                        MOVE      ISODate         ISONum
C                        MOVE      ISODate         ISOChar
```

If the result field is numeric, RPG will remove the separator characters from the date before moving it into the result. Otherwise, the result field should be long enough to accommodate the separators.

In the preceding examples, the result field values would be in *ISO format (the default). If you needed to change the date to a different format, you could specify the format in Factor 1, as in the following example:

```
*.. 1 ...+... 2 ...+... 3 ...+... 4 ...+... 5 ...+... 6 ...+... 7 ...+... 8
DName++++++++++ETDsFrom+++To/L+++IDc.Functions++++++++++++++++++++++++++++++++
CLØNØ1Factor1+++++++Opcode(E)+Factor2++++++Result++++++++Len++D+HiLoEq....
D ISODate        S                    D    DATFMT(*ISO)
D USANum         S                   8P Ø
D EURChar        S                  1ØA
D CYMDNum        S                   7   Ø

C     *USA               MOVE      ISODate         USANum
C     *EUR               MOVE      ISODate         EURChar
C     *CYMD              MOVE      ISODate         CYMDNum
```

Any valid date or time format will work, including *JOBRUN, *CYMD, and so on; however, the *USA format isn't allowed when you move between time and numeric data types. The following example would convert an *ISO format date to a numeric field in the job's runtime format.

```
*.. 1 ...+... 2 ...+... 3 ...+... 4 ...+... 5 ...+... 6 ...+... 7 ...+... 8
DName++++++++++ETDsFrom+++To/L+++IDc.Functions++++++++++++++++++++++++++++++++
CLØNØ1Factor1+++++++Opcode(E)+Factor2++++++Result++++++++Len++D+HiLoEq....
D ISODate        S                    D    DATFMT(*ISO)
D MDYNum         S                   6P Ø

C     *JOBRUN            MOVE      ISODate         MDYNum
```

Going in the other direction — from character or numeric to date/time — is just as easy. You can move legacy character/numeric fields representing dates/times to true date/time fields within your RPG program, perform date calculations on them, and then move them back to their original formats. The following example, repeated from the main text, shows how you might age an invoice record from a file that stores DueYMD as an eight-byte, packed-decimal field in *yyyymmdd* format.

```
*.. 1 ...+... 2 ...+... 3 ...+... 4 ...+... 5 ...+... 6 ...+... 7 ...+... 8
DName++++++++++ETDsFrom+++To/L+++IDc.Functions++++++++++++++++++++++++++++++++
CLØNØ1Factor1+++++++Opcode(E)+Factor2++++++Result++++++++Len++D+HiLoEq....
D DueDate        S                    D
D TodayDate      S                    D
D AgeDays        S                   5P Ø
C     *JOBRUN            MOVE      UDate           TodayDate
C     *ISO               MOVE      DueYMD          DueDate
C     TodayDate          SUBDUR    DueDate         AgeDays:*D
```

continued ...

Maintaining a Legacy: MOVE Operations ... *Continued*

Notice that these examples use Factor 1 to specify the format of the numeric date in Factor 2. Factor 1 specifies the format of the character or numeric field if it is the source (Factor 2) or target (result) of the operation. Remember that RPG treats UDATE (along with the other user date special values, such as *DATE and UYEAR) as a numeric field, not as a date field; in this sense, UDATE is a legacy field.

Let's take a look at a fixed-format version of the departure-date calculation from the main text. Remember that we will use a numeric, eight-digit arrival date (ArrDat) in *yyyymmdd* format and add a number of nights stayed (Nights) to it. The result will be a departure date (DepDat), also an eight-digit numeric field.

```
*.. 1 ...+... 2 ...+... 3 ...+... 4 ...+... 5 ...+... 6 ...+... 7 ...+... 8
DName++++++++++ETDsFrom+++To/L+++IDc.Functions++++++++++++++++++++++++++++++++
CLØNØ1Factor1+++++++Opcode(E)+Factor2++++++Result+++++++Len++D+HiLoEq....
D DateWork        S              D    DATFMT(*ISO)

C                    MOVE      ArrDat        DateWork
C                    ADDDUR    Nights:*D     DateWork
C                    MOVE      DateWork      DepDat
```

Because our numeric data was already in *yyyymmdd* format, we could forego specifying *ISO format in the calculations.

In addition to numeric legacy dates, the RPG IV MOVEx operations work for converting character fields to and from date/time fields. The date format in Factor 1 must be followed by a separator character for character fields — *ISO– or *USA/, for example. If your legacy dates are in character format but do not include separators, follow the date format in Factor 1 with a zero (0): *ISO0, *USA0, and so on.

When you use a MOVE operation to move a date to a timestamp field, the time and microsecond portion of the timestamp remain unaffected. When you move a time to a timestamp field, the date portion of the timestamp remains unaffected and the microseconds are set to 000000. In either case, the result must be a valid timestamp, or RPG will generate an error.

The TIME opcode supports date/time/timestamp result fields. This opcode to puts the current program date or time into a native date, time, or timestamp:

```
*.. 1 ...+... 2 ...+... 3 ...+... 4 ...+... 5 ...+... 6 ...+... 7 ...+... 8
DName++++++++++ETDsFrom+++To/L+++IDc.Functions++++++++++++++++++++++++++++++++
CLØNØ1Factor1+++++++Opcode(E)+Factor2++++++Result+++++++Len++D+HiLoEq....
D CurrDate        S              D
D CurrTime        S              T
D Now             S              Z

C                    TIME                    CurrDate
C                    TIME                    CurrTime
C                    TIME                    Now
```

✔ **You can determine day-of-week using RPG's date operations.**

Miscellaneous Date/Time Topics

RPG includes no direct function to determine the day of the week from a date field. But you can simplify that calculation, too, by using the date functions. By comparing a date with any known Sunday, you can easily find the day of the week. The following code yields a number 0 through 6, representing Sunday through Saturday, for any date (VarDate):

```
*.. 1 ...+... 2 ...+... 3 ...+... 4 ...+... 5 ...+... 6 ...+... 7 ...+... 8
DName++++++++++ETDsFrom+++To/L+++IDc.Functions++++++++++++++++++++++++++++++
CLØNØ1Factor1+++++++Opcode(E)+Factor2+++++++Result++++++++Len++D+HiLoEq....
D VarDate        S              D
D DayOfWeek      S              1 Ø

 /FREE
    DayOfWeek = %REM(%DIFF(VarDate:D'1899-12-31':*DAYS) : 7);
 /END-FREE
```

Or, at V4R4 or V4R5:

```
D VarDate        S              D
D WorkField      S              5 Ø
D DayOfWeek      S              1 Ø

C         VarDate      SUBDUR    D'1899-12-31' WorkField:*D
C                      EVAL      DayOfWeek = %REM(Workfield:7)
```

Or, for earlier releases:

```
D VarDate        S              D
D WorkField      S              5 Ø
D DayOfWeek      S              1 Ø

C         VarDate      SUBDUR    D'1899-12-31' WorkField:*D
C                      DIV       7             WorkField
C                      MVR                     DayOfWeek
```

You can determine the last day of any month using RPG IV's date operations. The following code calculates EOMonth for any date contained in VarDate:

```
*.. 1 ...+... 2 ...+... 3 ...+... 4 ...+... 5 ...+... 6 ...+... 7 ...+... 8
DName++++++++++ETDsFrom+++To/L+++IDc.Functions++++++++++++++++++++++++++++++
CLØNØ1Factor1+++++++Opcode(E)+Factor2+++++++Result++++++++Len++D+HiLoEq....
D VarDate        S              D
D EOMonth        S              D

 /FREE
    EOMonth = VarDate + %MONTHS(1);
    EOMonth = EOMonth - %DAYS(%SUBDT(EOMonth:*DAYS));
 /END-FREE
```

Or, before Version 5:

```
D VarDate        S              D
D EOMonth        S              D
D WorkDays       S              3 Ø

C         VarDate      ADDDUR    1:*M          EOMonth
C                      EXTRCT    EOMonth:*D    WorkDays
C                      SUBDUR    WorkDays:*D   EOMonth
```

Supporting Dates in Display Files

If you incorporate date/time/timestamp fields into your interactive programs, you'll almost certainly run into annoying problems relating to DDS. Most notably, if an operator enters an invalid date, time, or timestamp on a screen, the data-management routines won't let the display return to the program until the data is fixed on the screen.

One technique you can use to overcome the display files' lack of usable date support is to employ the date-related BIFs to convert between numeric or character fields and date/time/timestamp fields. You can represent dates on the screen in a DDS-supported data type (i.e., character or numeric) and then convert the data to and from date fields in your program.

The other method for supporting dates on screens uses the OVERLAY keyword to map the individual components of a date over the date itself. These components can be either character or numeric data consistent with DDS requirements. But the RPG program automatically shares the same storage between the date field and its components, thus avoiding the need for any conversion operations:

```
*.. 1 ...+... 2 ...+... 3 ...+... 4 ...+... 5 ...+... 6 ...+... 7 ...+... 8
DName++++++++++ETDsFrom+++To/L+++IDc.Functions++++++++++++++++++++++++++++++
CLØN01Factor1+++++++Opcode(E)+Factor2++++++Result+++++++Len++D+HiLoEq....
D                        DS
D  WorkDate                     D   DATFMT(*ISO) INZ
D  DspYear                     4S Ø OVERLAY(WorkDate:1)
D  DspMonth                    2S Ø OVERLAY(WorkDate:6)
D  DspDay                      2S Ø OVERLAY(WorkDate:9)
```

If you use this method, be sure to use the TEST operation to validate any values.

Chapter 10

New Data Types

In Chapter 9, we discussed RPG's new date, time, and timestamp data types. RPG IV supports several other new data types, which we'll talk about in this chapter.

RPG IV now supports a rich complement of data types — most of those supported by other AS/400 languages, including Java. Figure 10.1 lists the data types supported by RPG IV at Version 5.

FIGURE 10.1
RPG IV Data Types

Data class	Data type	Code
Character	Character	A
	UCS-2 (Unicode)	C
	Graphic	G
	Indicator	N
Numeric	Binary	B
	Floating point	F
	Integer	I
	Packed decimal	P
	Zoned	S
	Unsigned integer	U
Date	Date	D
	Time	T
	Timestamp	Z
Object	Object (Java)	O
Pointer	Pointer	*

Indicator Data Type

Indicator data (data type N) is a special type of character data, sometimes called Boolean data in other languages. Indicator data fields are one byte long and can contain only the value '1' (on) or '0' (off).

You're already familiar with RPG's 99 numbered indicators, as well as a few special-purpose indicators, that have long been a part of the RPG landscape. Now, you can define your own indicators, setting their values and testing their values to signal true/false conditions. This support can greatly improve the readability of your RPG programs.

When you define a named indicator, there is no need to specify the length of the field. To set the value of a named indicator, use the EVAL operation. You can test the named indicator's value within logical expressions. Here are two examples:

```
*.. 1 ...+... 2 ...+... 3 ...+... 4 ...+... 5 ...+... 6 ...+... 7 ...+... 8
DName++++++++++ETDsFrom+++To/L+++IDc.Keywords+++++++++++++++++++++++++++++++
D ProcessDone    S              N
D OverTime       S              N

 /FREE
    DOW NOT ProcessDone;
      ...
      ProcessDone = *ON;
    ENDDO;

    Overtime = (HoursWorked > 40);
    IF Overtime;
      ...
    ENDIF;
 /END-FREE
```

In the first example above, the DOW loop tests to see whether the ProcessDone indicator is on ('1'); once the indicator is on, the loop will terminate. In the second example, the value of HoursWorked is compared with 40; if the logical expression is true (i.e., if HoursWorked is greater than 40), Overtime is set on.

Chapter 4 shows you how to use named indicators in a data structure to map numbered indicators from a DDS-described workstation file and then use the named indicators instead of the numbered indicators to test and set conditions.

Using Variable-Length Fields

RPG IV provides direct support for variable-length character fields (as well as Unicode and graphic fields). When declaring variable-length fields in D-specs, define them with a maximum length; then use the VARYING keyword to indicate that the length can be shorter than the declared length. With I-specs or O-specs, use the *VAR data attribute.

Variable-length fields always have a maximum length (the declared length) and a current length that can change during the execution of the program. The current length depends on the value of the field. The default initial length for a variable-length field is zero.

To get the current length for a variable-length field, use the %LEN built-in function (BIF). You can also use %LEN on the left side of an expression to set the current length of a variable-length field.

Using variable-length fields can improve the performance of string operations and parameter passing, as well as make the code more readable, by eliminating the need for %TRIM functions. The %CHAR and %REPLACE functions also work with variable-length fields (see Chapter 8 for examples).

New Numeric Data Types

RPG IV recognizes several new numeric data types that expand its capabilities to store numbers in binary representations.

☑ Integers allow a wider range of values than binary numbers.

Integers (type I) and unsigned integers (U) efficiently provide a greater range of values than was previously available with the binary (B) data type. The following table details the allowable byte lengths, digit lengths, and ranges for the three data types.

Data type	Bytes	Digits	Lowest value	Highest value
Binary (B)	2	4	−9,999	9,999
	4	9	−999,999,999	999,999,999
Integer (I)	1	3	−128	127
	2	5	−32,768	32,767
	4	10	−2,147,483,648	2,147,483,647
	8	20	−9,223,372,036,854,775,808	9,223,372,036,854,775,807
Unsigned (U)	1	3	0	255
	2	5	0	65,535
	4	10	0	4,294,967,295
	8	20	0	18,446,744,073,709,551,615

Integers and unsigned integers allow no decimal places.

In general, you can safely substitute integers or unsigned integers for binary numbers in your RPG programs to gain the greater range of values that integers provide.

When you define any of these numeric data types as standalone fields in D-specs, specify the length by coding the number of digits. When you define them as data structure subfields, specify the number of digits if you're using length notation; specify the number of bytes if you're using from/to positions. In the following example, ArrayCounter, Counter, and Counter2 are all two-byte, five-digit unsigned integers.

```
*.. 1 ...+... 2 ...+... 3 ...+... 4 ...+... 5 ...+... 6 ...+... 7 ...+... 8
DName++++++++++ETDsFrom+++To/L+++IDc.Keywords+++++++++++++++++++++++++++++++++
D ArrayCounter    S              5U 0
D                 DS
D Counter                   1     2U 0
D Counter2                        5U 0
```

Using Floating-Point Numbers for Scientific Notation

In addition to integers, RPG IV supports floating-point numbers (type F), which you can use when you need to store very small numbers or very large numbers that the other numeric data types can't support. Floating-point numbers are generally used in scientific applications, not in business arithmetic. You should avoid their use when they're not absolutely necessary, because the value stored in a floating-point number may not exactly match the same number stored as a packed-decimal number. If you need to have a number accurate to a specific number of decimal places, as with currency amounts, do not use floating point for the number.

Floating-point numbers are represented by a mantissa and an exponent. To determine the value of a floating-point number, multiply the mantissa by 10 raised to the power of the exponent — for example, 1.2345 E5 = 123450. Floating-point numbers are always defined by the number of *bytes*, not the number of digits; they can be four bytes or eight bytes long. The following table shows the respective ranges.

Bytes	Lowest value	Highest value
4	1.175 494 4 E–38	3.402 823 5 E+38
8	2.225 073 858 507 201 E–308	1.797 693 134 862 315 E+308

You'll recall that negative exponents indicate smaller numbers (closer to zero), while positive exponents indicate larger numbers. Both positive and negative floating-point numbers have the same range, with a negative sign going left of the mantissa.

You can process floating-point numbers using two BIFs. The %EDITFLT function returns a character representation of a floating-point number. For example, %EDITFLT(16) would return a character string of +1.600000000000000E+001 to your program. The %FLOAT function converts an expression to the float numeric format.

Pointer Support

RPG IV provides new support for pointer data types. Although pointers may be a foreign concept to many RPG programmers, they are a familiar sight in many other computer languages. In particular, C makes heavy use of pointers; Cobol also supports a pointer data type.

A pointer is a symbolic representation of an address. A pointer "points" to a location in memory, telling you, for example, *where* a piece of data is found, not what is stored there. Just as a character variable always has a character as a value and a numeric variable always has a number as a value, so a pointer variable always has a memory address as a value.

Computer programs use pointers to pass data indirectly from one process to another. Actually, RPG has used pointers all along, probably without your even realizing it. When you use the CALL opcode in an RPG program and pass variable parameters to the CALLed program, the AS/400 passes pointers to those parameters, not the values of the parameters (this is also referred to as *pass-by-reference*). When you manipulate the value of a parameter in the CALLed program, you are also changing the value of the same parameter in the CALLing program, because both programs use the same memory location. Heretofore, RPG's use of pointers has been transparent to programmers, and you couldn't evaluate, manipulate, or even easily observe the pointers at work in your programs. Now, RPG IV offers these capabilities.

What good are pointers? As an RPG programmer, you've probably gotten along quite well without pointers for some time now, and you can probably continue to do without them for most business applications. An increasing number of AS/400 system application programming interfaces (APIs), however, require the use of pointers for some of their parameters. If you want to take the best advantage of some of these lower-level functions available from the operating system, you'll need to know how to define pointers and use them in your programs.

Defining Pointer Data Types

RPG IV supports two flavors of pointers: *basing* pointers and *procedure* pointers. Basing pointers point to data, while procedure pointers point to procedures or functions. Pointers are 16 bytes long, and they are always aligned on a 16-byte boundary in storage. The compiler will pad a data structure if necessary to ensure that the pointer begins at a 16-byte boundary.

To define a pointer, you can simply specify data type * in the D-specs, as the following example shows:

```
*.. 1 ...+... 2 ...+... 3 ...+... 4 ...+... 5 ...+... 6 ...+... 7 ...+... 8
DName++++++++++ETDsFrom+++To/L+++IDc.Keywords++++++++++++++++++++++++++++++++
D Pointer1        S                *
```

This example defines a pointer but does not point to any particular data. The initial value of the pointer is *NULL (the default). You need not specify a field length, because all pointers are 16 bytes long.

To put a valid memory address into the pointer defined in the example above, you can use the %ADDR built-in function. The following example initializes the value of Pointer1 to the address of the DaysOfWeek array:

```
*.. 1 ...+... 2 ...+... 3 ...+... 4 ...+... 5 ...+... 6 ...+... 7 ...+... 8
DName++++++++++ETDsFrom+++To/L+++IDc.Keywords++++++++++++++++++++++++++++++++
D DaysOfWeek      DS             9   DIM(7)
D Pointer1        S                * INZ(%ADDR(DaysOfWeek))
```

You also can implicitly define a basing pointer when you define the data on which the pointer is based. When you use the BASED keyword with a data structure or stand-alone field, RPG IV creates a basing pointer to hold the address of the storage space that holds the defined data component. The following example uses the BASED keyword:

```
*.. 1 ...+... 2 ...+... 3 ...+... 4 ...+... 5 ...+... 6 ...+... 7 ...+... 8
DName++++++++++ETDsFrom+++To/L+++IDc.Keywords++++++++++++++++++++++++++++++++
D TodayName       S             9   BASED(Pointer1)
```

This example defines field TodayName. The BASED keyword also defines a pointer, Pointer1, which will point to the TodayName field. There is no need to define Pointer1 separately (although good coding standards would dictate that you do so). Before you can use the component, however, its basing pointer must contain a valid address. If your program changes the value of Pointer1, the contents of TodayName will also automatically change because TodayName is BASED on Pointer1. The BASED keyword is valid with standalone fields, data structures, and runtime arrays.

To define a procedure pointer, you use the PROCPTR keyword in the D-specs:

```
*.. 1 ...+... 2 ...+... 3 ...+... 4 ...+... 5 ...+... 6 ...+... 7 ...+... 8
DName++++++++++ETDsFrom+++To/L+++IDc.Keywords+++++++++++++++++++++++++++++++++
D Pointer1        S              *    PROCPTR
```

This example defines Pointer1 as a procedure pointer, with an initial default value of *NULL. As defined, this pointer doesn't point to a procedure. Usually, you'll want to assign an initial value to a procedure pointer, as in the following example:

```
*.. 1 ...+... 2 ...+... 3 ...+... 4 ...+... 5 ...+... 6 ...+... 7 ...+... 8
DName++++++++++ETDsFrom+++To/L+++IDc.Keywords+++++++++++++++++++++++++++++++++
D Pointer1        S              *    PROCPTR
D                                     INZ(%PADDR('AddCust'))
```

Here, we define Pointer1 as a procedure pointer with a value that points to the AddCust procedure. The %PADDR function supplies the address value. AddCust might be a procedure that we will later call using the CALLB (Call a Bound Procedure) opcode. For the remainder of this chapter, we'll concentrate on basing pointers, leaving procedure pointers to the ILE discussion in Chapter 13.

RPG IV Pointer Manipulation

Now that you can define a pointer in an RPG program, what can you do with it? RPG IV lets you set the value of a pointer using free-form expressions, usually in conjunction with the %ADDR and %PADDR BIFs. You also can test pointers for equality, including testing for *NULL values. And you can perform pointer arithmetic — that is, you can add and subtract pointers.

When you use an assignment expression to set a pointer value, both sides of the expression must be the same data type: either both basing pointers or both procedure pointers. Although the compiler will generate special pointer-handling code when you set a pointer, your source statement will look like any other expression:

```
*.. 1 ...+... 2 ...+... 3 ...+... 4 ...+... 5 ...+... 6 ...+... 7 ...+... 8
DName++++++++++ETDsFrom+++To/L+++IDc.Keywords+++++++++++++++++++++++++++++++++
D Days            S              9    DIM(7)
D Pointer1        S              *    INZ(%ADDR(Days))
D Pointer2        S              *

 /FREE
    Pointer2 = Pointer 1;
    Pointer1 = *NULL;
 /END-FREE
```

In this example, Pointer1 will be initialized with a value corresponding to the address of the Days array, while Pointer2 will have a null value (the default). In the calculations, we assign the value of Pointer1 to Pointer2 and then change Pointer1 to a null value. When the code has been executed, the values of Pointer1 and Pointer2 will be reversed from the way they began: Pointer2 will now point to the Days array.

Don't forget that you can use the %ADDR and %PADDR BIFs in an expression. In the example above, we could have used %ADDR, as the following code shows:

```
*.. 1 ...+... 2 ...+... 3 ...+... 4 ...+... 5 ...+... 6 ...+... 7 ...+... 8
DName++++++++++ETDsFrom+++To/L+++IDc.Keywords+++++++++++++++++++++++++++++++
D Days            S             9    DIM(7)
D Pointer1        S             *    INZ(%ADDR(Days))
D Pointer2        S             *

 /FREE
    Pointer2 = %ADDR(Days);
    Pointer1 = *NULL;
 /END-FREE
```

You can test pointers for equality or for a *NULL value in your RPG C-specs. Here are some examples of pointer testing:

```
*.. 1 ...+... 2 ...+... 3 ...+... 4 ...+... 5 ...+... 6 ...+... 7 ...+... 8
DName++++++++++ETDsFrom+++To/L+++IDc.Keywords+++++++++++++++++++++++++++++++
D Days            S             9    DIM(7)
D Pointer1        S             *    INZ(%ADDR(Days))
D Pointer2        S             *

 /FREE
    IF Pointer1 = Pointer2;
      Pointer1 = *NULL;
    ENDIF;

    IF Pointer2 = *NULL;
      Pointer2 = %ADDR(Days);
    ENDIF;

    IF Pointer1 = %ADDR(Days);
      Pointer1 = *NULL;
    ENDIF;
 /END-FREE
```

In the first example, we test to see whether Pointer1 and Pointer2 are pointing to the same piece of data — that is, whether the pointers are equal. If they are equal, we set Pointer1 to a null value.

In the second example, we check to see whether Pointer2 is null; if it is, we set its value to the address of the Days array. Last, we check to see whether Pointer1 is pointing to the Days array — that is, whether its value is equal to the address of Days. If it is, we set Pointer1 to null.

Remember that when we talked about the BASED keyword earlier, we said you can change the value of a pointer to change the contents of a field if the field is BASED on the pointer. Figure 10.2 shows an example of manipulating pointers in this way.

FIGURE 10.2

An Example of Manipulating Pointers

```
*...+... 1 ...+... 2 ...+... 3 ...+... 4 ...+... 5 ...+... 6 ...+... 7 ...+... 8
    DName+++++++++++ETDsFrom+++To/L+++IDc.Keywords++++++++++++++++++++++++++++++++
    D Days            S              9        DIM(7)
    D                                         CTDATA
    D                                         PERRCD(7)

    D DayPtr          S              *        INZ(%ADDR(Days))
    D DayOfWeek       S              9        BASED(DayPtr)

    D BaseDate        S              D        INZ(D'1899-12-31')
    D VarDate         S              D
    D WorkField       S              5 0

     /FREE
        WorkField = %REM(%DIFF(VarDate:BaseDate:*DAYS) : 7);

        DayPtr = %ADDR(Days(WorkField + 1));       // DayOfWeek now has day name
     /END-FREE

**CTDATA Days
Sunday    Monday    Tuesday  WednesdayThursday Friday    Saturday
```

In the example in the figure, the Days array contains the spelled-out days of the week. We define DayOfWeek as a field BASED on DayPtr. We can manipulate the value of DayPtr to point to any value in the Days array, using an expression. In this case, we've borrowed some Version 5 code from Chapter 9 to determine the day of the week for VarDate. Without ever directly changing the contents of DayOfWeek, we can change its value by manipulating the address (in DayPtr) on which DayOfWeek is BASED.

Remember that the basing pointer must contain a valid address before your program can reference a BASED field. The following code would ensure that you could use the DayOfWeek variable:

```
*.. 1 ...+... 2 ...+... 3 ...+... 4 ...+... 5 ...+... 6 ...+... 7 ...+... 8
DName+++++++++++ETDsFrom+++To/L+++IDc.Keywords++++++++++++++++++++++++++++++++
D DayChar         S              9
D DayOfWeek       S              9        BASED(DayPtr)

 /FREE
    IF DayPtr <> *NULL;
      DayChar = DayOfWeek;
    ELSE;
      DayChar = *BLANKS;
    ENDIF;
 /END-FREE
```

By testing pointer DayPtr for a null value, we can alleviate the possibility of a pointer error at runtime when we refer to DayOfWeek. If DayPtr does not contain a valid address, the program will end with error message "MCH3601 Pointer not set" and/or "RNQ0222 Pointer or parameter error."

☑ **Some APIs require pointers.**

Using Pointers with APIs

IBM has provided hundreds of APIs with OS/400 to let you access functions that might otherwise be unavailable or difficult to implement. Many of these APIs require the use of pointers, so they previously have been useless to RPG programmers. Now that RPG IV supports pointers, you can take advantage of some APIs that were out of reach in prior releases. Even if an API doesn't require pointers, you can sometimes use pointers to enhance its performance and/or function.

The incomplete code example in Figure 10.3 shows the use of pointers with APIs; the code relevant to pointers is highlighted. (Coding these examples using free-form specifications requires the use of prototypes, which we won't discuss until Chapter 14; therefore, Figures 10.3 and 10.4 are shown with fixed-format C-specs.)

FIGURE 10.3
Using Pointers with APIs

```
*.. 1 ...+... 2 ...+... 3 ...+... 4 ...+... 5 ...+... 6 ...+... 7 ...+... 8
DName++++++++++ETDsFrom+++To/L+++IDc.Keywords+++++++++++++++++++++++++++++++
CLØNØ1Factor1++++++Opcode(E)+Factor2++++++Result+++++++Len++D+HiLoEq....
D QDBQ            DS                    BASED(QDBQPtr)
 ... (Data structure subfields go here)

 * Create a user space
C                   CALL      'QUSCRTUS'
C                   PARM                 SpaceName
C                   PARM      *BLANKS    SpaceAttr
C                   PARM      1Ø24       SpaceSize
C                   PARM                 SpaceInit
C                   PARM      '*CHANGE'  SpaceAut
C                   PARM      'QDBRTVFD' SpaceText
C                   PARM      '*YES'     SpaceRepl
C                   PARM                 ErrStruct
C                   PARM      '*USER'    SpaceDom

 * Get a resolved pointer to the user space
C                   CALL      'QUSPTRUS'
C                   PARM                 SpaceName
C                   PARM                 QDBQPtr
C                   PARM                 ErrStruct

 * Call QDBRTVFD, passing the address of the user space as the receiver
C                   CALL      'QDBRTVFD'
C                   PARM                 QDBQ
C                   PARM      16776704   SpaceSize
C                   PARM                 FileUsed
C                   PARM      'FILDØ1ØØ' Format
C                   PARM                 FileName
C                   PARM                 FormatName
C                   PARM                 Overrides
C                   PARM                 System
C                   PARM                 Format1
C                   PARM                 ErrStruct
```

This example uses the QDBRTVFD (Retrieve File Description) API to place file description information into a user space. Normally, QDBRTVFD returns file information to a receiver variable within a program. In this case, we want to return the information into a user space so the information will be in a permanent object on the system. We would then be able to use this format definition with the QQQQRY (Query) API. If the definition does not exist when QQQQRY runs, QQQQRY will build a definition; if the definition already exists, QQQQRY will run faster.

In Figure 10.3, we first define a data structure, QDBQ, which is BASED on the pointer QDBQPtr (the subfields for QDBQ can be found in the IBM-supplied file QSYSINC/QRPGLESRC, member QDBRTVFD). Next, we create a user space, using the QUSCRTUS (Create User Space) API; this API does not require the use of pointers. After creating the user space, we can retrieve a pointer to the address of the user space, using the QUSPTRUS (Retrieve Pointer to User Space) API; this API will return the value of the pointer to QDBQPtr.

Last, we execute the QDBRTVFD API to retrieve the file description. By specifying QDBQ as the receiver variable, we effectively return the file description information to the user space, instead of to a program variable. Because the QDBQPtr pointer is the address of *both* the user space and the return variable, we have successfully used a pointer to redirect the output of the API to a user space.

The code in Figure 10.3 provides a condensed overview of the process, highlighting the use of pointers in RPG IV. You can find a more complete example of retrieving a file description to a user space in IBM's AS/400 manual *OS/400 System API Programming* (SC41-3800).

Using Pointers to Process Lists

You also can use pointers to process simple lists that you store in user spaces. The partial code in Figure 10.4 can get you started.

FIGURE 10.4
Using Pointers to Process a List

```
*.. 1 ...+... 2 ...+... 3 ...+... 4 ...+... 5 ...+... 6 ...+... 7 ...+... 8
DName++++++++++ETDsFrom+++To/L+++IDc.Keywords+++++++++++++++++++++++++++++++++
CLØNØ1Factor1+++++++Opcode(E)+Extended-factor2+++++++++++++++++++++++++++++++++
D EntryPtr        S               *
D ListData        S             35      BASED(EntryPtr)

 * Get a resolved pointer to the user space
C                     CALL      'QUSPTRUS'
C                     PARM                    SpaceName
C                     PARM                    EntryPtr
C                     PARM                    ErrStruct

* Process the list
C                     DOW       %SUBST(ListData:1:1) <> '*'
                      ... (Process ListData)
C                     EVAL      EntryPtr = EntryPtr + %SIZE(ListData)
C                     ENDDO
```

In this program, we're assuming that a list of data already exists in a user space on the system; the list consists of 35-byte entries, with the final entry beginning with an asterisk (*). The code uses the QUSPTRUS API to resolve a pointer to the user space; the address is placed in pointer EntryPtr. The ListData variable is BASED on the EntryPtr pointer. When we use the QUSPTRUS API to retrieve the value of EntryPtr, we will have effectively moved to the first entry in the list. After we process the ListData variable, we add the byte size of ListData to EntryPtr, thus "bumping" our position in the list up one entry (35 bytes). In this manner, we can easily move through the list, processing each entry in order.

Chapter 11

Output Specification Changes

Of all the changed specifications in RPG IV, the output specifications (O-specs) have changed the least. Columnar areas have been expanded to accommodate longer field names, but IBM has made virtually no other changes in the O-specs. The only notable enhancement is support for new data types (as well as variable-length fields) in program-described O-specs; this support follows the same format and logic in the O-specs as it does in the I-specs (Chapter 5).

As with I-specs, an increasing number of RPG programmers prefer to use externally described output files, which greatly reduce the need for O-specs in an RPG IV program. RPG IV still supports program-described output files, however. Figures 11.1A and 11.1B illustrate the specification for both externally described and program-described file output.

FIGURE 11.1A
Output Specification Layout: Externally Described Files

```
*.. 1 ...+... 2 ...+... 3 ...+... 4 ...+... 5 ...+... 6 ...+... 7 ...+... 8
ORcdname+++D...N01N02N03Excnam++++.......................................
ORcdname+++DAddN01N02N03Excnam++++.......................................
O.........And..N01N02N03Excnam++++.......................................
O.............N01N02N03Field++++++++++.B.................................
```

Record Identifier Specifications

Columns	Description
1–5	Sequence number
6	O
7–16	Record name
16–18	Logical relationship: AND, OR
17	Type of record to write: D Detail E Exception (EXCEPT) H Detail (header) T Total
18	Release record after output: R, blank
18–20	Record addition/deletion: ADD, DEL
21–29	Output conditioning indicators: Blank, 01–99, H1–H9, KA–KN, KP–KY, L1–L9, U1–U8, LR, MR, RT, 1P
30–39	EXCEPT name
40–80	(Blank)
81–100	Comments

continued ...

FIGURE 11.1A *CONTINUED*

Field Description Specifications

Columns	Description
1–5	Sequence number
6	O
7–20	(Blank)
21–29	Output conditioning indicators: Blank, 01–99, H1–H9, KA–KN, KP–KY, L1–L9, U1–U8, LR, MR, RT, 1P
30–43	Field name or *ALL
44	(Blank)
45	Reset field contents after writing record: Blank, B
46–80	(Blank)
81–100	Comments

FIGURE 11.1B
Output Specification Layout: Program-Described Files

```
*.. 1 ...+... 2 ...+... 3 ...+... 4 ...+... 5 ...+... 6 ...+... 7 ...+... 8
OFilename++DF..N01N02N03Excnam++++B++A++Sb+Sa+.............................
OFilename++DAddN01N02N03Excnam++++.........................................
O.........And.N01N02N03Excnam++++.........................................
O.............N01N02N03Field+++++++++YB.End++PConstant/editword/DTformat++
O...........................................Constant/editword-continues+
```

Record Identifier Specifications

Columns	Description
1–5	Sequence number
6	O
7–16	File name
16–18	Logical relationship: AND, OR
17	Type of record to write: D Detail E Exception (EXCEPT) H Detail (header) T Total
18	Fetch overflow/release for printer files: Blank Do not fetch overflow F Fetch overflow R Release device after write
18–20	Record addition/deletion: ADD, DEL
21–29	Output conditioning indicators: Blank, 01–99, H1–H9, KA–KN, KP–KY, L1–L9, OA–OG, OV, U1–U8, LR, MR, RT, 1P

continued ...

FIGURE **11.1B** *CONTINUED*

(Record Identifier Specifications…)	
Columns	**Description**
30–39	EXCEPT name
40–42	Space before: Blank, 0–255 lines
43–45	Space after: Blank, 0–255 lines
46–48	Skip before: Blank, 1–255 lines
49–51	Skip after: Blank, 1–255 lines
52–80	(Blank)
81–100	Comments

Field Description Specifications	
Columns	**Description**
1–5	Sequence number
6	O
7–20	(Blank)
21–29	Output conditioning indicators: Blank, 01–99, H1–H9, KA–KN, KP–KY, L1–L9, OA–OG, OV, U1–U8, LR, MR, RT, 1P
30–43	Field to write: Blank, field name, table, array, element, named constant, data structure, PAGE, PAGE1–PAGE7, *PLACE, UDATE, *DATE, UDAY, *DAY, UMONTH, *MONTH, UYEAR, *YEAR, *IN, *INxx, *IN(xx)
44	Edit code: Blank, 1–9, A–D, J–Q, X, Y, Z
45	Reset field contents after writing record: Blank, B
46	(Blank)
47–51	End: position, +nnnn, –nnnn, K1–K8

52	External data format:
	  Blank Use default format
	  A Character
	  B Binary
	  C Unicode
	  D Date
	  F Float
	  G Graphic
	  I Signed integer
	  L Preceding (left) minus sign
	  N Indicator
	  P Packed decimal
	  R Following (right) minus sign
	  S Zoned decimal
	  T Time
	  U Unsigned integer
	  Z Timestamp

53–80	Constant, edit word, format name, date/time format (see Chapter 2 for valid date/time entries)
81–100	Comments

Here are some examples of using RPG IV O-specs for a program-described printer file. Because RPG IV brings no significant changes to the O-specs, we present these examples without comment.

```
*.. 1 ...+... 2 ...+... 3 ...+... 4 ...+... 5 ...+... 6 ...+... 7 ...+... 8
OFilename++DF..N01N02N03Excnam++++B++A++Sb+Sa+.............................
O..............N01N02N03Field++++++++YB.End++PConstant/editword/DTformat++
OQPRINT     E             Heading     2  6
O                                            25 'Objects in Library - '
O                         ODLBNM              36
O           E             Heading     2
O                                             6 'Object'
O                                            18 'Type'
O                                            30 'Attribute'
O                                            42 'Last used'
O           E             Detail      1
O                         ODOBNM              10
O                         ODOBTP              19
O                         ODOBAT              33
O                         LSTUSD          Y   41
```

Chapter 12

Converting and Compiling Programs

Now that you understand RPG IV syntax, you'll want to begin using your newfound knowledge to write RPG IV applications. Such an undertaking isn't a trivial task. As you've seen, the source specification layouts differ significantly from RPG III source, columnar positions have changed, and the types of specifications have changed. But you'll be happy to know that you don't need to rewrite all your code from scratch; IBM has provided a migration utility that will make most of the changes necessary to convert your RPG III program code to RPG IV syntax. In this chapter, we take a look at how to migrate from RPG III to RPG IV.

Keep in mind that RPG IV application conversion need not be an "all or nothing" proposition. Most people will adopt one of three strategies to gradually move their applications to RPG IV syntax:

Strategy #1: Use RPG IV only for new application development, leaving existing applications in RPG III. This approach results in new RPG IV applications but leaves existing applications as they are.

Strategy #2: Use RPG IV for all new RPG programming, including code maintenance. With this approach, you would convert existing programs as you maintain them but leave alone those programs that don't require maintenance. This strategy results in a hybrid of RPG III and RPG IV syntax within an application.

Strategy #3: Convert existing applications to RPG IV one at a time, converting all existing RPG programs within an application to the new syntax.

Your strategy may be dictated by whether or not you need to take advantage of the Integrated Language Environment (ILE). Earlier RPG syntaxes don't participate in ILE, so if your RPG application requires ILE-specific features, RPG IV will be necessary. Yet another issue may be whether your application requires features that only RPG IV supports, such as date data types; if you have an application that uses date arithmetic heavily, you may be able to make the application more reliable and efficient by converting it to RPG IV.

If your operating system is at Version 5 or later, you also need to decide whether you'll use the free-form specification wherever possible.

Changes in Source File Members

The RPG III syntax was based on an 80-column specification, a legacy from the days when all RPG source code was stored on 80-column paper punch cards. RPG IV, on the other hand, is based on a 100-column specification, with right-hand comments in columns 81–100. Until now, the typical source record on the AS/400 has been 92 bytes long: 80 bytes for the actual source statement, six bytes for Source Entry Utility (SEU) sequence numbers, and six bytes for the SEU change date. To store complete RPG IV source, you need a source file with 112-byte records. To create this source file, use the CRTSRCPF (Create Source Physical File) command:

```
CRTSRCPF  FILE(QRPGLESRC) +
          RCDLEN(112)
```

You must specify the record length because the CRTSRCPF command still defaults to a record length of 92. The default source file name for RPG IV source is QRPGLESRC, but you can use any valid AS/400 file name. In addition, you can store other types of source statements (e.g., display files, RPG III source) in the same source file as the RPG IV source. Those other source types will tolerate the longer record length without a problem. RPG IV statements will also work with shorter record lengths (they must be at least 92 bytes), but you'll lose the comment area of the specifications.

Right-hand source comments may be of limited value, however, because SEU won't readily display them on most displays. Because of this limitation, using right-hand comments may lead to situations in which the comments are "out of synch" with the actual code. You might change code but forget to change the undisplayed comments, which then become irrelevant or confusing. Many RPG experts recommend that your shop standards dictate that you simply not use right-hand comments. Without them, the 92-byte source record will work just fine. The free-form specification alleviates some of the concerns about right-hand comments by letting you code end-of-line comments, beginning with // characters, without respect to specific columnar restrictions.

✓ RPG IV source uses the RPGLE source member type.

When you use SEU and/or Programming Development Manager (PDM) to enter RPG IV source, use a source member type of RPGLE. When you edit RPGLE source members, SEU will use the RPG IV syntax checker, and PDM will use the RPG IV compiler. When the compiler creates RPG IV programs and modules, RPGLE will also be the object attribute type.

Using the CVTRPGSRC Command

Your first stop in converting existing programs to RPG IV should be the CVTRPGSRC (Convert RPG Source) command. This conversion aid will convert nearly all RPG III source into workable RPG IV syntax. The converted code may not exhibit the best coding techniques, and you'll probably want to tweak it, but much of the "grunt work" of converting source can be eliminated by this utility.

Figure 12.1A shows an example of some RPG III code, and Figure 12.1B shows the same program after the CVTRPGSRC tool has converted it.

FIGURE 12.1A
RPG III Code to Be Converted

```
*.. 1 ...+... 2 ...+... 3 ...+... 4 ...+... 5 ...+... 6 ...+... 7 ...+... 8
FQAJBACG IF  E              DISK
FQPRINT  O   F    132    OF PRINTER
E                       JOBT    1 10 1   JOB2    8
C            *ENTRY     PLIST
C                       PARM            STRTIM 60
C                       PARM            ENDTIM 60
C                       Z-ADD1          JX     30
C            JOBTYP     LOKUPJOBT,JX                   20
C    20                 MOVE JOB2,JX    JOBDES  8
C                       MOVELTIME6      HRS    20
C            3600       MULT HRS        SECS   50
C                       MOVE TIME6      WORK4   4
C                       MOVELWORK4      MINS   20
C            60         MULT MINS       WORK50 50
C                       ADD  WORK50     SECS
C                       MOVE WORK4      SEC    20
C                       ADD  SEC        SECS
C    01N02 03           Z-ADD50         JX
```

FIGURE 12.1B
RPG IV Converted Code

```
*.. 1 ...+... 2 ...+... 3 ...+... 4 ...+... 5 ...+... 6 ...+... 7 ...+... 8
F*ilename++IPEASFRLen+LKLen+AIDevice+.Functions++++++++++++++++++++++++++++++
FQAJBACG  IF  E              DISK
FQPRINT   O   F    132       PRINTER OFLIND(*INOF)
D*ame+++++++++++ETDsFrom+++To/L+++IDc.Functions+++++++++++++++++++++++++++++++
D JOBT         S            1    DIM(10) CTDATA PERRCD(1)
D JOB2         S            8    DIM(10) ALT(JOBT)
C*ØN01Factor1++++++Opcode(E)+Factor2++++++Result+++++++Len++D+HiLoEq....
C     *ENTRY     PLIST
C                PARM            STRDAT         6 0
C                PARM            ENDDAT         6 0
C                Z-ADD  1        JX             3 0
C     JOBTYP     LOOKUP JOBT(JX)                        20
C     20         MOVE   JOB2(JX) JOBDES         8
C                MOVEL  TIME6    HRS            2 0
C     3600       MULT   HRS      SECS          5 0
C                MOVE   TIME6    WORK4          4
C                MOVEL  WORK4    MINS           2 0
C     60         MULT   MINS     WORK50         5 0
C                ADD    WORK50   SECS
C                MOVE   WORK4    SEC            2 0
C                ADD    SEC      SECS
C     01
CANNØ2
CAN 03           Z-ADD  50       JX
```

As you can see in these examples, the CVTRPGSRC tool does a good job of migrating RPG III source specifications to pre–Version 5 RPG IV syntax: assigning new columnar locations and appropriate keywords; creating D-specs for arrays, data structures, and named constants; and changing opcodes and array references. But the migration aid doesn't perform more intricate conversions, such as moving C-spec field definitions to D-specs, creating EVAL expressions where appropriate, or using date opcodes when it could. Nor does it convert the C-specs to free-form specifications. You should think of CVTRPGSRC as a first step toward RPG IV but by no means a full conversion; you'll want to analyze and reengineer the program to fully take advantage of the new features in the language.

☑ **RPG IV does not support auto-report.**

The CVTRPGSRC command will convert the following source member types to RPGLE syntax: RPG, RPT, RPG38, RPT38, SQLRPG, and blank. It will not convert RPG36, RPT36, or other source member types. It's also important to note that RPG IV doesn't support the auto-report function; RPT members will be converted to RPGLE members. SQLRPG members will be converted to a comparable SQLRPGLE type.

To use the CVTRPGSRC command, type it at an AS/400 command line. The command supports the following parameters:

```
CVTRPGSRC   FROMFILE(library/file)       +
            FROMMBR(source-member)        +
            TOFILE(library/file)          +
            TOMBR(source-member)          +
            EXPCPY(*NO|*YES)              +
            CVTRPT(*YES|*NO)             +
            SECLVL(*NO|*YES)             +
            INSRTPL(*NO|*YES)            +
            LOGFILE(library/log-file) +
            LOGMBR(log-member)
```

CVTRPGSRC Parameters

Here's a closer look at the parameters that make up the CVTRPGSRC command.

From file (FROMFILE)

Qualified name of source file containing the RPG III source code to be converted (required).

Library: *LIBL (default), *CURLIB, name.

From member (FROMMBR)

Name(s) of the source member(s) to be converted (required): name, *ALL, generic*.

You can convert one, some, or all of the members in a source file, depending on your conversion strategy.

To file (TOFILE)

Qualified name of the source file to contain the converted RPG IV source members (cannot be the same as FROMFILE): QRPGLESRC (default), *NONE, name.

Library: *LIBL (default), *CURLIB, name.

Specifying TOFILE(*NONE) and CVTRPT(*YES) lets you print a conversion report without generating a converted source member.

To member (TOMBR)

Name(s) of the RPG IV source member(s) in the TOFILE: *FROMMBR (default), name.

The TOMBR must not already exist in TOFILE. If you specify more than one member in the FROMMBR parameter, you must specify TOMBR(*FROMMBR); the RPG IV member names will then match the original RPG III member names.

Expand copy member (EXPCPY)

Expand /COPY member(s) into the RPG IV source member: *NO (default), *YES.

You may find that the conversion tool will be able to convert more /COPY schemes if you expand the original /COPY member so that its contents actually become hard-coded specifications in the converted RPG IV source. You should, however, try the default EXPCPY(*NO) first.

Print conversion report (CVTRPT)

Print a conversion report: *YES (default), *NO.

Include second-level text (SECLVL)

Include second-level message text in the conversion report: *NO (default), *YES.

Insert specification template (INSRTPL)

Insert RPG IV specification templates into the RPG IV source at the beginning of each section (H-, F-, D-, I-, C- and/or O-specs): *NO (default), *YES.

The converted code in Figure 12.1B includes examples of inserted templates.

Log file (LOGFILE)

Qualified name of the log file used to track conversion information: QRNCVTLG (default), *NONE, name.

Library: *LIBL (default), name.

The log file must already exist, unless you specify LOGFILE(*NONE). To create the QRNCVTLG log file, use the CRTDUPOBJ (Create Duplicate Object) command, specifying the following parameters:

```
CRTDUPOBJ   OBJ(QARNCVTLG)    +
            LIB(QRPGLE)       +
            OBJTYPE(*FILE)    +
            TOLIB(library)    +
            NEWOBJ(QRNCVTLG)
```

Log file member (LOGMBR)

Name of LOGFILE member used to track conversion information. The new information is added to the existing data in the member: *FIRST (default), *LAST, name.

Solving Conversion Problems

The CVTRPGSRC command assumes that the RPG III source to be converted can already be compiled correctly. The conversion aid performs a line-by-line conversion of the code without any semantic checking from one line to another.

There may be some code combinations that CVTRPGSRC can't handle. In these cases, the conversion report will indicate the problem, and you'll have to convert that section of code manually. Figure 12.2 shows part of a sample conversion report, with some representative messages.

FIGURE 12.2
Sample Conversion Report

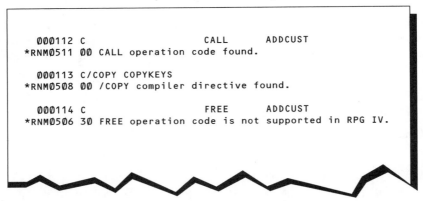

```
    000112 C                        CALL        ADDCUST
  *RNM0511 00 CALL operation code found.

    000113 C/COPY COPYKEYS
  *RNM0508 00 /COPY compiler directive found.

    000114 C                        FREE        ADDCUST
  *RNM0506 30 FREE operation code is not supported in RPG IV.
```

While some of the messages (e.g., RNM0506) will represent errors (severity 30), others (e.g., RNM0508, RNM0511) are simply informational messages (severity 00). Figure 12.3 lists some of the messages that CVTRPGSRC will generate.

FIGURE 12.3
CVTRPGSRC Messages

Message ID	Severity	Description
RNM0501	30	Unable to determine RPG specification type.
RNM0502	10	Comment has been truncated.
RNM0503	30	Corresponding F-spec is missing.
RNM0504	30	Corresponding E-spec is missing.
RNM0505	30	Corresponding L-spec is missing.
RNM0506	30	FREE opcode is not supported.
RNM0507	30	Auto-report is not supported.
RNM0508	0	/COPY compiler directive found.

continued ...

FIGURE 12.3 *CONTINUED*

Message ID	Severity	Description
RNM0509	30	Specification not valid or out of sequence.
RNM0510	10	/TITLE compiler removed.
RNM0511	0	CALL opcode found.
RNM0512	30	Not enough compile-time data records found.
RNM0513	10	Too many compile-time data records found.
RNM0514	30	Too many source records for SEU (more than 32,764).
RNM0516	10	Packed field larger than 30 digits in program-described file.
RNM0517	30	DEBUG operation is not supported.
RNM0518	30	Compile-time array definitions merged with a data structure subfield.

What types of problems can you expect to encounter when converting RPG III code? In general, the following situations may open up the possibility of conversion problems:

- RPG III compilation errors
- use of RPG III features not supported by RPG IV (e.g., FREE opcode and auto-report feature)
- /COPY statement sequencing problems in RPG III source
- externally described data structures in RPG III source

For most common programming techniques, you should encounter no problems converting your RPG III code to RPG IV syntax. Once the original code is in RPG IV syntax, you will need to manually address only style and standards issues. When the RPG IV code is acceptable, you can compile it into a bound program or a module.

Informational message RNM0508 is printed on the conversion report whenever CVTRPGSRC encounters a /COPY compiler directive. To compile the RPG IV source correctly, you must ensure that all /COPY source members included in this source member have also been converted to RPG IV. In general, you should convert all /COPY source members before converting their dependent RPG programs.

The conversion tool also highlights all the CALL opcodes that it finds in the RPG III source, marking them with informational message RNM0511. If you want to take advantage of static program calls using the new CALLB (Call a Bound Procedure) or CALLP (Call a Prototyped Procedure or Program) opcode, you can easily scan the conversion report to find all those instances where CALL occurs (for more information about CALLB and CALLP, see Chapter 13).

Compiling RPG IV Programs

Once you've converted your RPG program source to RPG IV syntax, it's time to compile the source into executable programs. Previously, this step meant that you would execute the CRTRPGPGM (Create RPG Program) command against the source code to invoke the RPG/400 compiler, which in turn would create a complete, callable program. ILE has introduced a two-step approach to creating callable programs:

1. Create one or more module (*MODULE) objects.
2. Bind one or more modules together into a single callable program (*PGM) object.

The *MODULE object is not executable unless you bind it (with or without other modules) into a program (*PGM) object. This binding step is similar to the link/edit step that may be familiar to you if you have created applications on hardware platforms other than the AS/400.

The CRTRPGMOD (Create RPG Module) command invokes the ILE RPG/400 compiler to create a non-executable module. PDM offers a new option 15 (Create module) to create modules; this option uses the CRTRPGMOD command. The OS/400 CRTPGM (Create Program) command binds together one or more modules and creates a callable program. The modules must exist when you use the CRTPGM command. The modules need not be RPG modules; you can mix and match modules from any ILE language (ILE RPG, ILE Cobol, ILE C, and ILE CL) into a single program. For more information about combining modules into a single program, see Chapter 13.

Initially, most of your RPG IV programs will probably be single-module programs, consisting solely of the specifications in a single source member. For this situation, the ILE RPG/400 compiler offers a single-step compilation command: CRTBNDRPG (Create Bound RPG Program). This command creates a temporary *MODULE object from RPG IV program source and then binds the module into a program; after the *PGM object is created, the *MODULE object is automatically deleted.

This is the command that PDM uses with its option 14 (Compile) when you invoke that option with an RPGLE source member. The CRTBNDRPG command offers close functionality and parameters similar to the familiar CRTRPGPGM command. Some ILE issues crop up when you compile a program with the CRTBNDRPG command, however. The two-step method, using the CRTRPGMOD and CRTPGM commands, is generally recommended to create ILE programs (for more information, see Chapter 13).

✓ **Modularize your application development with nested /COPY statements and new compiler directives.**

Nested /COPY and Conditional Compiles

RPG allows nested /COPY statements; that is, you can now code a /COPY within a /COPY member, enhancing your ability to modularize your RPG code effectively. The default nesting level is 32; if you need to adjust that level, you can use the COPYNEST H-spec keyword.

Nested /COPY statements can be useful with procedures as well as with another new RPG option: conditional compilation. Several new compiler directives let you control which statements are to be compiled, depending on conditions you can define. These are the new directives:

- /DEFINE condition-name
- /UNDEFINE condition-name
- /IF {NOT} DEFINED(condition-name)
- /ELSEIF {NOT} DEFINED(condition-name)
- /ENDIF
- /EOF

Among other things, you can use these directives to maintain a common source for different versions of an RPG program. In addition to defining conditions within the source code, you can define them with the CRTBNDRPG and CRTRPGMOD commands.

At Version 5, the compiler supports several predefined conditions to cover some of the situations that commonly occur:

- *ILERPG
- *CRTBNDRPG
- *CRTRPGMOD
- *VxRxMx

You need not set these conditions explicitly; the compile command will properly set them. The *ILERPG condition is true when you are using the ILE RPG/400 compiler to compile the source (instead of, for example, the VisualAge RPG compiler). The *CRTBNDRPG and *CRTRPGMOD conditions refer to the particular compile command being used to compile the source, and the *VxRxMx condition lets you maintain common source for different releases of the language (e.g., V4R4M0 or V5R1M0). The *VxRxMx condition is true when you're compiling to the specified target release or later.

Here are a couple of examples of how you might use conditional compilation:

```
*.. 1 ...+... 2 ...+... 3 ...+... 4 ...+... 5 ...+... 6 ...+... 7 ...+... 8
DName++++++++++ETDsFrom+++To/L+++IDc.Functions++++++++++++++++++++++++++++++++
CLØNØ1Factor1+++++++Opcode(E)+Factor2+++++++Result++++++++Len++D+HiLoEq....
CLØNØ1Factor1+++++++Opcode(E)+Extended-factor2+++++++++++++++++++++++++++++++
 /IF DEFINED(*CRTBNDRPG)
H DFTACTGRP(*NO) ACTGRP(*CALLER)
 /ENDIF

D VarDate          S              D
D DayOfWeek        S              1 Ø


 /IF DEFINED(*V5R1MØ)
 /FREE
    DayOfWeek = %REM(%DIFF(VarDate:D'1899-12-31':*DAYS) : 7);
 /END-FREE
 /ELSEIF DEFINED(*V4R4MØ)
C      VarDate      SUBDUR    D'1899-12-31' WorkField:*D
C                   EVAL      DayOfWeek = %REM(Workfield:7)
 /ELSE
C      VarDate      SUBDUR    D'1899-12-31' WorkField:*D
C                   DIV       7             WorkField
C                   MVR                     DayOfWeek
 /ENDIF
```

Here, the H-spec is included only if the short-cut CRTBNDRPG command is used to compile the source (the DFTACTGRP and ACTGRP keywords are not valid with the CRTRPGMOD command). In the calculations, the compiler will use one of three sets of code, depending on the TGTRLS (Target release) parameter value of the compiler command; the *V4R4M0 condition will be true for *both* Version 4 Release 4 and for Version 4 Release 5.

Chapter 13

RPG and ILE

With V2R3 of the OS/400 operating system, IBM introduced the Integrated Language Environment (ILE); with V3R1, IBM introduced the ILE RPG/400 compiler, which lets RPG IV participate in ILE. The other ILE compilers offered for the AS/400 are ILE Cobol/400, ILE C/400, and ILE CL. In this chapter, we briefly discuss ILE, as well as RPG's role in an ILE application. A complete discussion of ILE is beyond the scope of this "jump start," but the overview should give you a good basic understanding of ILE and its relationship to RPG IV.

ILE presents a single runtime model for all programs, regardless of which language the programs are written in. Using the ILE model offers many benefits, including

- better call performance
- program modularity and reusable components
- inter-language consistency in applications
- better control over job environment

Calling Programs in ILE

RPG III has always included the capability to call internal subroutines or external programs. Executing a subroutine (using the EXSR opcode) is a relatively fast process, but you have no way to break an application into separate modules using this approach. Calling an external program (using the CALL opcode) lets you take advantage of modular programming techniques, but this option carries with it a high performance cost. ILE now offers you more choices for calling programs. These choices not only improve call performance but also encourage programming modularity.

The traditional type of program call is the dynamic program call, which uses a CALL opcode to transfer control to a *PGM object outside the program that's currently running. RPG IV supports this type of call, just as RPG III did before it. The first time a program must CALL an external program, it must find the called program, create an internal system pointer, and build a number of internal structures to support the execution of the called program. Subsequent calls take fewer steps, but they are still relatively expensive in terms of machine instructions and performance. If an application makes heavy use of external program calls, the dynamic call can prove to have a significant and noticeable performance impact. Dynamic calls do offer a major advantage: You can make changes to a called program and then simply recompile it without touching the program(s) that call it (as long as there is no change in the number and type of parameters passed between the programs).

☑ **ILE's bound procedure calls execute much faster than dynamic calls.**

ILE introduces a new type of call, the bound procedure call (also called the static procedure call). Instead of calling a separate program, bound calls execute *procedures* within a single program. ILE gives you tools to build those procedures within the same program(s) that will call them or in separate source members and modules that you can develop apart from the program(s) that will call the procedures. (Chapter 14 discusses procedures and how to code them.)

Bound calls execute much faster than dynamic calls; the trade-off for better performance is that you lose some or all of the dynamic call's flexibility in changing the called procedure. RPG IV's new CALLB (Call a Bound Procedure) and CALLP (Call a Prototyped Procedure or Program) operations implement the bound procedure call:

```
*.. 1 ...+... 2 ...+... 3 ...+... 4 ...+... 5 ...+... 6 ...+... 7 ...+... 8
CLØNØ1Factor1+++++++Opcode(E)+Factor2+++++++Result++++++++Len++D+HiLoEq....
 * Call PROCA as a bound procedure (static call)
C                    CALLB     'PROCA'
C                    PARM                CompNbr
C                    PARM                Division
```

or

```
C                    CALLP     PROCA(CompNbr:Division)
```

As you can see, the syntax for the CALLB opcode is nearly identical to the familiar CALL opcode. CALLP, however, is a free-format operation; we'll discuss the CALLP operation further in Chapter 14.

The difference between a program and a procedure may be unclear to you if you've worked only with RPG. Other languages, such as C and Pascal, are procedure-oriented. You can think of a procedure as a distinct piece of related executable code within a program, similar to a subroutine. Unlike a subroutine, however, procedures can exist in separate modules by themselves, or within a service program (which we'll discuss later). You cannot use the CALL command to execute a procedure. You must use one of the bound procedure call operations, such as RPG's CALLB or CALLP or CL's CALLPRC (Call Procedure) command.

Bound procedure calls also require an additional step when you create the main calling program. First, you must compile the calling program and each of the called procedures into separate non-executable *MODULE objects using the new CRTRPGMOD (Create RPG Module) command. This command works similarly to the familiar CRTRPGPGM (Create RPG Program) command, but it creates a module instead of an executable program. After you have compiled each of the modules, you must "bind" them into a single callable program, using OS/400's CRTPGM (Create Program) command.

☑ **CRTRPGPGM doesn't work with RPG IV source.**

Note that you cannot use the CRTRPGPGM command to create a callable program from RPG IV source. You must first create a module and then bind one or more modules into a program. The ILE RPG/400 compiler does offer a command that combines the functions of the CRTRPGMOD and the CRTPGM commands into a single effort. If your program consists of just one module, you can use the CRTBNDRPG (Create Bound RPG Program) command, described in Chapter 12.

There are two kinds of bound procedure calls: bound by copy and bound by reference. With bound-by-copy calls, the actual code from the called procedures (programs) is included in the main executable program; thus, the compiler resolves all references to modules and generates all the start-up code for the called procedures at the time the executable program is created. This process can result in larger program objects because many copies of the code for called procedures may exist within the programs that make up an application.

Bound-by-copy calls offer all the same performance advantages that RPG III subroutine calls offer, but with the added benefit that you can build the called procedures in a modular fashion, separate from the main calling program. If you make a change in a called procedure, however, you will have to "re-bind" all the programs that use the procedure.

Bound-by-reference calls offer most of the execution speed of bound-by-copy calls, and they add much of the flexibility and memory conservation of the dynamic call. Bound-by-reference calls introduce a new type of AS/400 object: the service program (*SRVPGM). A service program is a collection of procedures that can be called only using a bound procedure call; you cannot use the CALL opcode, nor can you use the CALL CL command to invoke a service program or its procedures. You create a service program by first creating *MODULE objects for each of the procedures that are to be called. You then use the CRTSRVPGM (Create Service Program) command to bind the modules into a single *SRVPGM object.

To call a module in a service program, you simply use the CALLB or CALLP opcode, naming the procedure you want to run. A calling program can use modules in one or more service programs and can also include modules that are bound by copy, as described earlier. When you first load a program, the system activates all the service programs that it will need, causing a one-time performance hit. But after the program has started, there is little difference in the performance between a bound-by-copy call and a bound-by-reference call.

Because the module code exists in only one place (the *SRVPGM object), the bound-by-reference architecture is a better steward of memory than the bound-by-copy model, which "glues" a copy of the called code into each calling program. Service programs also offer you the advantage of changing the called module in one place without rebinding all the calling programs; in some instances, you can even change the number and type of parameters passed between the programs without recompiling the calling programs.

Implementing Bound Procedure Calls

RPG IV implements the bound procedure call with the new CALLB and CALLP opcodes. CALLB works in almost the same way as the familiar CALL opcode, except that it executes a bound call, either to a module copied into the program object or to a module in a service program. In Factor 2, you can either name the procedure to be called (a literal or a constant) or designate a procedure pointer that specifies the address of the procedure to be called. The optional result field can contain a parameter list, or you can follow the

CALLB operation with PARM statements. The following examples illustrate the use of the CALLB opcode to issue a bound procedure call:

```
*.. 1 ...+... 2 ...+... 3 ...+... 4 ...+... 5 ...+... 6 ...+... 7 ...+... 8
DName++++++++++ETDsFrom+++To/L+++IDc.Keywords+++++++++++++++++++++++++++++++++
CL0N01Factor1+++++++Opcode(E)+Factor2+++++++Result+++++++++Len++D+HiLoEq....
D ListCust         C                         'LSTCUST'
D CrtSpcPtr        S              *          PROCPTR
D                                            INZ(%PADDR('CreateSpace'))
C                      CALLB      'DLTCUST'                               99
C                      CALLB      ListCust
C                      CALLB      CrtSpcPtr
```

In the first CALLB example above, we simply name the procedure to be called. If the procedure ends in error, indicator 99 will be set on. The next example uses a constant to specify the procedure to call. In the final example, we use the procedure pointer CrtSpcPtr to point to a procedure to be called — in this case, procedure CreateSpace. Using a procedure pointer call will usually be somewhat faster than using either a literal or a constant.

Note that the procedure to be called can be a module created in any ILE language. To create RPG modules, you use the CRTRPGMOD command. Cobol, C, and CL have similar commands to create *MODULE objects. Any of these modules can be bound and called by an RPG program. In fact, after the CRTPGM command creates a *PGM object, you need not know or care which ILE language(s) the modules were originally written in. The CRTPGM command is a generic command that encompasses all ILE languages.

By now, you should have a good idea of the factors involved in choosing between bind-by-copy and bind-by-reference procedure calls. But RPG IV uses the same CALLB or CALLP syntax to address either type of call; so how do you implement one or the other in your ILE applications? The answer lies outside of RPG IV, in the CRTPGM command that actually binds modules together into an executable program.

Once you've created the *MODULE objects using CRTRPGMOD and created any service programs using CRTSRVPGM, you can bring all the parts together into a callable program with the CRTPGM command:

```
CRTPGM  PGM(library/program)              +
        MODULE(module-list)               +
        ENTMOD(entry-module)              +
        BNDSRVPGM(service-program-list)   +
        ACTGRP(activation-group)
```

The CRTPGM command has other parameters, but these are the main ones that will concern you. Notice the MODULE parameter. Here, you can list all the *MODULE objects that will be copied and bound into the program; when the program calls the procedures in these modules, the calls will be bound by copy. You can list up to 300 qualified module names (or generic names) to include in the program.

For example, the following command would bind together several modules to create a single program:

```
CRTPGM    PGM(CUSTLIB/WRKCUST)      +
          MODULE(CUSTLIB/WRKCUST    +
                 CUSTLIB/ADDCUST    +
                 CUSTLIB/CHGCUST    +
                 CUSTLIB/DLTCUST    +
                 CUSTLIB/DSPCUST    +
                 CUSTLIB/LSTCUST)   +
          ENTMOD(CUSTLIB/WRKCUST)
```

The optional ENTMOD parameter indicates which module contains the program entry point; that is, the module that is invoked when the program is dynamically called. The default is *FIRST, meaning the first module in the MODULE list that has a program entry procedure specification.

To include bound-by-reference calls in the program, you must name the service programs that contain the modules to be thus called. You list the service programs in the BNDSRVPGM parameter of the CRTPGM command:

```
CRTPGM    PGM(CUSTLIB/WRKCUST)        +
          MODULE(CUSTLIB/WRKCUST      +
                 CUSTLIB/ADDCUST      +
                 CUSTLIB/CHGCUST      +
                 CUSTLIB/DLTCUST      +
                 CUSTLIB/DSPCUST      +
                 CUSTLIB/LSTCUST)     +
          ENTMOD(CUSTLIB/WRKCUST)     +
          BNDSRVPGM(QGPL/VFYCUST      +
                    QGPL/VFYLEDG)
```

In this program, we include common routines from the service programs VFYCUST and VFYLEDG, which might contain routines to verify customer information and ledger information. The CRTPGM command won't copy these programs into the main program; instead, it will set up all the "hooks" the program will need at runtime to perform a bound-by-reference static call. You can name up to 50 service programs for the BNDSRVPGM parameter.

ILE Activation Groups

Another important ILE concept to be aware of is that of activation groups. An activation group is a substructure (or "run unit") within a job that controls the resources an application uses. An activation group isolates such resources as open data paths and file overrides inside logical boundaries within a job.

By using activation groups, you can segregate applications within the same job. For example, you can use shared open data paths for all files in both an accounts payable application and a general ledger application that will run in the same job. Accounts payable could run in the PAYABLES activation group, while general ledger could run in the LEDGER activation group. Even though both applications may use shared open data paths for the same file, each application will use a shared data path separate from the other application. Using activation groups can also make it easier to end an application within a job, because you reclaim only the resources (e.g., open files, active programs) for a single application, without disturbing other applications. You can explicitly name an activation group in the ACTGRP parameter if you want to control the name. For example, you could specify ACTGRP(PAYABLES) for all accounts payable programs in an application.

Normally, when you create a *PGM object, the CRTPGM command will default to ACTGRP(*NEW), which tells the system to create a new activation group (of its own naming) whenever this program is called. Creating an activation group is expensive in terms of the time it takes to build it. Instead of using the default, you should always run an ILE program in a named activation group (or use *CALLER, discussed below). Using a named activation group — for example, by specifying ACTGRP(QILE) — will improve program start-up performance.

☑ **When you use the CRTBNDRPG command, always specify DFTACTGRP(*NO).**

There's nothing magic about the name QILE; it's simply a name you can give to an activation group that will run all your ILE RPG programs. Coincidentally, QILE is the name of the activation group that the CRTBNDRPG command will use if you specify DFTACTGRP(*NO). To help performance, you should always specify this non-default option when you're using the single-step command to create single-module programs.

☑ **Consider changing the defaults for the CRTPGM and CRTSRVPGM commands to use ACTGRP(*CALLER).**

☑ **When you use the CRTBNDRPG command, consider specifying ACTGRP(*CALLER) along with DFTACTGRP(*NO).**

If you specify ACTGRP(*CALLER), the called program will run in the same activation group as the program that called it. You may want to use this option for subprograms within an application. This option is perhaps the easiest, most reliable activation group option. Even if you don't plan to use activation groups to segment your applications, you should consider changing the default for the CRTPGM and CRTSRVPGM commands, so that major "driver" programs use a named activation group, and subprograms use ACTGRP(*CALLER), instead of creating a new activation group each time you load the program.

Separate ILE from RPG IV

Learning RPG IV and learning ILE should be seen as two separate tasks. Although there are a few ILE-specific features to learn in RPG IV (the bound program call, subprocedures, and pointer support being probably the most notable), you can and should learn most of RPG IV's syntax and language features separately from learning the features and benefits of ILE.

And don't be put off by the word "environment" in Integrated Language Environment; ILE is poorly named. It is not an "environment" in the same sense that the System/36 and System/38 environments are (where "environment" implies "emulation"). Rather, ILE is a new programming model. It replaces both OS/400's Original Program Model (OPM), which provided support for languages such as RPG and Cobol, and its Extended Program Model (EPM), which provided support for C and Pascal. IBM added ILE primarily to provide a better C language environment. However, RPG, Cobol, and CL will also benefit from the new features ILE provides.

Before ILE, OS/400's OPM supported only one type of external program call — the dynamic program call. ILE's primary feature is that it offers two new ways to execute program calls: bound-by-copy and bound-by-reference static program calls. Unlike dynamic calls, which are resolved at runtime (i.e., the program is found, its name resolved to a system pointer, and authorities checked at runtime), static calls are resolved at link, or bind, time (a new step that follows the compile step). IBM claims that the performance of a static program call will be on a par with that of a local sub-routine call.

Beyond static program calls, ILE offers a single runtime model for all ILE languages. Thus, the promise of ILE is that you'll be able to call one program from another with effective exception and error handling, but without regard for either program's source language. Activation groups, which provide new ways for applications to manage resources, and service programs, which provide common services for all ILE languages, are other ILE features.

As you can see, there is a lot to learn about ILE, but you don't need to be an ILE expert before you start writing RPG IV. With just overview knowledge of ILE, you can begin. However, the better you understand ILE, the better you can exploit the ILE architecture of the AS/400.

Consider boning up on ILE by spending some time with the IBM publication *AS/400 ILE Concepts* (SC41-5606). With clear non–language-specific explanations, a comprehensive glossary, and a good index, this small manual lays a solid foundation for understanding ILE and wringing the most out of your AS/400.

Chapter 14

Procedures, Subprocedures, and Prototypes

In this chapter, you'll see how you can use procedures to help you build modular code, to localize variables, and to create your own built-in functions (BIFs) for your RPG applications. Using procedures goes beyond adding new subroutine function, helping you build truly reusable RPG components.

What Is a Procedure?

Up to now, RPG programs have always been single-procedure programs with a single entry point into the program. No more. With the latest enhancements, you can write an RPG IV program that consists of one main procedure and, optionally, one or more subprocedures. You can think of subprocedures as functional groupings of code: subroutines with a life of their own.

Procedures can exist in a module (*MODULE) object apart from the program that uses them. You can pass arguments (parameters) to procedures, and procedures can have their own local variables that won't interfere with variables in any other part of the program. In the main procedure, you call subprocedures using a syntax that's similar to that of RPG IV's BIFs. Usually, a subprocedure will return a value to the main procedure.

Subprocedures can be local to the main procedure; that is, they can be in the same program. On the other hand, you can code and compile subprocedures in a separate source member for other programs to use, thus making them more modular than subroutines could ever be. The terms "procedure" and "subprocedure" are often used interchangeably. Technically, a program consists of a main procedure and optional subprocedures, but you need not be overly concerned with the distinction.

From Subroutine to Procedure

To explain procedures and help you see where you can use them, let's look at an example. In this example, we'll convert an RPG IV subroutine into a procedure so that you can compare and contrast the syntax. Figure 14.1 shows the subroutine from Chapter 9 that calculates the day of the week (0 = Sunday, 1 = Monday, and so on) within an RPG IV program fragment.

FIGURE 14.1

Day of Week Subroutine

```
*.. 1 ...+... 2 ...+... 3 ...+... 4 ...+... 5 ...+... 6 ...+... 7 ...+... 8
DName++++++++++ETDsFrom+++To/L+++IDc.Functions+++++++++++++++++++++++++++++++
CLØNØ1Factor1++++++Opcode(E)+Factor2+++++++Result++++++++Len++D+HiLoEq....
CLØNØ1Factor1++++++Opcode(E)+Extended-factor2+++++++++++++++++++++++++++++++
D VarDate        S              D
D DayOfWeek      S              1 Ø

 /FREE
    DayOfWeek = %REM(%DIFF(VarDate:D'1899-12-31':*DAYS) : 7);
 /END-FREE
```

Or, at V4R4 or V4R5:

```
D VarDate        S              D
D WorkField      S              5 Ø
D DayOfWeek      S              1 Ø

C        VarDate      SUBDUR    D'1899-12-31' WorkField:*D
C                     EVAL      DayOfWeek = %REM(Workfield:7)
```

Or, for earlier releases:

```
D VarDate        S              D
D WorkField      S              5 Ø
D DayOfWeek      S              1 Ø

C        VarDate      SUBDUR    D'1899-12-31' WorkField:*D
C                     DIV       7             WorkField
C                     MVR                     DayOfWeek
```

Figure 14.2 shows the same subroutine (Version 5), now written as a procedure that returns a value of the day of the week. At first glance, the code looks like a normal RPG IV program, but if you scrutinize it, you'll see that the routine has several key differences that make it a procedure.

First, the source includes a NOMAIN H-spec to indicate that there is no main procedure in this source module; the source consists only of subprocedure code. When the RPG compiler builds the module from this source, it will not include any RPG cycle-related logic. (We've also included a COPYRIGHT H-spec to give you an idea of where you might use one.)

Next, the source may include D-specs for any variables that are global within this module or program. Every procedure in a module can access and manipulate all of the module's global variables. In our simple case, we don't have global work variables, but we must declare a special structure called a *procedure prototype*.

FIGURE 14.2
Day of Week Procedure

```
*.. 1 ...+... 2 ...+... 3 ...+... 4 ...+... 5 ...+... 6 ...+... 7 ...+... 8
DName++++++++++ETDsFrom+++To/L+++IDc.Functions+++++++++++++++++++++++++++++++
PName++++++++++..T..................Functions+++++++++++++++++++++++++++++++
H NOMAIN
H COPYRIGHT('(c) 2001, Bryan Meyers. All rights reserved.')

 * --------------------------------------------- Declare procedure prototype
D GetDOW         PR              1 0
D                                D

 * --------------------------------------------------- Begin procedure
P GetDOW         B                       EXPORT

 * ------------------------------------------------ Procedure interface
D                PI              1 0
D VarDate                        D

/FREE
    RETURN %REM(%DIFF(VarDate:D'1899-12-31':*DAYS) : 7);
/END-FREE

P GetDOW         E
 * --------------------------------------------------------- End of procedure
```

Declaring Prototypes

A special declaration called a procedure prototype must be present for every subprocedure that is used in the module. This special type of definition, which has a PR coded in columns 24–25, identifies any procedures included in the module. In addition to naming the procedure, the first prototype D-spec identifies the attributes (data type and length) of the value that the procedure will return to its caller. Following the prototype header are additional D-specs that tell the compiler the attributes of any parameters that will be passed to the procedure when it is executed.

The definition in Figure 14.2 indicates that any time the program calls the GetDOW procedure, the caller must pass GetDOW a date variable and should expect back a single-byte packed number in return.

The purpose of a prototype definition may not be familiar to you. A prototype lists the procedure's parameters in order, describing the attributes of the returned value, along with the attributes of any parameters passed to the procedure. Prototypes provide a "sanity check" between procedures, letting the RPG compiler perform validity checking on the procedure's calls. Without a prototype definition, it would be easy to create mysterious program bugs by passing invalid data to a procedure or by assuming the wrong return type.

Prototypes appear in two places: in the main program that will use a subprocedure and in the subprocedure itself. For each subprocedure a program uses, one prototype definition should exist. You must include the prototype in every "calling" procedure, as well as in the module for the procedure itself. The prototype need be coded only once within each module.

You'll normally want to code the prototype definition in a /COPY source member, so that you can easily include the same code in both the calling procedure and the subprocedure. You could, in fact, group all your prototype definitions for all your procedures into a single source member and then /COPY that member into your programs; the compiler would overlook the unreferenced prototypes.

Prototypes Provide Compiler Rules

If you've never encountered a language that uses prototyping, the prototype's purpose may seem fuzzy. It may help to understand prototypes in terms of traditional RPG operation codes.

When IBM developers first wrote the RPG compiler, they included support for a number of opcodes and hard-coded into the compiler the rules for using those opcodes. For example, with the ADD opcode, IBM made these requirements:

- The result field is required and must be numeric.
- Factor 1 is optional. If it is present, it must be a numeric field or literal.
- Factor 2 is required and must be a numeric field or literal.

If you try to write an RPG program that violates any of these rules, the compile will fail.

With subprocedures, you essentially are writing your own user-defined functions (your own opcodes), and the RPG IV compiler doesn't know the rules that it must use in determining whether you're coding the subprocedure correctly. The prototype serves the purpose of providing those rules to the compiler. If your code violates the rules that the prototype defines, the compile will fail. The prototype is the means that the compiler uses to ensure that the parameters and result value will work properly when the program is run.

If IBM developers had used D-specs (or at least a rough equivalent) in providing the rules for the ADD opcode, they might have coded something similar to this:

```
DName++++++++++ETDsFrom+++To/L+++IDc.Functions++++++++++++++++++++++++++++
D ADD              PR            P
D  Factor1                       P    OPTIONAL
D  Factor2                       P
```

Although these are not "real" (or even valid) D-specs, they illustrate the relationship between the rules listed above and their appearance in a prototype.

Coding a Subprocedure

The source code for a subprocedure follows the code for the main procedure, if there is one (in Figure 14.2, there is no main procedure). A new specification, the *procedure specification* (P-spec), defines the beginning and ending boundaries of the procedure. You can think of procedure specifications as taking the place of the BEGSR and ENDSR operations in a subroutine. Figure 14.3 describes the P-spec. P-specs currently support only one keyword, EXPORT, which is described in Figure 14.4.

FIGURE 14.3
Procedure Specification Layout

```
*.. 1 ...+... 2 ...+... 3 ...+... 4 ...+... 5 ...+... 6 ...+... 7 ...+... 8
PName+++++++++++..T.................Functions++++++++++++++++++++++++++++++++
```

Columns	Description
1–5	Sequence number
6	P
7–21	Procedure name (optional if column 24 contains an E)
22–23	Reserved
24	Begin/end procedure: B Begin procedure E End procedure
25–43	Reserved
44–80	Keywords

FIGURE 14.4
Procedure Specification Keyword

Keyword	Description
EXPORT	Makes a procedure available to be called by another procedure in another module.

Following the beginning P-spec, we must define a *procedure interface*, which is somewhat analogous to an *ENTRY parameter list. The procedure interface (PI) D-spec defines the data type and size of the value that the procedure will return, followed by a list defining each of the input parameters that the procedure will use. The data described in this area must match the prototype definition in data type and length.

You use D-specs to code procedure interfaces. Specify PI for the structure type (columns 24–25). On the same line, you also define the length, data type, and decimal positions of the value to be returned by the procedure (in this case, a single-digit packed numeric field with zero decimal places). Any subsequent fields (in this case, VarDate) define the parameters to be passed to the procedure and name the variables to which the procedure will assign those parameters. These variables are *local variables*; that is, they exist only within the context of the procedure.

Following the procedure interface definition are the D-spec entries for any other local variables that the procedure will require. Because these variables are defined between the boundaries of the procedure, they are local variables, specific to the procedure. Should any other procedure in the program (including the main procedure) happen to define an identically named field, it would represent a completely different variable. The Version 5 procedure in Figure 14.2 does not require any local work definitions beyond the procedure interface, but if there were any, they would appear following the prodecure interface.

Local variables normally allocate automatic storage and are reinitialized each time the procedure is executed. The system will not save the values of local variables across procedure calls, nor will values from prior invocations of the procedure be available if you call the procedure recursively. If you need to retain the value of a local variable, declare it in static storage by specifying the STATIC keyword in the D-spec for the variable.

The C-specs in Figure 14.2 are straightforward RPG IV C-specs. In fact, at Version 5 only one statement is necessary. Notice, however, that the RETURN operation now has a newly added function. The new function not only provides an exit from the procedure but also identifies the value that the procedure should return to its caller. You can return the value of a variable, an expression, or a literal. In this case, the procedure will return the value of the expression

```
REM(%DIFF(VarDate:D'1899-12-31':*DAYS) : 7)
```

A single procedure can also contain more than one RETURN operation, although it cannot return more than one value. The procedure will end when it encounters any RETURN operation.

How to Use Procedures

You can call a procedure using the same syntax that you use to call a built-in function. For the procedure in our example, we could code an expression similar to the following:

```
WeekDay = GetDOW(TodaysDate);
```

Or, we could use the procedure in an IF statement:

```
IF  GetDOW(TodaysDate) > 1;
```

You also can use prototypes with the new CALLP (Call a Prototyped Procedure or Program) opcode, which allows you some freedom in specifying parameters, using the extended Factor 2. CALLP takes the following syntax:

```
CALLP(E) Prototype(Parm1:Parm2:...ParmN);
```

Use CALLP to call programs or procedures that do not return a value. If you don't need to perform error checking with the E extender, you can omit coding CALLP on the free-form specification:

```
Prototype(Parm1:Parm2:...ParmN);
```

If there are no parameters to pass, the parentheses following the prototype name are optional:

```
Prototype();
```

or

```
Prototype;
```

Compiling Procedures

Recall from Chapters 12 and 13 that creating a callable ILE program is a two-step process:

1. Create one or more *MODULE objects.
2. Bind one or more modules into a single program (*PGM) object.

You cannot execute the module object until you bind it (with or without other modules) into a program. The CRTRPGMOD (Create RPG Module) command invokes the ILE RPG/400 compiler to create a non-executable module. Once you've used this command to compile your source, you must next bind together one or more modules using the CRTPGM (Create Program) command; this command creates the actual callable program. The CRTPGM command's MODULE parameter lets you list all the modules that the command must copy and bind together into the program.

Up to now, your RPG programs have probably consisted of only a single module, with the same name as your program. Now, with subprocedure support, you have two choices. First, you can code programs that will contain all the necessary code in a single compilation unit — that is, in the same source member. If you use this method, the source can contain /COPY statements to include various code components. However, you compile the source member as a single module and then bind it into a program just as you've always done. When you code subprocedures using this scheme, the code for the subprocedures follows the code for the main procedure.

As an alternative, you can now code each subprocedure within its own separate source member and compile it as a separate module. When you create the program, you then list each module so that the CRTPGM command can combine the components of the program into a callable unit. This method lets you maintain your subprocedure toolkit separate from the programs that use the subprocedures. You cannot employ the CRTBNDRPG "shortcut" command to build subprocedure modules separate from the programs that use them.

When you code procedures in separate source modules, be sure to include the EXPORT keyword when you begin the procedure. The EXPORT keyword ensures that you can access the procedure from other modules in the program.

Why Prototypes?

At first glance, the introduction of the prototype simply to declare parameter patterns seems like a cumbersome addition to the RPG language. But the prototype definition does more than enable the compiler to check the number of parameters passed on a call and the data attributes of those parameters. In addition, prototypes let RPG manage minor differences in parameter definitions. For example, if you code a procedure that expects a packed-decimal number as a parameter, you can write the prototype to accept an integer or a zoned number as well. Prototypes also afford you a great deal of flexibility in how you pass parameters.

Parameter-Passing Methods

Traditionally, RPG has always passed parameters from one program to another *by reference*. When you pass a parameter by reference, the caller passes a memory pointer to the called procedure (or program) and allows the called procedure access to the memory that corresponds to the parameter variable; the called procedure does not allocate its own storage for the parameter. If the called procedure makes a change to the value of that memory, the caller recognizes that change. This "two-way" parameter communication has been the only method of parameter passing available to RPG until the advent of prototypes. Passing parameters by reference is still the default method, and no special coding is necessary to use this method; the prototype examples shown earlier pass by reference.

If you want to protect the caller's parameter value from being changed by the called procedure, you now have the capability of passing parameters *by value*. When you pass a parameter by value, the called procedure allocates its own storage for the parameter, and the caller's storage is protected. If the called procedure makes a change to the parameter, the caller will not be aware of the change and thus will ignore it. Passing parameters by value lets you communicate information between procedures while at the same time isolating and localizing the storage used by individual procedures in a modular application.

To specify that you want to pass a parameter by value, you code the VALUE keyword for that parameter in the prototype and the procedure interface:

```
*.. 1 ...+... 2 ...+... 3 ...+... 4 ...+... 5 ...+... 6 ...+... 7 ...+... 8
DName++++++++++ETDsFrom+++To/L+++IDc.Functions+++++++++++++++++++++++++++++++
D CalcPmt         PR             13  2
D                               15  2 VALUE
D                                7  7 VALUE
D                                3  0 VALUE

D                 PI             13  2
D LoanAmt                        15  2 VALUE
D Interest                        7  7 VALUE
D Term                            3  0 VALUE
```

You can mix parameter-passing methods within a single prototype, passing some parameters by reference and others by value.

In addition to protecting storage, one other advantage of passing parameters by value is that you can code expressions and literals as parameters when calling the procedure; when you pass parameters by reference, you're limited to passing parameters within variables. For example, we could call the procedure in the preceding example using the following code:

```
*.. 1 ...+... 2 ...+... 3 ...+... 4 ...+... 5 ...+... 6 ...+... 7 ...+... 8
 /FREE
    Payment = CalcPmt(Balance + Fees:IntRate:360);
 /END-FREE
```

In this example, when the RPG procedure calls the CalcPmt procedure, it will evaluate the Balance + Fees expression before passing the value to CalcPmt as the first parameter. The second parameter will be the value contained in variable IntRate, and the third parameter will be the number 360, outside the context of any variable.

When you pass parameters by value, you need not be overly concerned about passing exactly the same data type that the called procedure is expecting for a parameter. For example, you can pass an integer variable or a zoned-decimal variable instead of a packed-decimal variable, as long as the value of the variable will fit into the called procedure's "slot" for that parameter.

A third parameter-passing method, *read-only reference*, is used primarily when proto-typing calls to external programs. External programs do not allow parameter passing by value, so you normally cannot code expressions and literals as parameters. Specifying read-only reference, by coding the CONST keyword for a parameter in the prototype and procedure interface, however, will let you code expressions and literals as parameters for the call. (See "Other Uses for Prototypes," page 164, for an example of read-only reference.) When you pass parameters using CONST, the system may make an internal copy of the parameter and then pass the pointer to that copy; should the called procedure or program make a change to the parameter, the caller should not depend on recognizing that change.

Additional Parameter-Passing Options

A few other parameter-passing options are worth noting, although these options are seldom used. Specifying OPTIONS(*NOPASS) for a parameter makes the parameter optional; if you code OPTIONS(*NOPASS), all subsequent parameters in the prototype and procedure interface must also be optional. In the called procedure (or program), you can use the %PARMS built-in function to find out how many parameters have been passed to a proce-dure and then process the parameters accordingly.

Specifying OPTIONS(*OMIT) for a parameter is similar to OPTION(*NOPASS) in that it gives you some flexibility in whether to pass a parameter. With OPTIONS(*OMIT), the caller will pass the special value *OMIT in place of the parameter. The called procedure (or program) should then use the %ADDR function to determine whether the parameter variable is pointing to a *NULL value; if the address of a parameter variable is null, the parameter was omitted. OPTIONS(*OMIT) can appear anywhere in the parameter list and need not be followed by other omissible parameters.

Last, OPTIONS(*VARSIZE) lets a parameter be shorter than the prototype specifies. For an example of using a variable-length parameter, see "Other Uses for Prototypes."

The Last Word on Procedures

You can use procedures to build your own toolkit of everyday routines that you can easily snap into your applications without worrying about field-naming crashes or indicator conflicts.

Use subprocedures to build functions that you feel are missing from the standard IBM-issue RPG. Sub-procedures could open up a whole new RPG industry: providing specialized toolkits that less technical AS/400 workshops could piece together into complete applications.

Other Uses for Prototypes

RPG IV uses the prototype definition to ensure accurate procedure interfaces between calling procedures and subprocedures. It's worth pointing out that this prototyping capability also can be used to ensure that the right number and type of parameters are passed when you do a call to any program, procedure, or API. If you use a prototype in this manner, you can then use the BIF-like calling syntax to call the program or API.

The example in Figure A illustrates using a prototype for the QCMDEXC CL command execution program. Your program can then call QCMDEXC, using a simple CALLP free-format syntax to execute the WRKACTJOB (Work with Active Jobs) CL command (or any other command). Note the use of the EXTPGM keyword to relate the ExeCL prototype to the QCMDEXC external program; whenever you invoke the prototype, the system will call QCMDEXC.

In addition to RPG procedures and external programs, you can use prototyping to incorporate C language functions into your RPG programs. Even if you don't have the C compiler on your system, you can access the standard C functions. The code in Figure B (page 165) makes use of C's srand and rand functions to generate random numbers.

In the figure, we first include an H-spec BNDDIR keyword to aim the compiler toward the IBM-supplied QC2LE binding directory to find the C functions. In the SeedRand and Rand prototypes, the EXTPROC keyword relates the RPG prototype names (SeedRand and Rand) to the C functions that we want to use (srand and rand). Because C is a case-sensitive language, we must code the C function names as quoted strings to maintain the correct case. C functions require you to pass all parameters by value, hence the use of the VALUE keyword in the prototypes shown in Figure B.

FIGURE A
Prototyping QCMDEXC

```
DName++++++++++ETDsFrom+++To/L+++IDc.Functions++++++++++++++++++++++++++++++
D ExeCL           PR                  EXTPGM('QCMDEXC')
D   Cmd                         512   OPTIONS(*VARSIZE)
D                                     CONST
D   CmdLen                    15P 5   CONST

D WrkActJob       S             512   INZ('WRKACTJOB')

  ...

  /FREE
     CALLP(E) ExeCL(%TRIM(WrkActJob):%LEN(%TRIM(WrkActJob)));
     IF %ERROR;
        ...
     ENDIF;
  /END-FREE
```

continued ...

Other Uses for Prototypes ... *Continued*

FIGURE B
Prototyping C Functions

```
DName++++++++++ETDsFrom+++To/L+++IDc.Functions+++++++++++++++++++++++++++++
H BNDDIR(QC2LE)

D SeedRand        PR                        EXTPROC('srand')
D   Seed                        10U 0 VALUE

D Rand            PR            10I 0 EXTPROC('rand')

D SysTime         S                Z   INZ(*SYS)
D RandNbr         S            10I 0
D Seed            S            10U 0

 /FREE
    // Set starting point for random number generator
    Seed = %DIFF(SysTime:%TIMESTAMP(%DATE):*MSECONDS) / 10;
    SeedRand(Seed);

    // Get next 10 random numbers
    FOR X=1 TO 10;
     RandNbr = Rand;
    ENDDO;
 /END-FREE
```

Chapter 15

Rethinking RPG Standards

Professional programmers appreciate the importance of standards in developing programs that are readable, understandable, and maintainable. The issue of programming style goes beyond any one language, but the introduction of the RPG IV syntax demands that you re-examine standards of RPG style. Now would be a great time to begin thinking about how your own shop's RPG standards might change as you move into application development with RPG IV. Make no mistake: Your existing RPG standards are now obsolete. This chapter presents some issues to think about before you start feeling your way around RPG IV.

Use Comments Judiciously

Good programming style can serve a documentary purpose in helping others understand the source code. If you practice good code-construction techniques, you'll find that "less is more" when it comes to commenting the source. Too many comments are as bad as too few.

Use comments to clarify — not echo — your code. Comments that merely repeat the code add to a program's bulk, but not to its value. In general, you should use comments for just three purposes:

- to provide a brief program or procedure summary
- to give a title to a subroutine, procedure, or other section of code
- to explain a technique that isn't readily apparent by reading the source

Always include a brief summary at the beginning of a program or procedure. This prologue should include the following information:

- a program or procedure title
- a brief description of the program's or procedure's purpose
- a chronology of changes that includes the date, programmer name, and purpose of each change
- a summary of indicator usage
- a description of the procedure interface (the return value and parameters)
- an example of how to call the procedure

Use consistent "marker line" comments to divide major sections of code. For example, you should definitely section off with lines of dashes (-) or asterisks (*) the declarations, the main procedure, each subroutine, and any subprocedures. Identify each section for easy reference.

Use blank lines to group related source lines and make them stand out. In general, you should use completely blank lines instead of blank comment lines to group lines of code, unless you're building a block of comments. Use only one blank line, though; multiple consecutive blank lines make your program hard to read.

Avoid right-hand "end-line" comments in columns 81–100. Right-hand comments tend simply to echo the code, can be lost during program maintenance, and can easily become "out of synch" with the line they comment. If a source line is important enough to warrant a comment, it's important enough to warrant a comment on a separate line. Version 5's support for end-of-line comments (starting with //) relaxes this rule somewhat, but if the comment merely repeats the code, eliminate it entirely.

Centralize Declarations

With RPG IV, we finally have an area of the program source in which to declare all variables and constants associated with the program. The D-specs organize all your declarations in one place.

RPG IV still supports the *LIKE DEFINE opcode, along with Z-ADD, Z-SUB, MOVEx, and CLEAR, to define program variables. But for ease of maintenance as well as program clarity, you'll want to dictate a standard that consolidates all data definition, including work fields, in D-specs.

Declare all variables within D-specs. Except for key lists and parameter lists, don't declare variables in C-specs — not even using *LIKE DEFINE. Define key lists and parameter lists in the first C-specs of the program, before any executable calculations. Use a prototype definition instead of an *ENTRY PLIST.

Whenever a literal has a specific meaning, declare it as a named constant in the D-specs. This practice helps document your code and makes it easier to maintain. One obvious exception to this rule is the allowable use of 0 and 1 when they make perfect sense in the context of a statement. For example, if you're going to initialize an accumulator field or increment a counter, it's fine to use a hard-coded 0 or 1 in the source.

Indent data item names to improve readability and document data structures. Unlike many other RPG entries, the name of a defined item need not be left-justified in the D-specs; take advantage of this feature to help document your code:

```
*.. 1 ...+... 2 ...+... 3 ...+... 4 ...+... 5 ...+... 6 ...+... 7 ...+... 8
DName++++++++++ETDsFrom+++To/L+++IDc.Functions+++++++++++++++++++++++++++++++
D ErrMsgDSDS      DS
D    ErrPrefix                 3
D    ErrMsgID                  4
D    ErrMajor                  2    OVERLAY(ErrMsgID:1)
D    ErrMinor                  2    OVERLAY(ErrMsgID:3)
```

Use length notation instead of positional notation in data structure declarations. D-specs let you code fields either with specific from and to positions or simply with the length of the field. To avoid confusion and to better document the field, use length notation consistently. For example, code

```
*.. 1 ...+... 2 ...+... 3 ...+... 4 ...+... 5 ...+... 6 ...+... 7 ...+... 8
DName++++++++++ETDsFrom+++To/L+++IDc.Functions+++++++++++++++++++++++++++++++
D RtnCode         DS
D    PackedNbr                15P 5
```

instead of

```
*.. 1 ...+... 2 ...+... 3 ...+... 4 ...+... 5 ...+... 6 ...+... 7 ...+... 8
DName+++++++++++ETDsFrom+++To/L+++IDc.Functions+++++++++++++++++++++++++++++++
D RtnCode         DS
D PackedNbr               1       8P 5
```

Use positional notation only when the actual position in a data structure is important. For example, when coding the program status data structure, the file information data structure, or the return data structure from an application programming interface (API), you'd use positional notation if your program ignores certain positions leading up to a field or between fields. Using positional notation is preferable to using unnecessary "filler" variables with length notation:

```
*.. 1 ...+... 2 ...+... 3 ...+... 4 ...+... 5 ...+... 6 ...+... 7 ...+... 8
DName+++++++++++ETDsFrom+++To/L+++IDc.Functions+++++++++++++++++++++++++++++++
D APIRtn          DS
D PackedNbr             145     152P 5
```

In this example, to better document the variable, consider overlaying the positionally declared variable with another variable declared with length notation:

```
*.. 1 ...+... 2 ...+... 3 ...+... 4 ...+... 5 ...+... 6 ...+... 7 ...+... 8
DName+++++++++++ETDsFrom+++To/L+++IDc.Functions+++++++++++++++++++++++++++++++
D APIRtn          DS
D Pos145                145     152
D PackNbr                       15P 5 OVERLAY(Pos145)
```

When defining overlapping fields, use the OVERLAY keyword instead of positional notation. Keyword OVERLAY explicitly ties the declaration of a "child" variable to that of its "parent." Not only does OVERLAY document this relationship, but if the parent moves elsewhere within the program code, the child will follow.

If your program uses compile-time arrays, use the **CTDATA form to identify the compile-time data. This form effectively documents the identity of the compile-time data, tying the data at the end of the program to the array declaration in the D-specs. The **CTDATA syntax also helps you avoid errors by eliminating the need to code compile-time data in the same order in which you declare multiple arrays.

Expand Naming Conventions

Perhaps the most important aspect of programming style deals with the names you give to data items (e.g., variables, named constants) and routines. Establish naming conventions that go beyond the traditional six characters, to fully identify variables and other identifiers. Those extra characters can make the difference between program "code" and a program "description."

When naming an item, be sure the name fully and accurately describes the item. The name should be unambiguous, easy to read, and obvious. Although you should exploit RPG IV's allowance for long names, don't make your names too long to be useful. Name lengths of 10 to 14 characters are usually sufficient, and longer names may not be practical in many specifications. When naming a data item, describe the item; when naming a subroutine or procedure, use a verb/object syntax (similar to a CL command) to describe the process. Maintain a dictionary of names, verbs, and objects, and use the dictionary to standardize your naming conventions.

When coding an RPG symbolic name, use mixed case to clarify the named item's meaning and use. RPG IV lets you type your source code in upper- and lowercase characters. Use this feature to clarify named data. For RPG-reserved words and operations, use all uppercase characters.

Avoid using special characters (e.g., @, #, $) when naming items. Although RPG IV allows an underscore (_) within a name, you can easily avoid using this "noise" character if you use mixed case intelligently.

Write Indicator-less Code

Historically, indicators have been an identifying characteristic of the RPG syntax, but with RPG IV they are fast becoming relics of an earlier era. Reducing a program's use of indicators may well be the single most important thing you can do to improve the program's readability.

Use indicators as sparingly as possible; go out of your way to eliminate them. At Version 5, RPG completely eliminates the need for conditioning indicators and resulting indicators and does not support them in any free-form specifications. In earlier releases, the only indicators present in a program should be resulting indicators for opcodes that absolutely require them (e.g., LOOKUP). Whenever possible, use built-in functions (BIFs) instead of indicators. Remember that you can indicate file exception conditions with error-handling BIFs (e.g., %EOF, %ERROR, %FOUND) and an E operation extender to avoid using indicators.

If you must use indicators, name them. V4R2 supports a Boolean data type (N) that serves the same purpose as an indicator. You can use the INDDS keyword with a display-file specification to associate a data structure with the indicators for a display or printer file; you can then assign meaningful names to the indicators.

Use the EVAL opcode with *Inxx and *ON or *OFF to set the state of indicators. Do not use the SETON or SETOFF operation, and never use MOVEA to manipulate multiple indicators at once.

Use indicators only in close proximity to the point where your program sets their condition. For example, it's bad practice to set an indicator and not test it until several pages later. If it's not possible to keep the related actions (setting and testing the indicator) together, move the indicator value to a meaningful variable instead.

Don't use conditioning indicators — ever. If a program must conditionally execute or avoid a block of source, explicitly code the condition with a structured comparison opcode, such as IF. If you're working with old System/36 code, get rid of the blocks of conditioning indicators in the source. The Version 5 free-form specification does not support conditioning indicators.

Include a description of any indicators you use. It's especially important to document indicators whose purpose isn't obvious by reading the program, such as indicators used to communicate with display or printer files or the U1–U8 external indicators, if you must use them.

Structured Programming Techniques

Give those who follow you a fighting chance to understand how your program works by implementing structured programming techniques at all times. The IF, DOU, DOW, FOR, and WHEN opcodes are positively elegant. Banish IF*xx*, DOU*xx*, DOW*xx*, and WH*xx* from your RPG IV code forever. By the way, you'd never use indicators to condition structured opcodes, would you? Good!

Don't use GOTO, CABxx, or COMP. Instead, substitute a structured alternative, such as nested IF statements, or status variables to skip code or to direct a program to a specific location. To compare two values, use the structured opcodes IF and ELSE. To perform loops, use DOU, DOW, and FOR. Never code your loops by comparing and branching with COMP (or even IF) and GOTO. Employ ITER to repeat a loop iteration, and use LEAVE for premature exits from loops or LEAVESR to prematurely exit subroutines.

Don't use the obsolete IFxx, DOUxx, DOWxx, or WHxx opcodes. The newer forms of these opcodes — IF, DOU, DOW, and WHEN — support free-format expressions, making those alternatives more readable. In general, if an opcode offers a free-format alternative, use it. This rule applies to the DO opcode as well; the free-format FOR operation is usually a better choice, if you're at V4R4 or later.

Perform multipath comparisons with SELECT/WHEN/OTHER/ENDSL. Deeply nested IF*xx*/ELSE/ENDIF code blocks are hard to read and result in an unwieldy accumulation of ENDIFs at the end of the group. Don't use the obsolete CAS*xx* opcode; instead, use the more versatile SELECT/WHEN/OTHER/ENDSL construction.

Always qualify END opcodes. Use ENDIF, ENDDO, ENDFOR, ENDSL, or ENDCS as applicable. This practice can be a great help in deciphering complex blocks of source.

Avoid programming tricks and hidden code. Such maneuvers aren't so clever to someone who doesn't know the trick. If you think you must add comments to explain how a block of code works, consider rewriting the code to clarify its purpose. Use of the obscure "bit-twiddling" opcodes (BITON, BITOFF, M*xx*ZO, TESTB, and TESTZ) may be a sign that your source needs updating.

Modular Programming Techniques

The RPG IV syntax, along with the AS/400's Integrated Language Environment (ILE), encourages a modular approach to application programming. Modularity offers a way to organize an application, facilitate program maintenance, hide complex logic, and efficiently reuse code wherever it applies.

Use RPG IV's prototyping capabilities to define parameters and procedure interfaces. Prototypes (PR definitions) offer many advantages when you're passing data between modules and programs. For example, they avoid runtime errors by giving the compiler the ability to check the data type and number of parameters. Prototypes also let you code literals and expressions as parameters, declare parameter lists (even the *ENTRY PLIST) in the D-specs, and pass parameters by value and by read-only reference, as well as by reference.

Store prototypes in /COPY members. For each module, code a /COPY member containing the procedure prototype for each exported procedure in that module. Then include a reference to that /COPY module in each module that refers to the procedures in the called module. This practice saves you from typing the prototypes each time you need them and reduces errors.

Include constant declarations for a module in the same /COPY member as the prototypes for that module. If you then reference the /COPY member in any module that refers to the called module, you've effectively "globalized" the declaration of those constants.

Use IMPORT and EXPORT only for global data items. The IMPORT and EXPORT keywords let you share data among the procedures in a program without explicitly passing the data as parameters — in other words, they provide a "hidden interface" between procedures. Limit use of these keywords to data items that are truly global in the program — usually values that are set once and then never changed.

Hone Your Modular Programming Skills

Creating effective modular programs requires two things: an architecture that offers high-performance calls with a uniform runtime model for high-level languages, and a language (or languages) capable of harnessing that architecture. With ILE, the AS/400 has the necessary program/procedure call environment, and with RPG IV, the RPG programmer has a language that can exploit that environment. RPG's support for subprocedures (covered in Chapter 14) is an especially welcome tool as you work on modularizing applications and creating repositories of reusable code.

As you write new ILE applications, you'll probably find yourself using program and/or procedure calls far more often than in the past. Consider a date conversion routine required by six fields in a one-million-record file. If you were to add that routine to an RPG/400 program as an external call, the six million times the routine is called could significantly degrade performance.

In the past, your only real option for this scenario was to code the routine as an internal subroutine. With ILE's static call mechanisms, though, you'll be able to code it as a subprocedure or a called program, with the effective performance of a subroutine call. This means you'll be able to rethink the structure of all your monolithic, inline RPG programs and achieve a substantial level of modularity without a trade-off in speed.

As you increasingly exploit the benefits of modular procedure calls, you'll need to know how best to carve up your code. Robust modular programming isn't achieved by butchering old code into random chunks; rather, it requires "filleting" code into planned, manageable, reusable pieces. You'll need to engineer each module so that it does one thing well and so that your call interfaces are simple, yet flexible enough to do the job.

Free the Factor 2

You can mix and match RPG III style, RPG IV fixed-form style, and RPG IV free-form style in your C-specs, but the result is inconsistent and difficult to read. Take full advantage of the more natural order and expanded space afforded by the free-form specification (or, previous to Version 5, the extended Factor 2). When you're coding loops and groups, you'll find that the code looks and feels better in free-form.

Use free-form expressions (or EVAL) wherever possible. Instead of Z-ADD and Z-SUB, use assignment expressions. Use expressions for any arithmetic in your program. Instead of CAT and SUBST, use string expressions. Use expressions to set indicators (if you need them).

But don't completely abandon columnar alignment as a tool to aid readability in expressions. Especially when an expression must continue onto subsequent lines, align the expression to make it easier to understand (see Chapter 7 for examples).

Character String Manipulation

IBM has greatly enhanced RPG IV's ability to easily manipulate character strings. Many of the tricks you had to use with earlier versions of RPG are now obsolete. Modernize your source by exploiting these new features.

Use a named constant to declare a string constant instead of storing it in an array or table. Declaring a string (such as a CL command string) as a named constant lets you refer to it directly instead of forcing you to refer to the string through its array name and index. Use a named constant to declare any value that you don't expect to change during program execution.

Avoid using arrays and data structures to manipulate character strings and text. Use the new string manipulation opcodes and/or built-in functions instead.

Use EVAL's free-form assignment expressions whenever possible for string manipulation. When used with character strings, EVAL is usually equivalent to a MOVEL(P) opcode. When you don't want the result to be padded with blanks, use %SUBST or %REPLACE functions.

Use variable-length fields to simplify string handling. Use variable-length fields as CONST or VALUE parameters to every string-handling subprocedure, as well as for work fields. Not only does the code look better (eliminating the %TRIM function, for example), but it's also faster than using fixed-length fields. For example, code

```
*.. 1 ...+... 2 ...+... 3 ...+... 4 ...+... 5 ...+... 6 ...+... 7 ...+... 8
DName++++++++++ETDsFrom+++To/L+++IDc.Functions++++++++++++++++++++++++++++++
D QualName        S             33    VARYING
D Library         S             10    VARYING
D File            S             10    VARYING
D Member          S             10    VARYING

/FREE
   QualName = Library + '/' + File + '(' + Member + ')';
/END-FREE
```

instead of

```
*.. 1 ...+... 2 ...+... 3 ...+... 4 ...+... 5 ...+... 6 ...+... 7 ...+... 8
DName++++++++++ETDsFrom+++To/L+++IDc.Functions+++++++++++++++++++++++++++++++
D QualName        S             33
D Library         S             10
D File            S             10
D Member          S             10

 /FREE
    QualName = %TRIM(Library) + '/' + %TRIM(File)
             + '(' + %TRIM(Member) + ')';

 /END-FREE
```

Avoid Obsolescence

RPG is an old language. After 30 years, many of its original, obsolete features are still available. Don't use them.

Don't sequence program line numbers in columns 1–5. Chances are you'll never again drop that deck of punched cards, so the program sequence area is unnecessary. In RPG IV, the columns are commentary only. You may use them to identify changed lines in a program or structured indentation levels, but be aware that these columns may be subject to the same hazards as right-hand comments.

Avoid program-described files. Instead, use externally defined files whenever possible.

If an opcode offers a free-format syntax, use it instead of the fixed-format version. Opcodes to avoid include CAB*xx*, CAS*xx*, CAT, DO (at V4R4), DOU*xx*, DOW*xx*, IF*xx*, and WH*xx*. At Version 5, avoid any opcode that the free-form specification doesn't support (Figure 6.4 in Chapter 6 lists them).

If a BIF offers the same function as an opcode, use the BIF instead of the opcode. With some opcodes, you can substitute a built-in function for the opcode and use the function within an expression. At V4R1, the SCAN and SUBST opcodes have virtually equivalent built-in functions, %SCAN and %SUBST. In addition, you can usually substitute the concatenation operator (+) in combination with the %TRIM*x* BIFs in place of the CAT opcode. The free-format versions are preferable if they offer the same functionality as the opcodes.

Use the date operations to operate on dates. Get rid of the clever date and time routines that you have gathered and jealously guarded over the years. The RPG IV operation codes and built-in functions are more efficient, clearer, and more modern. Even if your database includes dates in "legacy" formats, you can use the date opcodes to manipulate them.

Shun obsolete opcodes. In addition to the opcodes mentioned earlier, some opcodes are no longer supported or have better alternatives:

- CALL, CALLB — The prototyped calls (CALLP or a function call) are just as efficient as CALL and CALLB and offer the advantages of prototyping and parameter passing by value. Neither CALL nor CALLB can accept a return value from a procedure.

- DEBUG — With OS/400's advanced debugging facilities, this opcode is no longer supported.

- DSPLY — You should use display file I/O to display information or to acquire input.

- FREE — This opcode is no longer supported.

- PARM, PLIST — If you use prototyped calls, these opcodes are no longer necessary.

Miscellaneous Guidelines

Here's an assortment of other style guidelines that can help you improve your RPG IV code.

In all specifications that support keywords, observe a one-keyword-per-line limit. Instead of spreading multiple keywords and values across the entire specification, your program will be easier to read and let you more easily add or delete specifications if you limit each line to one keyword, or at least to closely related keywords (e.g., DATFMT and TIMFMT).

Begin all H-spec keywords in column 8, leaving column 7 blank. Separating the keyword from the required H in column 6 improves readability.

Relegate mysterious code to a well-documented, well-named procedure. Despite your best efforts, on extremely rare occasions you simply will not be able to make the meaning of a chunk of code clear without extensive comments. By separating such heavily documented, well-tested code into a procedure, you'll save future maintenance programmers the trouble of deciphering and dealing with the code unnecessarily.

Final Advice

Sometimes good style and efficient runtime performance don't mix. Wherever you face a conflict between the two, choose good style. Hard-to-read programs are hard to debug, hard to maintain, and hard to get right. Program correctness must always win out over speed. Keep in mind these admonitions from Brian Kernighan and P. J. Plauger's *The Elements of Programming Style*:

- Make it right before you make it faster.
- Keep it right when you make it faster.
- Make it clear before you make it faster.
- Don't sacrifice clarity for small gains in efficiency.

Appendix A

RPG IV Operation Code and Function Summary

This appendix contains a summary of all the RPG operation codes and built-in functions (BIFs) — both those that already existed in the RPG III syntax and the ones that are new with RPG IV. For each operation code, both the free-form (Version 5) and the fixed-form syntax are shown; for functions, the syntax is noted. Following the syntax description, we briefly describe the operation or function and the entries needed to perform it, as follows:

%Function and Name

Function: %Function(<u>required-entry</u>:optional-entry)

Operation Code and Name

Free-form: Opcode(optional extenders) <u>required-entry</u> optional-entry

Factor 1		Factor 2	Result	HI	LO	EQ
Optional entry (not underlined)	Opcode (with optional extenders)	<u>Required entry (underlined)</u>		<u>Req</u> <u>Ind</u>	Opt Ind	

Note: In the examples above, the required and optional entries are underlined or not underlined, respectively, as examples of how the syntax descriptions will look.

Following each syntax example, you'll find a description of the operation code or function, followed by descriptions of each of the syntax description's entries. If an operation code has a newer equivalent operation code or built-in function, the operation code will be labeled "Obsolete" and the new operation code or function will be noted.

Except where otherwise noted, level indicators (columns 7–8) and conditioning indicators (columns 9–11) are allowed for the fixed-form syntax of each operation code. The free-form syntax does not allow level indicators or conditioning indicators for any operation.

%ABS Absolute value

Function: %ABS(<u>numeric-expression</u>)

Returns absolute value of expression, removing sign if negative.

Numeric Expression to evaluate.
expression

ACQ Acquire a program device for a WORKSTN file

Free-form: ACQ(E) <u>device-name</u> <u>workstn-file</u>

Factor 1		Factor 2	Result	HI	LO	EQ
<u>Device name</u>	ACQ(E)	<u>WORKSTN file</u>			ER	

Attaches a device to a workstation file.

Device name Name of the program device to be acquired.

WORKSTN file The multiple-device file to be associated with the program device.

ER or **(E)** Operation not completed successfully.

ADD Add two values together

Free-form: Not supported

Factor 1		Factor 2	Result	HI	LO	EQ
Addend 1	ADD(H)	<u>Addend 2</u>	<u>Sum</u>	+	–	Z

If there is a value in Factor 1, adds that value to the value in Factor 2. If there is not a value in Factor 1, adds the value in Factor 2 to the result. The sum is always placed in the result field.

Addend 1 If Factor 1 is specified, the ADD operation adds it to Factor 2 and places the sum in the result field.

(H) Result will be half-adjusted (rounded).

Addend 2 If Factor 1 is not specified, the ADD operation adds Factor 2 to the sum field.

Sum The summation of the ADD operation.

+ Set on if the result field is greater than 0.

– Set on if the result field is less than 0.

Z Set on if the result field is equal to 0.

Note: *Obsolete.* Use + operator instead.

ADDDUR Add duration
Free-form: Not supported

Factor 1		Factor 2	Result	HI	LO	EQ
Date/Time 1	ADDDUR(E)	Duration:code	Date/Time 2		ER	

Adds a duration (e.g., a number of days) to a date, time, or timestamp.

<table>
<tr><td>Date/Time 1</td><td>Date, time, or timestamp field, subfield, array, array element, literal, or constant. If Factor 1 is not specified, the duration is added to the field specified in the result field.</td></tr>
<tr><td><u>Duration</u></td><td>Numeric field, array element, or integer constant with zero decimal positions. If the duration is negative, it is subtracted from the date.</td></tr>
<tr><td><u>Code</u></td><td>A special value that indicates the type of duration.</td></tr>
<tr><td>Date/Time 2</td><td>Date, time, or timestamp field, subfield, array, or array element.</td></tr>
<tr><td>ER or (E)</td><td>Invalid operand, or other error performing operation.</td></tr>
</table>

Note: The system places a 15-digit limit on durations. *Obsolete.* Use + operator with duration function (e.g., %DAYS, %MONTHS, %YEARS) instead.

%ADDR Get address pointer
Function: %ADDR(variable(index-expression))

Returns a basing pointer representing the storage address of the specified variable. On the left-hand side of an assignment expression, assigns a storage address to a pointer.

<table>
<tr><td><u>Variable</u></td><td>The variable for which the address should be returned/assigned. May include an array or table index or an occurrence for a multiple-occurrence data structure.</td></tr>
</table>

%ALLOC Allocate storage
Function: %ALLOC(length)

Returns a pointer to uninitialized storage of the specified length.

<table>
<tr><td><u>Length</u></td><td>Amount of storage to allocate. Must be a numeric literal constant or field with a value between 1 and 16,776,704.</td></tr>
</table>

ALLOC Allocate storage

Free-form: Not supported

Factor 1		Factor 2	Result	HI	LO	EQ
	ALLOC(E)	Length	Pointer		ER	

Allocates uninitialized storage of the specified length, setting a pointer to the new storage.

Length   Amount of storage to allocate. Must be a numeric literal constant or field with a value between 1 and 16,776,704.

Pointer   Basing pointer to set to new storage.

ER or (E)   Invalid operand or other error performing operation.

Note: *Obsolete.* Use %ALLOC function instead.

ANDxx And operation

Free-form: Not supported

Factor 1		Factor 2	Result	HI	LO	EQ
Compare value 1	ANDxx	Compare value 2				

ANDxx is an optional operation, used to specify a complex condition. When used, it must immediately follow a DOUxx, DOWxx, IFxx, ORxx, or WHENxx operation. In the ANDxx operation, the relationship xx can be

GT	Factor 1 >	Factor 2
LT	Factor 1 <	Factor 2
EQ	Factor 1 =	Factor 2
NE	Factor 1 <>	Factor 2
GE	Factor 1 >=	Factor 2
LE	Factor 1 <=	Factor 2

Compare value 1   Must contain a literal, a named constant, a table name, an array element, a data structure name, or a field name.

Compare value 2   Must contain a literal, a named constant, a table name, an array element, a data structure name, or a field name.

Note: Conditioning indicators are not valid. *Obsolete.* Use AND operator instead.

BEGSR Begin a subroutine

Free-form: BEGSR subroutine-name

Factor 1		Factor 2	Result	HI	LO	EQ
Subroutine name	BEGSR					

Identifies the beginning of a subroutine.

Subroutine name   A unique symbolic name that identifies an RPG IV subroutine.

Note: The keyword *PSSR used in Factor 1 specifies that this is an exception/error subroutine. The keyword *INZSR specifies a subroutine to be run during the initialization step. Conditioning indicators are not valid.

BITOFF Set bits off

Free-form: Not supported

Factor 1		Factor 2	Result	HI	LO	EQ
	BITOFF	Bit numbers	Character field			

Causes bits identified in Factor 2 to be set off (set to 0) in the result field.

Bit numbers   The bits to be set off are identified by the numbers 0–7 (0 is the leftmost bit). The bit numbers must be enclosed in apostrophes ('). Can be a field name, a one-byte hexadecimal literal, or a named constant.

Character field   One-position character field.

BITON Set bits on

Free-form: Not supported

Factor 1		Factor 2	Result	HI	LO	EQ
	BITON	Bit numbers	Character field			

Causes bits identified in Factor 2 to be set on (set to 1) in the result field.

Bit numbers   The bits to be set on are identified by the numbers 0–7 (0 is the leftmost bit). The bit numbers must be enclosed in apostrophes ('). Can be a field name, a one-byte hexadecimal literal, or a named constant.

Character field   One-position character field.

CAB*xx* Compare and branch

Free-form: Not supported

Factor 1		Factor 2	Result	HI	LO	EQ
Compare value 1	CAB*xx*	Compare value 2	Label	HI	LO	EQ

Compares the two values specified by the *xx* portion of the operation and branches to the TAG or ENDSR operation. In the CAB*xx* operation, the *xx* can be

GT	Factor 1	>	Factor 2
LT	Factor 1	<	Factor 2
EQ	Factor 1	=	Factor 2
NE	Factor 1	<>	Factor 2
GE	Factor 1	>=	Factor 2
LE	Factor 1	<=	Factor 2

Compare value 1 Must contain a character literal, a numeric literal, a named constant, a figurative constant, a field name, a table name, an array element, or a data structure name.

Compare value 2 Must contain a character literal, a numeric literal, a named constant, a figurative constant, a field name, a table name, an array element, or a data structure name.

Label The label specified in the result field must be associated with a unique TAG operation.

HI Set on if Factor 1 is greater than Factor 2.

LO Set on if Factor 1 is less than Factor 2.

EQ Set on if Factor 1 equals Factor 2.

Note: The Factor 1 and the Factor 2 entries must be both character data or both numeric. *Obsolete.* Use free-form expressions instead.

CALL Call a program
Free-form: Not supported

Factor 1		Factor 2	Result	HI	LO	EQ
	CALL(E)	Program name	Plist name		ER	LR

Passes control to the program specified in Factor 2.

Program name   Character entry that specifies the name of the program to be called.

Plist name   Parameter list name used to communicate values between calling program and called program.

ER or **(E)**   Set on if error returned from the called program.

LR   Set on if called program is RPG program that returns with the LR indicator on.

Note: *Obsolete.* Use CALLP instead.

CALLB Call a bound procedure
Free-form: Not supported

Factor 1		Factor 2	Result	HI	LO	EQ
	CALLB(DE)	Procedure name or procedure pointer	Plist name		ER	LR

Passes control to the program specified in Factor 2.

(D)   Include operational descriptors of character or graphic strings passed.

Procedure name   A literal or a constant character entry that specifies the name of the procedure to be called.

Procedure pointer   The address of the procedure to be called.

Plist name   Parameter list name used to communicate values between calling program and called program.

ER or **(E)**   Set on if error returned from the called program.

LR   Set on if called program is RPG program that returns with the LR indicator on.

Note: *Obsolete.* Use CALLP instead.

CALLP Call a prototyped procedure or program

Free-form: CALLP(EMR) <u>name</u>(parm1:parm2:...)

Factor 1		Extended Factor 2
	CALLP(EMR)	<u>Name</u> (Parm1:Parm2 ...)

Passes control to the procedure or program specified in the extended Factor 2 using any parameters specified in the extended Factor 2. You must include a prototype definition for the procedure or program to call.

(E)	Sets on %ERROR function if error returned from the called program or procedure.
(M/R)	Use *MAXDIGITS or *RESDECPOS precision rules when evaluating expression.
<u>Name</u>	Prototype name of the prototyped procedure or program to call.
<u>Parm1:Parm2...</u>	Optional parameters to pass to the procedure or program. Use a colon (:) to separate parameters.

CASxx Conditionally invoke subroutine

Free-form: Not supported

Factor 1		Factor 2	Result	HI	LO	EQ
Compare value 1	CASxx	Compare value 2	<u>Subroutine name</u>	HI	LO	EQ

Conditionally invokes a subroutine. In the CAS*xx* operation, the *xx* relationship can be defined as

GT	Factor 1	>	Factor 2
LT	Factor 1	<	Factor 2
EQ	Factor 1	=	Factor 2
NE	Factor 1	<>	Factor 2
GE	Factor 1	>=	Factor 2
LE	Factor 1	<=	Factor 2
(Blank)	(No comparison made)		

Compare value 1	Must contain a literal, a named constant, a table name, an array element, a data structure name, or a field name.
Compare value 2	Must contain a literal, a named constant, a table name, an array element, a data structure name, or a field name.
<u>Subroutine name</u>	Unique symbolic name that identifies RPG subroutine.

HI Set on if Factor 1 is greater than Factor 2.

LO Set on if Factor 1 is less than Factor 2.

EQ Set on if Factor 1 equals Factor 2.

Note: *Obsolete.* Use SELECT and WHEN instead.

CAT Concatenate two character strings

Free-form: Not supported

Factor 1		Factor 2	Result	HI	LO	EQ
Source string 1	CAT(P)	Source string 2: number of blanks	Target string			

Concatenates the character string specified in source string 2 to the end of the character string specified in source string 1. The concatenated string is placed in the target string in the result field.

Source string 1	A character string that can be one of the following: a field name, an array element, a named constant, a data structure name, a table name, or a literal. If Factor 1 is not specified, the result field is used.
(P)	Pad result field with blanks.
Source string 2: number of blanks	Must contain a character string, and may optionally contain the number of blanks to be inserted between the concatenated strings.
Target string	The target string must be character and can contain the following: a field name, an array element, a data structure name, or a table name.

Note: *Obsolete.* Use free-form expressions instead.

CHAIN Random retrieval from a file based on key value or record number

Free-form: CHAIN(EN) <u>search-argument</u> <u>file-format-name</u> data-structure

Factor 1		Factor 2	Result	HI	LO	EQ
<u>Search argument</u>	CHAIN(EN)	<u>File name</u> or <u>format name</u>	Data structure	<u>NR</u>	ER	

Randomly retrieves a file based on key value or record number.

<u>**Search argument**</u>	If access is by key, Factor 1 can be a field name, a named constant, a figurative constant, a literal, or, for an externally described file, a KLIST name. If access is by relative record number, Factor 1 must contain an integer literal or numeric field with zero decimal fields.
(N)	Do not lock record.
<u>**File name**</u> or <u>**format name**</u>	File name or format name from externally described file.
Data structure	Data structure into which the record will be placed (valid only with a program-described file).
<u>**NR**</u>	Set on if no record in the file matches the search argument.
ER or **(E)**	Operation not completed successfully.

Note: Requires a full procedural file (F in position 22 of F-spec).

%CHAR Convert to character data

Function: %CHAR(<u>expression</u>:format)

Converts an expression (numeric, date, time, timestamp, graphic, or UCS-2 data) to character data.

<u>**Expression**</u>	Expression to convert.
Format	Date or time format to use.

%CHECK Check characters

Function: %CHECK(<u>compare-string</u>:<u>base-string</u>:start)

Verifies that each character in the base string is among the valid characters indicated in the compare string. Returns leftmost position of character in base string that is not in compare string.

<u>**Compare string**</u>	A character string that can be one of the following: a field name, an array element, a named constant, a data structure name, a literal, or a table name.

Base string:start Must contain either the source string or the source string followed by a colon followed by the start location. Must be a character string that can be one of the following: a field name, an array element, a named constant, a data structure name, a literal, or a table name.

CHECK Check characters
Free-form: Not supported

Factor 1		Factor 2	Result	HI	LO	EQ
Compare string	CHECK(E)	Base string:start	Left position(s)		ER	FD

Verifies that each character in the base string is among the valid characters indicated in the compare string.

Compare string A character string that can be one of the following: a field name, an array element, a named constant, a data structure name, a literal, or a table name.

Base string:start Must contain either the source string or the source string followed by a colon followed by the start location. Must be a character string that can be one of the following: a field name, an array element, a named constant, a data structure name, a literal, or a table name.

Left position(s) Can be a numeric variable, a numeric position(s) array element, a numeric table name, or a numeric array. No decimal positions should be defined. If not specified, the found indicator must be specified.

ER or **(E)** Operation not completed successfully.

FD Invalid characters found.

Note: *Obsolete.* Use %CHECK function instead.

%CHECKR Check characters (reversed)
Function: %CHECKR(compare-string:base-string:start)

Verifies that each character in the base string is among the valid characters indicated in the compare string. Checking begins with the rightmost character. Returns rightmost position of character in base string that is not in compare string.

Compare string A character string that can be one of the following: a field name, an array element, a named constant, a data structure name, a literal, or a table name.

Base string:start Must contain either the source string or the source string followed by a colon followed by the start location. Must be a character string that can be one of the following: a field name, an array element, a named constant, a data structure name, a literal, or a table name.

CHECKR Check characters (reversed)

Free-form: Not supported

Factor 1		Factor 2	Result	HI	LO	EQ
Compare string	CHECKR(E)	Base string:start	Right position(s)		ER	FD

Verifies that each character in the source string is among the valid characters indicated in the compare string. Checking begins with the rightmost character.

Compare string — A character string that can be one of the following: a field name, an array element, a named constant, a data structure name, a literal, or a table name.

Base string:start — Must contain either the source string or the source string followed by a colon followed by the start location. Must be a character string that can be one of the following: a field name, an array element, a named constant, a data structure name, a literal, or a table name.

Right position(s) — Can be a numeric variable, a numeric array element, a numeric table name, or a numeric array. No decimal positions should be defined. If not specified, the found indicator must be specified.

ER or **(E)** — Operation not completed successfully.

FD — Invalid characters found.

Note: *Obsolete.* Use %CHECKR function instead.

CLEAR Clear data structure, variable, or record format

Free-form: CLEAR *NOKEY *ALL structure-variable

Factor 1		Factor 2	Result	HI	LO	EQ
*NOKEY	CLEAR	*ALL	Structure or variable			

Clears a data structure, variable, or record format, setting it to its default value.

*NOKEY — Indicates that all fields except key fields are to be cleared. Valid only if the data structure or the variable contains a DISK record format name.

*ALL — If specified, and the result field contains a multiple-occurrence data structure or a table name, all occurrences or table elements will be cleared and the occurrence level will be set to 1.

Structure or **variable** — Contains the structure or variable to be cleared. It can be one of the following: a field name, an array element or name, a data structure name, or a table name.

CLOSE Close files

Free-form: CLOSE(E) <u>file-name</u>

Factor 1		Factor 2	Result	HI	LO	EQ
	CLOSE(E)	<u>File name</u>			ER	

Closes one or more files or devices and disconnects them from the program.

<dl>

File name Names the file to be closed. The keyword *ALL can be specified to close all the files at once.

ER or **(E)** Close operation not completed successfully.

COMMIT Commit group

Free-form: COMMIT(E) boundary

Factor 1		Factor 2	Result	HI	LO	EQ
Boundary	COMMIT(E)				ER	

Makes all the changes to files that have been specified in output operations since the previous COMMIT or ROLBK operation. Releases all the record locks for files under commitment control.

Boundary Identifier of the boundary between the changes made by the COMMIT operation and subsequent changes.

ER or **(E)** Operation not completed successfully.

COMP Compare two values

Free-form: Not supported

Factor 1		Factor 2	Result	HI	LO	EQ
Compare value 1	COMP	Compare value 2		HI	LO	EQ

Compares two values, setting result indicators on or off depending upon the comparison.

Compare value 1   Must contain a literal, a named constant, a table name, an array element, a data structure name, or a field name.

Compare value 2   Must contain a literal, a named constant, a table name, an array element, a data structure name, or a field name.

HI   Set on if Factor 1 is greater than Factor 2.

LO   Set on if Factor 1 is less than Factor 2.

EQ   Set on if Factor 1 equals Factor 2.

Note: At least one of the resulting indicators must be specified. You should not use the same indicator for all three conditions. Compare values must be both character or both numeric. *Obsolete*. Use free-form expressions instead.

%DATE Convert to date

Function: %DATE(expression:format)

Converts expression (numeric, character, or timestamp data type), returning a date in *ISO format.

Expression   Expression to be converted (may be *DATE or UDATE). If omitted, %DATE returns the current system date.

Format   Date format of character or numeric expression (%DATE always returns date in *ISO format). Do not specify for *DATE, UDATE, or timestamp expression.

%DAYS Number of days

Function: %DAYS(number)

Converts a number to a duration representing a number of days that can be added or subtracted to a date or timestamp.

Number   Number to be converted to days.

Note: You can use %DAYS only on the right-hand side of an assignment expression. The result must be a date or timestamp.

DEALLOC Free storage

Free-form: DEALLOC(EN) <u>pointer</u>

Factor 1		Factor 2	Result	HI	LO	EQ
	DEALLOC(EN)		<u>Pointer</u>		ER	

Frees storage previously allocated by ALLOC operation.

(N)	Set pointer to null after successful operation.
Pointer	Basing pointer pointing to storage to be freed.
ER or **(E)**	Operation not completed successfully.

%DEC Convert to packed decimal
%DECH Convert to packed decimal with half-adjust

Function: %DEC(<u>numeric-expression</u>:precision:decimals)
%DECH(<u>numeric-expression:precision:decimals</u>)

Converts a numeric expression to packed-decimal format (optionally with half-adjusting) with the specified precision and number of decimal places.

Numeric expression	Expression to convert.
Precision	Total number of digits in result.
Decimals	Number of decimal places in result.

Note: %DECH requires entries for precision and decimals; if not specified for %DEC, precision and decimals are determined by attributes of expression.

%DECPOS Get number of decimal positions

Function: %DECPOS(<u>numeric-expression</u>)

Returns the number of decimal positions in the numeric expression or variable.

Numeric expression	Expression or variable to inspect.

DEFINE Field definition

Free-form: Not supported

Factor 1		Factor 2	Result	HI	LO	EQ
*LIKE	DEFINE	Referenced field	Defined field			
*DTAARA	DEFINE	External data area	Internal field			

Defines a field based on the attributes of another field (*LIKE), or defines a field as a data area (*DTAARA), depending on the entry in Factor 1.

*LIKE	The keyword *LIKE defines a field based upon the attributes of another field.
Referenced field	Must contain the name of the field being referenced. This field provides the attributes for the field being defined.
Defined field	The name of the field being defined.
*DTAARA	The keyword *DTAARA associates the internal program area with an external data area.
External data area	Specifies the external name of the data area. Use *LDA for local data area, *PDA for the PIP data area, or blank if the result field is both the RPG IV name and the external name of the data area.
Internal field	Must contain the name of the data area being defined.

Note: You can use positions 64–70 to define the length and number of decimal positions for the entry in the result field. Conditioning indicators are not valid. *Obsolete.* Use definition specifications (D-specs) with the LIKE or DTAARA keyword instead.

DELETE Delete record

Free-form: DELETE(E) search-argument <u>file-format-name</u>

Factor 1		Factor 2	Result	HI	LO	EQ
Search argument	DELETE(E)	File name or Format name		NR	ER	

Deletes a record from a database file. The file must be specified as an update file.

<dl>

Search argument Can contain a key or relative record number that identifies the record to be deleted. If blank, the DELETE operation deletes the current record.

File name or **format name** File name or format name from externally described file.

NR Record not found.

ER or **(E)** Operation not completed successfully.

</dl>

%DIFF Difference between two dates/times/timestamps

Function: %DIFF(<u>date1:date2:duration-code</u>)

Returns the difference (duration) between two date, time, or timestamp values.

Date1 Date, time, or timestamp value.

Date2 Date, time, or timestamp value. Must be same data type as Date1, or must be timestamp data.

Duration code Code representing type of duration to return. Must be *YEARS (*Y), *MONTHS (*M), *DAYS (*D), *HOURS (*H), *MINUTES (*MN), *SECONDS (*S), or *MSECONDS (*MS).

Note: Duration is rounded down, and remainder is discarded.

%DIV Integer division

Function: %DIV(<u>dividend:divisor</u>)

Returns integer portion of quotient when dividing dividend by divisor.

Dividend Number to be divided by divisor.

Divisor Number by which to divide dividend.

DIV Divide operation

Free-form: Not supported

Factor 1		Factor 2	Result	HI	LO	EQ
Dividend	DIV(H)	Divisor	Quotient	+	–	Z

If there is a value in Factor 1, divide that value by the value in Factor 2. If there is not a value in Factor 1, the result is divided by the value in Factor 2. The quotient is always placed in the result field.

Dividend	If specified, the DIV operation divides the dividend field by the divisor. Must contain a literal, a named constant, an array, an array element, a data structure name, a field name, a subfield, or a table name.
(H)	Result will be half-adjusted (rounded).
Divisor	Must contain a literal, a named constant, an array, an array element, a data structure name, a field name, a subfield, or a table name.
Quotient	The result of the DIV operation is placed in this field.
+	Set on if the result field is greater than 0.
–	Set on if the result field is less than 0.
Z	Set on if the result field is equal to 0.

Note: *Obsolete.* Use / operator or %DIV function instead.

DO Begin a DO group

Free-form: Not supported

Factor 1		Factor 2	Result	HI	LO	EQ
Starting value	DO	Limit value	Index value			

Begins a DO group of operations and indicates the number of times the group is processed.

Starting value	Must be a numeric value with no decimal positions using a numeric literal, a named constant, or a field name. If not specified, defaults to 1.
Limit value	Must be a numeric value with no decimal positions using a numeric literal, a named constant, or a field name. If not specified, defaults to 1.
Index value	Contains the current index value.

Note: To close a DO group, use ENDDO. *Obsolete.* Use FOR instead.

DOU Do until

Free-form: DOU(MR) <u>logical-expression</u>

Factor 1		Extended Factor 2
	DOU(MR)	<u>Logical expression</u>

Begins a group of operations you want to process at least one time, and usually more than once, until a logical expression is true.

(M/R)	Use *MAXDIGITS or *RESDECPOS precision rules when evaluating expression.
<u>Logical expression</u>	The operations controlled by the DOU operation are performed until the expression in Factor 2 is true. Factor 1 must be blank.

Note: To close a DOU group, use ENDDO.

DOU*xx* Do until *xx*

Free-form: Not supported

Factor 1		Factor 2	Result	HI	LO	EQ
<u>Compare value 1</u>	DOU*xx*	<u>Compare value 2</u>				

Begins a group of operations you want to process at least one time, and usually more than once, until a condition is satisfied. In the DOU*xx* operation, the *xx* can be

GT	Factor 1	>	Factor 2
LT	Factor 1	<	Factor 2
EQ	Factor 1	=	Factor 2
NE	Factor 1	<>	Factor 2
GE	Factor 1	>=	Factor 2
LE	Factor 1	<=	Factor 2

<u>Compare value 1</u>	Must contain a literal, a named constant, a table name, an array element, a data structure name, or a field name.
<u>Compare value 2</u>	Must contain a literal, a named constant, a table name, an array element, a data structure name, or a field name.

Note: Compare values must be both character or both numeric. To close a DOU*xx* group, use ENDDO. *Obsolete.* Use DOU instead.

DOW Do while

Free-form: DOW(MR) <u>logical-expression</u>

Factor 1		Extended Factor 2
	DOW(MR)	<u>Logical expression</u>

Begins a group of operations you want to process while the logical expression is true.

> **(M/R)** Use *MAXDIGITS or *RESDECPOS precision rules when evaluating expression.
>
> **Logical** The operations controlled by the DOW operation are performed as long
> **expression** as the expression in Factor 2 is true. Factor 1 must be blank.

Note: To close a DOW group, use ENDDO.

DOW*xx* Do while *xx*

Free-form: Not supported

Factor 1		Factor 2	Result	HI	LO	EQ
<u>Compare value 1</u>	DOW*xx*	<u>Compare value 2</u>				

Begins a group of operations you want to process while the relationship *xx* exists. In the DOW*xx*, *xx* can be

GT	Factor 1	>	Factor 2
LT	Factor 1	<	Factor 2
EQ	Factor 1	=	Factor 2
NE	Factor 1	<>	Factor 2
GE	Factor 1	>=	Factor 2
LE	Factor 1	<=	Factor 2

> **Compare value 1** Must contain a literal, a named constant, a table name, an array element, a data structure name, or a field name.
>
> **Compare value 2** Must contain a literal, a named constant, a table name, an array element, a data structure name, or a field name.

Note: Compare values must be both character or both numeric. To close a DOW*xx* group, use ENDDO. *Obsolete.* Use DOW instead.

DSPLY Display function

Free-form: DSPLY(E) message message-queue response

Factor 1		Factor 2	Result	HI	LO	EQ
Message	DSPLY(E)	Message queue	Response		ER	

Lets the program communicate with a display workstation that requested the program.

Message	Can contain a field name, a literal, a named constant, a table name, an array element whose value is used to create the message, or *M followed by a message identifier.
Message queue	The symbolic name of the object to receive the message and from which the optional response can be sent.
Response	May contain a field name, a table name, or an array element into which the response is placed.
ER or **(E)**	Operation not completed successfully.

DUMP Program dump

Free-form: DUMP(A) identifier

Factor 1		Factor 2	Result	HI	LO	EQ
Identifier	DUMP(A)					

Provides a detailed listing of the values for all fields, files, indicators, data structures, arrays, and tables, to aid in debugging a program. The DUMP is performed if DEBUG(*YES) is specified in H-specs or if the A extender is coded.

Identifier	Identifies the DUMP operation. It must contain a character entry that can be one of the following: a field name, a literal, a named constant, a table name, or an array element whose contents identify the dump. It cannot be a figurative constant.
(A)	Perform dump even when DEBUG(*NO) is specified in H-specs.

%EDITC Apply an edit code

Function: %EDITC(numeric-expression:edit-code:fill)

Returns a character result representing the edited number after applying an edit code to it.

Numeric expression	Numeric expression or variable to edit.
Edit code	Edit code to use (constant).
Fill	Optional floating currency symbol, *CURSYM, or *ASTFILL.

%EDITFLT Convert to floating point
Function: %EDITFLT(<u>numeric-expression</u>)

Converts a numeric expression to the external character display format for a floating-point number.

<u>**Numeric expression**</u>	Numeric expression or variable to convert.

%EDITW Apply an edit word
Function: %EDITW(<u>numeric-expression:edit-word</u>)

Returns a character result representing the edited number after applying an edit word to it.

<u>**Numeric expression**</u>	Numeric expression or variable to edit.
<u>**Edit word**</u>	Edit word to use. Must be a character constant.

%ELEM Number of elements
Function: %ELEM(<u>data-item</u>)

Returns the number of elements in a table, array, or multiple-occurrence data structure.

<u>**Data item**</u>	Name of table, array, or multiple-occurrence data structure.

ELSE
Free-form: ELSE

Factor 1		Factor 2	Result	HI	LO	EQ
	ELSE					

Used optionally with the IF and IF*xx* operations to indicate a block of code to process when the IF condition is not satisfied.

Note: To close an IF/ELSE group, use ENDIF. Conditioning indicators are not valid.

ELSEIF Else if

Free-form: ELSEIF(MR) <u>logical-expression</u>

Factor 1		Extended Factor 2
	ELSEIF(MR)	Logical expression

Lets a group of calculations be processed if a logical expression is true and if the logical expression for the previous IF/ELSEIF statement(s) in the IF block was false.

(M/R)   Use *MAXDIGITS or *RESDECPOS precision rules when evaluating expression.

Logical   The operations controlled by the IF operation are performed if the
expression   expression in Factor 2 is true.

Note: Do not individually close each ELSEIF group; close the entire IF group with ENDIF. Conditioning indicators are not valid.

END*yy* End a structured group

Free-form: END*yy* increment-value

Factor 1		Factor 2	Result	HI	LO	EQ
	END*yy*	Increment value				

Used to end a structured group of code. Use one of the following values in place of *yy*:

(Blank)   Ends any structured group. Not supported by free-form syntax. *Obsolete.*
CS   Ends a CAS*xx* group. Not supported by free-form syntax.
DO   Ends a DO, DOU, DOW, DOU*xx*, or DOW*xx* group
FOR   Ends a FOR group
IF   Ends an IF or IF*xx* group
MON   Ends a MONITOR group
SL   Ends a SELECT group

Increment value   Used with ENDDO to specify a value by which to increment the index. Must be a numeric value with no decimal positions using a numeric literal, a named constant, or a field name. It can be positive or negative; if not specified, defaults to 1.

Note: You can specify conditioning indicators for ENDDO, but they are not allowed for ENDCS, ENDFOR, ENDIF, ENDMON, and ENDSL.

ENDSR End of subroutine

Free-form: ENDSR return-point

Factor 1		Factor 2	Result	HI	LO	EQ
Label	ENDSR	Return point				

Marks the end of a subroutine.

Label A symbolic name that represents a specific location in a program. A label can serve as the destination point of two or more branching operations. Not supported by free-form syntax.

Return point Contains an entry that specifies where control is going to be returned following the processing of the subroutine. Not allowed in a subroutine that appears within a subprocedure.

Note: Level and conditioning indicators are not valid.

%EOF End of file

Function: %EOF(file-name)

Returns the end-of-file (or beginning-of-file) condition — *ON or *OFF — after a read operation or a write to a subfile. %EOF applies to READ, READE, READP, READPE, READC, and WRITE (subfile only) operations and, with restrictions, to CHAIN, SETLL, SETGT, and OPEN operations.

File name Name of file. If omitted, %EOF applies to most recent file operation.

Note: CHAIN, SETLL, SETGT, and OPEN operations will set %EOF to *OFF if they are successful and if you specify a file name; if they are unsuccessful, or if a file name is omitted, %EOF will not be affected by these operations.

%EQUAL Equal match

Function: %EQUAL(file-name)

Returns *ON if the most recent LOOKUP or SETLL operation found an exact match; otherwise, returns *OFF.

File name Name of file. If omitted, %EQUAL applies to most recent operation.

Note: %EQUAL is equivalent to the EQ (Equal) resulting indicator.

%ERROR Error
Function: %ERROR

Returns *ON if the most recent operation code with an E extender resulted in an error condition; otherwise, returns *OFF.

> **Note:** %ERROR is usually used in conjunction with the %STATUS function to identify the specific error condition.

EVAL Evaluate expression
Free-form: EVAL(HMR) <u>assignment-statement</u>

Factor 1		Extended Factor 2
	EVAL(HMR)	<u>Assignment statement</u>

Assigns to a variable the result of an expression. With non-numeric (character, graphic, or UCS-2) expressions, the result will be left-adjusted, and padded or truncated on the right, if necessary.

(H)	Half-adjust (rounding) for numeric expressions.
(M/R)	Use *MAXDIGITS or *RESDECPOS precision rules when evaluating expression.
<u>Assignment statement</u>	Result must be a field name, an array name, an array element, a data structure, a data structure subfield, or a string using the %SUBST built-in function.

> **Note:** EVAL may be omitted when using free-form syntax, if extenders are not required.

EVALR Evaluate expression, right-adjust
Free-form: EVALR(MR) <u>assignment-statement</u>

Factor 1		Extended Factor 2
	EVALR(MR)	<u>Assignment statement</u>

Evaluates a non-numeric (character, graphic, or UCS-2) expression and assigns the result to a variable, right-adjusting the result, and padding or truncating on the left, if necessary.

(M/R)	Use *MAXDIGITS or *RESDECPOS precision rules when evaluating expression.
<u>Assignment statement</u>	Result must be a field name, an array name, an array element, a data structure, a data structure subfield, or a string using the %SUBST built-in function.

EXCEPT Calculation time output

Free-form: EXCEPT name

Factor 1		Factor 2	Result	HI	LO	EQ
	EXCEPT	Name				

Writes one or more output records during calculations.

Name A symbolic name that represents the specific output record(s) to write.

EXFMT Write then read format

Free-form: EXFMT(E) format-name

Factor 1		Factor 2	Result	HI	LO	EQ
	EXFMT(E)	Format name			ER	

The EXFMT operation is a combination of a WRITE followed by a READ to the same display record format.

Format name Name of record format to be written and then read.

ER or **(E)** Operation not completed successfully.

EXSR Invoke subroutine

Free-form: EXSR subroutine-name

Factor 1		Factor 2	Result	HI	LO	EQ
	EXSR	Subroutine name				

Branches to a subroutine, then continues with the next calculation specification upon return from the subroutine.

Subroutine name Unique symbolic name of subroutine to be called. If *PSSR is used, the program exception/error subroutine is to be processed. If *INZSR is used, the program initialization subroutine is to be processed.

EXTRCT Extract date/time/timestamp

Free-form: Not supported

Factor 1		Factor 2	Result	HI	LO	EQ
	EXTRCT(E)	Date/Time: duration code	Target		ER	

Returns a segment of a date, time, or timestamp field.

Date/Time Date, time, or timestamp field, subfield, array, array element, literal, or constant.

Duration code A special value that indicates the type of duration (segment).

Target Any numeric or character field, subfield, array, or table element.

ER or **(E)** Invalid operand or other error performing operation.

Note: *Obsolete.* Use %SUBDT function instead.

FEOD Force end of data

Free-form: FEOD(E) file-name

Factor 1		Factor 2	Result	HI	LO	EQ
	FEOD(E)	File name			ER	

Signals the logical end of data for a primary, secondary, or full procedural file.

File name Name of file that will be forced to signal end of data.

ER or **(E)** Operation not completed successfully.

%FLOAT Convert to floating point

Function: %FLOAT(numeric-expression)

Converts a numeric expression to floating-point format.

Numeric expression Numeric expression to evaluate and convert.

FOR For

Free-form: FOR(MR) <u>index</u> = start BY increment TO|DOWNTO limit

Factor 1		Extended Factor 2
	FOR	<u>Index</u> = Start BY increment TO|DOWNTO limit

Begins a FOR group of operations and controls the number of times the group is processed.

(M/R) Use *MAXDIGITS or *RESDECPOS precision rules when evaluating expression. Not supported by fixed-form syntax.

Index Numeric variable containing the index value.

Start Must be a numeric value with no decimal positions using a numeric literal, a named constant, a field name, or an expression. If not specified, index will retain the value it had before the loop started.

Increment Non-zero numeric value used to increment index on each iteration. Must be a numeric literal, a named constant, a field name, or an expression. If not specified, defaults to 1.

Limit Numeric value used to determine index limit. Must be a numeric literal, a named constant, a field name, or an expression. If not specified, loop repeats indefinitely until a branching operation is encountered.

Note: The BY and TO/DOWNTO clauses can be specified in either order. To close a FOR group, use ENDFOR.

FORCE Force a certain file to be read next cycle

Free-form: FORCE <u>file-name</u>

Factor 1		Factor 2	Result	HI	LO	EQ
	FORCE	<u>File name</u>				

Selects the file from which the next record will be read.

File name The name of the file from which the next record will be selected.

Note: Level indicators are not valid.

%FOUND Found

Function: %FOUND(file-name)

Returns *ON if the most recent relevant operation found a record or element; otherwise, returns *OFF. %FOUND applies to CHAIN, DELETE, SETLL, and SETGT file operations; CHECK, CHECKR, and SCAN string operations; and the LOOKUP search operation.

> **File name** Name of file. If omitted, %FOUND applies to most recent operation.

Note: For file operations, %FOUND is opposite of the HI (No record) resulting indicator. For string operations, %FOUND is equivalent to the EQ (Found) resulting indicator. For LOOKUP, %FOUND is *ON if an element satisfies any search condition.

GOTO Go to label

Free-form: Not supported

Factor 1		Factor 2	Result	HI	LO	EQ
	GOTO	Label				

Branches to a specific location in a program, identified by a TAG operation.

> **Label** A symbolic name that represents a specific location in a program. A label can serve as the destination point of one or more branching operations.

%GRAPH Convert to graphic

Function: %GRAPH(expression:ccsid)

Converts a character, graphic, or UCS-2 expression to graphic format.

> **Expression** Expression to evaluate and convert.
>
> **CCSID** Character set identifier.

%HOURS Number of hours

Function: %HOURS(number)

Converts a number to a duration representing a number of hours that can be added to or subtracted from a time or timestamp.

> **Number** Number to be converted to hours.

Note: You can use %HOURS only on the right-hand side of an assignment expression. The result must be a time or timestamp.

IF If

Free-form: IF(MR) <u>logical-expression</u>

Factor 1		Extended Factor 2
	IF(MR)	<u>Logical expression</u>

Lets a group of calculations be processed if a logical expression is true.

(M/R) Use *MAXDIGITS or *RESDECPOS precision rules when evaluating expression.

<u>Logical expression</u> The operations controlled by the IF operation are performed if the expression in Factor 2 is true.

Note: To close an IF group, use ENDIF.

IF*xx* If *xx*

Free-form: Not supported

Factor 1		Factor 2	Result	HI	LO	EQ
<u>Compare value 1</u>	IF*xx*	<u>Compare value 2</u>				

Lets a group of calculations be processed if a given relationship exists between factors. The *xx* in the IF*xx* operation can be

GT	Factor 1	>	Factor 2
LT	Factor 1	<	Factor 2
EQ	Factor 1	=	Factor 2
NE	Factor 1	<>	Factor 2
GE	Factor 1	>=	Factor 2
LE	Factor 1	<=	Factor 2

<u>Compare value 1</u> Must contain a literal, a named constant, a table name, an array element, a data structure name, or a field name.

<u>Compare value 2</u> Must contain a literal, a named constant, a table name, an array element, a data structure name, or a field name.

Note: To close an IF*xx* group, use ENDIF. *Obsolete.* Use IF instead.

IN Retrieve a data area

Free-form: IN(E) *LOCK <u>data-area-name</u>

Factor 1		Factor 2	Result	HI	LO	EQ
*LOCK	IN(E)	<u>Data area name</u>			ER	

Retrieves a data area and lets you specify whether or not the data area is to be locked from update by another program.

> ***LOCK** Must be either the reserved word *LOCK or blank.
>
> <u>**Data area name**</u> Must be either the name of the area to be retrieved or the reserved word *DTAARA.
>
> **ER** or **(E)** Operation not completed successfully.

%INT Convert to integer format
%INTH Convert to integer format with half-adjust

Function: %INT(<u>numeric-expression</u>)
%INTH(<u>numeric-expression</u>)

Converts a numeric expression to integer format (optionally with half-adjusting).

> <u>**Numeric**</u> Expression to convert.
> <u>**expression**</u>

ITER Iterate

Free-form: ITER

Factor 1		Factor 2	Result	HI	LO	EQ
	ITER					

Transfers control within a DO group to the ENDDO statement of the DO group.

KFLD Define parts of a key

Free-form: Not supported

Factor 1		Factor 2	Result	HI	LO	EQ
	KFLD		<u>Key field</u>			

Defines a field in a list of fields (KLIST) that make up the key to a file.

> <u>**Key field**</u> Must be the name of the key field that is to be part of a search argument identified by a KLIST name.

Note: Conditioning indicators are not valid.

KLIST Define a composite key
Free-form: Not supported

Factor 1		Factor 2	Result	HI	LO	EQ
Klist name	KLIST					

Gives a name to a list of KFLDs. This list can be used as a search argument to retrieve records from files that have a composite key.

KLIST name Must be the name of the key field that is to be part of a search argument identified by a KLIST name.

Note: Conditioning indicators are not valid.

LEAVE Leave a DO group
Free-form: LEAVE

Factor 1		Factor 2	Result	HI	LO	EQ
	LEAVE					

Transfers control from within a DO group to the statement following the ENDDO operation.

LEAVESR Leave a subroutine
Free-form: LEAVESR

Factor 1		Factor 2	Result	HI	LO	EQ
	LEAVESR					

Transfers control to the ENDSR operation in a subroutine.

%LEN Get or set length
Function: %LEN(expression)

Returns the number of digits or characters in an expression, or sets the current length of a variable-length field.

Expression Expression or variable to inspect or set.

Note: When used on the right-hand side of an expression, %LEN returns the precision of a numeric expression, the number of characters in a character expression, or the current length of a variable-length field. When used on the left-hand side of an expression, %LEN sets the current length of a variable-length field.

%LOOKUP*xx* Look up element in an array

Function: %LOOKUP*xx*(<u>search-argument</u>:<u>array</u>:start:number-of-elements)

Searches an array for a specific element; returns the array index of the found element (or 0, if the search is unsuccessful). The *xx* in the %LOOKUP*xx* function can be

(Blank)	Find an exact match to search argument.
LT	Find element closest to but less than search argument.
LE	Find exact match, or element closest to but less than search argument.
GE	Find exact match, or element closest to but greater than search argument.
GT	Find element closest to but greater than search argument.

<u>**Search argument**</u>	The search argument can be a character or numeric literal, a named constant, an array element, a data structure name, or a field name.
<u>Array</u>	The name of the array that is to be searched.
Start	Number of index where search will start. Defaults to first element.
Number of elements	Number of elements to search. Defaults to entire array.

Note: %LOOKUP*xx* will *not* set the value of the %FOUND or %EQUAL function. %LOOKUP does not apply to tables; to search a table, use %TLOOKUP*xx*.

LOOKUP Look up element in an array or table

Free-form: Not supported

Factor 1		Factor 2	Result	HI	LO	EQ
<u>Search argument</u>	LOOKUP	<u>Array name</u>		HI	LO	EQ
<u>Search argument</u>	LOOKUP	<u>Table name</u>	Table name	HI	LO	EQ

Searches an array or table for a specific element.

<u>**Search argument**</u>	The search argument can be a character or numeric literal, a named constant, a table name, an array element, a data structure name, or a field name.
<u>Array name/ Table name</u>	The name of the array or table that is to be searched.
Table name	You can use the name of the second table to reference the element retrieved. The field must be blank if an array is being searched.
HI	Instructs the program to find the entry nearest to, yet higher in sequence than, the search argument.

LO   Instructs the program to find the entry nearest to, yet lower in sequence than, the search argument.

EQ   Instructs the program to find the entry equal to the search argument.

Note: *Obsolete.* Use %LOOKUP*xx* or %TLOOKUP*xx* function instead.

MHHZO Move high to high zone

Free-form: Not supported

Factor 1		Factor 2	Result	HI	LO	EQ
	MHHZO	Source field	Target field			

Moves the zone portion of a character from the leftmost zone of the source field to the leftmost zone of the target field.

    Source field   Must be a character field.

    Target field   Must be a character field.

MHLZO Move high to low zone

Free-form: Not supported

Factor 1		Factor 2	Result	HI	LO	EQ
	MHLZO	Source field	Target field			

Moves the zone portion of a character from the leftmost zone of the source field to the rightmost zone of the target field.

    Source field   Must contain a character field.

    Target field   Must contain a character field or a numeric field.

%MINUTES Number of minutes

Function: %MINUTES(number)

Converts a number to a duration representing a number of minutes that can be added or subtracted to a time or timestamp.

    Number   Number to be converted to minutes.

Note: You can use %MINUTES only on the right-hand side of an assignment expression. The result must be a time or timestamp.

MLHZO Move low to high zone
Free-form: Not supported

Factor 1		Factor 2	Result	HI	LO	EQ
	MLHZO	Source field	Target field			

Moves the zone portion of a character from the rightmost zone of the source field to the leftmost zone of the target field.

> **Source field**   Must contain a character field or a numeric field.
>
> **Target field**   Must contain a character field.

MLLZO Move low to low zone
Free-form: Not supported

Factor 1		Factor 2	Result	HI	LO	EQ
	MLLZO	Source field	Target field			

Moves the zone portion of a character from the rightmost zone of the source field to the rightmost zone of the target field.

> **Source field**   Must contain a character field or a numeric field.
>
> **Target field**   Must contain a character field or a numeric field.

MONITOR Begin a monitor group
Free-form: MONITOR

Factor 1		Factor 2	Result	HI	LO	EQ
	MONITOR					

Begins a group of statements to be processed with specific conditional error handling, based on the status code. In addition to the statements to be processed, the monitor group will include one or more on-error blocks, which will be processed if specific exceptions occur within the monitor group.

Note: To close a MONITOR block, use ENDMON.

%MONTHS Number of months

Function: %MONTHS(<u>number</u>)

Converts a number to a duration representing a number of months that can be added or subtracted to a date or timestamp.

> **Number**   Number to be converted to months.

> **Note:** You can use %MONTHS only on the right-hand side of an assignment expression. The result must be a date or timestamp.

MOVE Move characters from source field to target field

Free-form: Not supported

Factor 1		Factor 2	Result	HI	LO	EQ
Date/Time format	MOVE(P)	Source field	Target field	+	–	ZB

Transfers characters from a source field to a target field. The move starts with rightmost character of the source field. If the source field is longer than the target field, the excess leftmost characters are not moved.

> **Date/Time format**   If applicable, a specific value that indicates the type of date or time.

> **(P)**   Pad result field with blanks.

> **Source field**   Must be a character or a numeric literal, a named constant, a table name, an array element, a data structure name, or a field name.

> **Target field**   Must be a table name, an array element, a data structure name, or a field name.

> **+**   Set on if the result field is greater than 0.

> **–**   Set on if the result field is less than 0.

> **ZB**   Set on if the result field is equal to 0 or blank.

> **Note:** You cannot specify resulting indicators if the result field is an array. However, you can specify them if the result field is an array element or a non-array field. *Preferred alternative*: Use EVALR instead whenever possible.

MOVEA Move array
Free-form: Not supported

Factor 1		Factor 2	Result	HI	LO	EQ
	MOVEA(P)	Source	Target	+	–	ZB

Transfers character, graphic, or numeric values from the source to the target; either the source or the target must be an array. The source and the target cannot specify the same array even if the array is indexed.

(P)	Pad result field with blanks.
Source	Must contain the character-, graphic-, or numeric-based source field.
Target	Must contain the character-, graphic-, or numeric-based target field.
+	Set on if the result field is greater than 0.
–	Set on if the result field is less than 0.
ZB	Set on if the result field is equal to 0 or blank.

MOVEL Move left
Free-form: Not supported

Factor 1		Factor 2	Result	HI	LO	EQ
Date/Time format	MOVEL(P)	Source field	Target field	+	–	ZB

Transfers characters from the source to the target. The move begins with the leftmost character of the source field. If the source field is longer than the target field, the excess rightmost characters are not moved.

Date/Time format	If applicable, a specific value that indicates the type of date or time format used.
(P)	Pad result field with blanks.
Source field	Must be a character or a numeric literal, a named constant, a table name, an array element, a data structure name, or a field name.
Target field	Must be a table name, an array element, a data structure name, or a field name.
+	Set on if the result field is greater than 0.
–	Set on if the result field is less than 0.
ZB	Set on if the result field is equal to 0 or blank.

Note: You cannot specify the resulting indicators if the result is an array. However, you can specify them if the result field is an array element or a non-array field. *Preferred alternative*: Use EVAL instead whenever possible.

%MSECONDS Number of microseconds

Function: %MSECONDS(<u>number</u>)

Converts a number to a duration representing a number of microseconds that can be added or subtracted to a time or timestamp.

> **Number**   Number to be converted to microseconds.

> **Note:** You can use %MSECONDS only on the right-hand side of an assignment expression. The result must be a time or timestamp.

MULT Multiply

Free-form: Not supported

Factor 1		Factor 2	Result	HI	LO	EQ
Multiplicand	MULT(H)	<u>Multiplier</u>	<u>Product</u>	+	–	Z

Multiplies the value in the Factor 2 position by the value in Factor 1, if there is one. If there is not a value in Factor 1, the Factor 2 value is multiplied by the value in the result field. The product is always placed in the result field.

> **Multiplicand**   Must be numeric.
>
> **(H)**   Result will be half-adjusted (rounded).
>
> **Multiplier**   Must be numeric.
>
> **Product**   The product must be a numeric field.
>
> **+**   Set on if the result field is greater than 0.
>
> **–**   Set on if the result field is less than 0.
>
> **Z**   Set on if the result field is equal to 0.

> **Note:** *Obsolete.* Use * operator instead.

MVR Move remainder
Free-form: Not supported

Factor 1		Factor 2	Result	HI	LO	EQ
	MVR		Remainder	+	–	Z

Moves the remainder of the immediately previous DIV operation to a separate field named in the result field.

> **Remainder** Must be numeric and contain one of the following: an array, an array element, a subfield, or a table name.
>
> **+** Set on if the result field is greater than 0.
>
> **–** Set on if the result field is less than 0.
>
> **Z** Set on if the result field is equal to 0.

Note: *Obsolete.* Use %REM function instead.

NEXT Specify next input for multiple-device file
Free-form: NEXT(E) program-device file-name

Factor 1		Factor 2	Result	HI	LO	EQ
Program device	NEXT(E)	File name			ER	

Forces the next input for a multiple-device file to come from a specific program device.

> **Program device** Name of program device to be acquired.
>
> **File name** Multiple-device WORKSTN file to be associated with program device.
>
> **ER or (E)** Set on if an exception/error occurs on the NEXT operation.

%NULLIND Get or set null indicator
Function: %NULLIND(field)

On the right-hand side of an expression, returns the null indicator setting — *ON or *OFF — for a field; on the left-hand side of an expression, sets the null indicator for a field.

> **Field** Null-capable field to test or set.

%OCCUR Get or set occurrence of a data structure

Function: %OCCUR(data-structure)

On the right-hand side of an expression, returns the current occurrence number of a multiple-occurrence data structure; on the left-hand side of an expression, specifies which occurrence is to be used next.

> **Data structure** Name of the multiple-occurrence data structure.

OCCUR Get or set occurrence of a data structure

Free-form: Not supported

Factor 1		Factor 2	Result	HI	LO	EQ
Occurrence value 1	OCCUR(E)	Data structure	Occurrence value 2		ER	

Specifies which occurrence of a multiple-occurrence data structure is to be used next, or gets the current occurrence of a multiple-occurrence data structure.

> **Occurrence value 1** Numeric value used to set the occurrence of a data structure. May contain a numeric literal (no decimal places), a field name, a named constant, or a data structure name.
>
> **Data structure** Name of the multiple-occurrence data structure.
>
> **Occurrence value 2** Numeric field (no decimal places) to hold the occurrence of a data structure.
>
> **ER or (E)** Operation not completed successfully. Beyond range set for occurrence value.

Note: *Obsolete.* Use %OCCUR function instead.

ON-ERROR On error
Free-form: ON-ERROR exception-id1:exception-id2 ...

Factor 1		Extended Factor 2
	ON-ERROR	Exception-id1:exception-id2 ...

Specifies which error conditions are to be handled by an on-error block within a monitor group. After all the statements in the on-error block are processed, control passes to the statement following the monitor group's ENDMON statement.

Exception ID1: Exception identifiers that will signal that the on-error block is to
exception ID2 ... handle an error. May be a status code 00100–09999 or *PROGRAM, *FILE, or *ALL.

Note: Exception identifiers match the same codes as the %STATUS function, within the 00100–09999 range.

%OPEN Return open file condition
Function: %OPEN(file-name)

Returns *ON if the specified file is open; otherwise, returns *OFF.

File name Name of the file to report on.

OPEN Open file for processing
Free-form: OPEN(E) file-name

Factor 1		Factor 2	Result	HI	LO	EQ
	OPEN(E)	File name			ER	

Explicitly opens the file named in Factor 2. The file named cannot be designated as a primary, secondary, or table file and must specify UC in positions 73–74 of the file description specifications.

File name Name of the file to be opened explicitly.

ER or **(E)** Operation not completed successfully.

OR*xx* Or condition *xx*

Free-form: Not supported

Factor 1		Factor 2	Result	HI	LO	EQ
Compare value 1	ORxx	Compare value 2				

Specified immediately following a DOU*xx*, DOW*xx*, IF*xx*, WHEN*xx*, AND*xx*, or OR*xx* statement, to further specify a condition. The *xx* in OR*xx* can be

GT	Factor 1	>	Factor 2
LT	Factor 1	<	Factor 2
EQ	Factor 1	=	Factor 2
NE	Factor 1	<>	Factor 2
GE	Factor 1	>=	Factor 2
LE	Factor 1	<=	Factor 2

Compare value 1 Must contain a literal, a named constant, a table name, an array element, a data structure name, or a field name.

Compare value 2 Must contain a literal, a named constant, a table name, an array element, a data structure name, or a field name.

Note: Compare values must both be either numeric data or character data. Conditioning indicators are not valid. *Obsolete.* Use OR operator instead.

OTHER Otherwise select

Free-form: OTHER

Factor 1		Factor 2	Result	HI	LO	EQ
	OTHER					

Begins the sequence of operations to be processed if no WHEN*xx* or WHEN condition is satisfied in a SELECT group. The sequence ends with the ENDSL or END operation.

Note: Conditioning indicators are not valid.

OUT Write a data area

Free-form: OUT(E) *LOCK <u>data-area-name</u>

Factor 1		Factor 2	Result	HI	LO	EQ
*LOCK	OUT(E)	<u>Data area name</u>			ER	

Updates the data area named in Factor 2.

*LOCK	Factor 1 must either contain the reserved word *LOCK, in which case the data area remains locked until after it is updated, or be blank.
<u>Data area name</u>	Name of the data area, or the reserved word *DTAARA. When *DTAARA is used, all data areas in a program are used.
ER or **(E)**	Operation not completed successfully.

Note: The data area must also be specified in the result field of a *DTAARA DEFINE statement. The data area must have been locked previously by a *LOCK IN statement, or it must have been specified as a data-area data structure by a U in position 23 of the I-spec.

%PADDR Get procedure address

Function: %PADDR(<u>proc-name</u>)

Returns a procedure pointer representing the storage address of the specified procedure.

<u>Proc name</u>	The procedure for which the address should be returned. Must be a constant or a prototype name.

PARM Identify parameters

Free-form: Not supported

Factor 1		Factor 2	Result	HI	LO	EQ
Target field	PARM	Source field	<u>Parameter</u>			

Names a field as part of a parameter list. This operation must immediately follow a PLIST, CALL, or CALLB operation.

Target field	If a target is specified, the value of the parameter is placed in the target. The target can be character or numeric based.
Source field	If a source is specified, the value of the source field is placed into the parameter. The source can be character or numeric based.
<u>Parameter</u>	Must contain the name of the parameter.

Note: Conditioning indicators are not valid. *Obsolete.* Use prototype (PR) and procedure interface (PI) definitions instead.

%PARMS Number of parameters
Function: %PARMS

Returns the number of parameters passed to a procedure.

> **Note:** For the main procedure, the %PARMS function returns the same number as the *PARMS figurative constant.

PLIST Identify a parameter list
Free-form: Not supported

Factor 1		Factor 2	Result	HI	LO	EQ
Plist name	PLIST					

Defines a unique symbolic name for a parameter list to be specified in a CALL or CALLB operation.

> **PLIST name** Name of a parameter list of a called program. If the parameter list is the entry parameter list of a called program, Factor 1 must contain *ENTRY.

> **Note:** Conditioning indicators are not valid. *Obsolete.* Use prototype (PR) and procedure interface (PI) definitions instead.

POST Put information into a file information data structure
Free-form: POST(E) program-device file-name

Factor 1		Factor 2	Result	HI	LO	EQ
Program device	POST(E)	File name	INFDS name		ER	

Puts information into an INFDS. The information is either the status of a specific program device or I/O feedback information associated with a file.

> **Program device** Program device name to get information about.

> **File name** Name of file for which information is posted in the INFDS associated with this file. Required in free-form syntax.

> **INFDS name** Name of the information data structure that is to be posted. Not supported by free-form syntax.

> **ER or (E)** Operation not completed successfully.

READ Read a record

Free-form: READ(EN) file-format-name data-structure

Factor 1		Factor 2	Result	HI	LO	EQ
	READ(EN)	File name or record name	Data structure		ER	EOF

Reads the record that is currently pointed to from a full procedural file.

(N)	Do not lock record.
File name or **record name**	Name of the file or record name from an externally described file.
Data structure	Data structure (valid only with a program-described file).
ER or **(E)**	Set on if operation not successful.
EOF	Set on if end-of-file is reached.

Note: Requires a full procedural file (F in position 18 of F-specs).

READC Read next changed record

Free-form: READC(E) record-name

Factor 1		Factor 2	Result	HI	LO	EQ
	READC(E)	Record name			ER	EOF

Reads next changed record in a subfile. Can be used only with an externally described WORKSTN file.

Record name	Record format name (of subfile) from the externally described file that is to be read.
ER or **(E)**	Set on if operation not completed successfully.
EOF	Set on if end-of-file is reached.

READE Read equal key

Free-form: READE(EN) search-argument <u>file-record-name</u> data-structure

Factor 1		Factor 2	Result	HI	LO	EQ
Search argument	READE(EN)	File name or record name	Data structure		ER	EOF

Retrieves the next sequential record from a full procedural file if the key of the record matches the search argument.

Search argument	Search argument used to identify the record to be retrieved. It can be a field name, a literal, a named constant, or a figurative constant. You can specify a KLIST name for an externally described file.
(N)	Do not lock record.
File name or **record name**	Name of the file or record format to be retrieved.
Data structure	Data structure (valid only with a program-described file).
ER or **(E)**	Operation not completed successfully.
EOF	Set on if end-of-file is reached.

Note: Usage requires a full procedural file (F in position 18 of F-specs).

READP Read prior record

Free-form: READP(EN) <u>file-record-name</u> data-structure

Factor 1		Factor 2	Result	HI	LO	EQ
	READP(EN)	File name or record name	Data structure		ER	BOF

Retrieves the prior record from a full procedural file.

(N)	Do not lock record.
File name or **record name**	File name or record name from an externally described file.
Data structure	Data structure (valid only with a program-described file).
ER or **(E)**	Operation not completed successfully.
BOF	Set on if beginning-of-file is reached.

Note: Usage requires a full procedural file (F in position 18 of F-specs).

READPE Read prior equal

Free-form: READPE(EN) search-argument <u>file-record-name</u> data-structure

Factor 1		Factor 2	Result	HI	LO	EQ
Search argument	READPE(N)	<u>File name</u> or <u>record name</u>	Data structure		ER	BOF

Retrieves the next prior sequential record from a full procedural file if the key of the record matches the search argument.

<dl>
<dt>Search argument</dt>
<dd>Search argument used to identify the record to be retrieved. It can be a field name, a literal, a named constant, or a figurative constant. You can specify a KLIST name for an externally described file.</dd>
<dt>(N)</dt>
<dd>Do not lock record.</dd>
<dt><u>File name</u> or <u>record name</u></dt>
<dd>File name or record format name from an externally described file.</dd>
<dt>Data structure</dt>
<dd>Data structure into which the record is placed (valid only with a program-described file).</dd>
<dt>ER or (E)</dt>
<dd>Operation not completed successfully.</dd>
<dt>BOF</dt>
<dd>Set on if beginning-of-file is reached.</dd>
</dl>

Note: Requires a full procedural file (F in position 18 of F-specs).

%REALLOC Reallocate storage with new length

Function: %REALLOC(<u>pointer:length</u>)

Changes the length of the storage (previously allocated) pointed to by the pointer.

<dl>
<dt><u>Pointer</u></dt>
<dd>Basing pointer that points to the allocated storage.</dd>
<dt><u>Length</u></dt>
<dd>New length of storage to be allocated.</dd>
</dl>

REALLOC Reallocate storage with new length

Free-form: Not supported

Factor 1		Factor 2	Result	HI	LO	EQ
	REALLOC(E)	Length	Pointer		ER	

Changes the length of the storage (previously allocated by ALLOC) pointed to by the result field pointer.

Length New length of storage to be allocated.

Pointer Basing pointer that points to the allocated storage.

ER or **(E)** Operation not completed successfully.

Note: *Obsolete.* Use %REALLOC function instead.

REL Release program device

Free-form: REL(E) program-device file-name

Factor 1		Factor 2	Result	HI	LO	EQ
Program device	REL(E)	File name			ER	

Detaches the program device named in Factor 1 from a workstation file.

Program device The program device name can be a character field of length 10 or less, a character literal, or a named constant.

File name Name of the WORKSTN file.

ER or **(E)** Operation not completed successfully.

%REM Integer remainder

Function: %REM(dividend:divisor)

Returns integer remainder when dividing dividend by divisor.

Dividend Number to be divided by divisor. Must be numeric with no decimal places.

Divisor Number by which to divide dividend. Must be numeric with no decimal places.

%REPLACE Replace character string

Function: %REPLACE(<u>replacement:source</u>:start:length)

Returns character string that results from inserting a replacement string into a source string.

<u>**Replacement**</u>	String to insert into source string.
<u>**Source**</u>	String in which to insert replacement string.
Start	Position in source string at which replacement will start. Defaults to beginning.
Length	Number of characters to be replaced in source string. Defaults to length of replacement string. May be 0 (zero).

RESET Set variable to initial value

Free-form: RESET(E) *NOKEY *ALL <u>structure-variable</u>

Factor 1		Factor 2	Result	HI	LO	EQ
*NOKEY	RESET(E)	*ALL	<u>Structure</u> or <u>variable</u>		ER	

Resets a variable to the value it held after the *INIT phase of the program.

*NOKEY	If the result field contains a record format name, this entry can contain *NOKEY to indicate that key values are not to be reset.
*ALL	Reset all occurrences of a multiple-occurrence data structure and set the current occurrence to 1.
<u>**Structure** or</u> <u>**variable**</u>	The name of the data structure or variable to be reset to its initial value.
ER or **(E)**	Operation not completed successfully.

RETURN Return to caller

Free-form: RETURN(HMR) expression

Factor 1		Extended Factor 2	Result	HI	LO	EQ
	RETURN(HMR)	Expression				

Returns a program or procedure to its caller. If a value or expression is specified in the extended Factor 2, that value is returned to the calling procedure.

(H)	Half-adjust (rounding) for numeric expressions.
(M/R)	Use *MAXDIGITS or *RESDECPOS precision rules when evaluating expression.
Expression	The variable or expression to return to the calling procedure.

ROLBK Roll back

Free-form: ROLBK(E)

Factor 1		Factor 2	Result	HI	LO	EQ
	ROLBK(E)				ER	

Eliminates all changes made to files (under commitment control) that have been specified in output operations since the previous COMMIT or ROLBK operation.

ER or **(E)**   Operation not completed successfully.

%SCAN Scan character string

Function: %SCAN(search-argument:source:start)

Scans a character string for the specified substring; returns the leftmost position of the character string, or zero if the character string is not found.

Search argument   Character substring to find.

Source   Character string to search.

Start   Position in source string at which to start search. Defaults to 1.

SCAN Scan character string

Free-form: Not supported

Factor 1		Factor 2	Result	HI	LO	EQ
Search-arg: length	SCAN(E)	Source: start	Leftmost position		ER	FD

Scans a character string for the substring specified.

Search-arg:length   Character substring to find. Can include the length of the substring.

Source:start   Character string to search. Can include the starting position.

Leftmost position   Variable to contain numeric value of leftmost position of the compare string in the base string. If an array is specified, array will contain numeric value of *each* position of the compare string in the base string.

ER or **(E)**   Operation not completed successfully.

FD   Set on if the string is found.

Note: *Preferred alternative* is to use %SCAN function instead whenever possible (i.e., whenever result is not an array).

%SECONDS Number of seconds

Function: %SECONDS(number)

Converts a number to a duration representing a number of seconds that can be added to or subtracted from a time or timestamp.

Number   Number to be converted to seconds.

Note: You can use %SECONDS only on the right-hand side of an assignment expression. The result must be a time or timestamp.

SELECT Begin a select group

Free-form: SELECT

Factor 1		Factor 2	Result	HI	LO	EQ
	SELECT					

Conditionally processes one of several alternate sequences of operations. It includes a SELECT statement, zero or more WHEN*xx* or WHEN groups, an optional OTHER group, and an ENDSL or END statement.

SETGT Set greater than

Free-form: SETGT(E) search-argument file-name

Factor 1		Factor 2	Result	HI	LO	EQ
Search argument	SETGT(E)	File name		NR	ER	

Positions a file at the next record with a key or relative record number greater than the search argument.

Search argument   Search argument used to identify the record to be retrieved. It can be a field name, a literal, a named constant, or a figurative constant. You can specify a KLIST name for an externally described file. If the file is accessed by relative record number, you must use an integer value.

File name   File name or the format from an externally described file.

NR   Set on if no record is found.

ER or **(E)**   Operation not completed successfully.

SETLL Set lower limit

Free-form: SETLL(E) <u>search-argument</u> <u>file-name</u>

Factor 1		Factor 2	Result	HI	LO	EQ
<u>Search argument</u>	SETLL(E)	<u>File name</u>		NR	ER	EQ

Positions a file at the next record with a key or relative record number greater than or equal to the search argument.

<u>Search argument</u> Search argument used to identify the record to be retrieved. It can be a field name, a literal, a named constant, or a figurative constant. You can specify a KLIST name for an externally described file. If the file is accessed by relative record number, you must use an integer value.

<u>File name</u> File name or the format from an externally described file.

NR Set on if no record is found.

ER or (E) Operation not completed successfully.

EQ Set on if record is equal to search argument.

SETOFF Set indicator off

Free-form: Not supported

Factor 1		Factor 2	Result	HI	LO	EQ
	SETOFF			OF	OF	OF

Sets off any indicators specified in columns 71–76.

OF Indicator(s) to be set off.

Note: *Obsolete.* Use free-form expression (*IN*xx* = *OFF) instead.

SETON Set indicator on

Free-form: Not supported

Factor 1		Factor 2	Result	HI	LO	EQ
	SETON			ON	ON	ON

Sets on any indicators specified in positions 71–76.

ON Indicator(s) to be set on.

Note: *Obsolete.* Use free-form expression (*IN*xx* = *ON) instead.

%SHTDN Shut down

Function: %SHTDN

Returns *ON if the system operator has requested a shutdown; otherwise, returns *OFF.

SHTDN Shut down

Free-form: Not supported

Factor 1		Factor 2	Result	HI	LO	EQ
	SHTDN			ON		

Lets the program determine whether or not the system is shutting down.

> **ON**   Set on if system shutdown has been initiated.

Note: *Obsolete.* Use %SHTDN function instead.

%SIZE Size

Function: %SIZE(data-item:*ALL)

Returns the number of bytes occupied by a data item.

> **Data item**   Data item to inspect. May be a literal, named constant, data structure, data structure subfield, field, array, or table.
>
> ***ALL**   If the data item is an array, table, or multiple-occurrence data structure, specify *ALL to return the total size of all elements or occurrences; otherwise, %SIZE returns the size of a single element or occurrence.

Note: For variable-length fields, %SIZE returns the declared length plus two bytes.

SORTA Sort array

Free-form: SORTA array-name

Factor 1		Factor 2	Result	HI	LO	EQ
	SORTA	Array name				

Sorts an array into the sequence specified by position 45 of the definition specifications.

> **Array name**   Name of the array to be sorted.

Note: The array *IN cannot be specified in Factor 2 of the SORTA operation. A related array, such as a second array defined on the same D-spec, is not sorted.

%SQRT Square root

Function: %SQRT(numeric-expression)

Returns the square root of a numeric expression.

Numeric expression Expression to evaluate.

SQRT Square root

Free-form: Not supported

Factor 1		Factor 2	Result	HI	LO	EQ
	SQRT(H)	Value	Root			

Derives the square root of the field named in Factor 2.

(H) Result will be half-adjusted (rounded).

Value Must be numeric and can contain a literal, a named constant, a table name, an array element, a data structure name, or a field name.

Root Must be numeric and can contain one of the following: an array, an array element, a subfield, or a table element.

Note: *Obsolete.* Use %SQRT function instead.

%STATUS File or program status

Function: %STATUS(file-name)

Returns the most recent value for the file or program status. %STATUS is usually used in conjunction with the %ERROR function to identify a specific error condition.

File name If a file name is specified, %STATUS returns the value from the INFDS *STATUS field for the file. Otherwise, it returns the most recently changed program or file status (for any file).

Note: %STATUS is reset to 00000 whenever an operation code is specified with the E extender.

%STR Get or set null-terminated string

Function: %STR(pointer:length)

On the right-hand side of an expression, gets the string indicated by a pointer up to (but not including) the first null (x'00') character. On the left-hand side of an expression, creates a null-terminated string at the storage location indicated by a pointer.

Pointer The basing pointer to the storage containing the string.

Length The maximum length for the null-terminated string. Required when creating a string; optional when getting a string.

SUB Subtract

Free-form: Not supported

Factor 1		Factor 2	Result	HI	LO	EQ
Minuend	SUB(H)	Subtrahend	Difference	+	–	Z

Subtracts one or two numeric items.

Minuend The field must be numeric, and it can contain one of the following: an array, an array element, a subfield, or a table name. If not specified, the subtrahend is subtracted from the difference.

(H) Result will be half-adjusted (rounded).

Subtrahend The field must be numeric, and it can contain one of the following: an array, an array element, a subfield, or a table name.

Difference The field must be numeric, and it can contain one of the following: an array, an array element, a subfield, or a table name.

+ Set on if the difference is greater than 0.

– Set on if the difference is less than 0.

Z Set on if the difference is equal to 0.

Note: *Obsolete.* Use – operator instead.

%SUBDT Subset of a date, time, or timestamp

Function: %SUBDT(date:duration-code)

Extracts a portion of a date, time, or timestamp; returns a number representing the extracted portion.

Date Date, time, or timestamp value.

Duration code Code representing portion to return. Must be *YEARS (*Y), *MONTHS (*M), *DAYS (*D), *HOURS (*H), *MINUTES (*MN), *SECONDS (*S), or *MSECONDS (*MS).

SUBDUR Subtract duration

Free-form: Not supported

Factor 1		Factor 2	Result	HI	LO	EQ
Date/Time 1	SUBDUR(E)	Duration: duration code	Date/Time 2		ER	
Date/Time 1	SUBDUR(E)	Date/Time 2	Duration: duration code		ER	

Subtracts a duration to establish a new date, time, or timestamp; or calculates a duration (difference).

To subtract a duration:

Date/Time 1   Date, time, or timestamp field, subfield, array, array element, literal, or constant. If Factor 1 is not specified, the duration is subtracted from the field specified in the result field.

Duration: duration code   The amount of duration to subtract, along with a special value that indicates the type of duration.

Date/Time 2   Date, time, or timestamp field, subfield, array, or array element.

To calculate a duration:

Date/Time 1   (Minuend) Date, time, or timestamp field, subfield, array, array element, literal, or constant.

Date/Time 2   (Subtrahend) Date, time, or timestamp field, subfield, array, array element, literal, or constant.

Duration: duration code   The resulting duration, along with a special value that indicates the type of duration.

ER or (E)   Operation not completed successfully.

Note: The system places a 15-digit limit on durations. *Obsolete.* Use – operator with duration function (e.g., %DAYS, %MONTHS, %YEARS), or use the %DIFF function instead.

%SUBST Get or set substring

Function: %SUBST(<u>string</u>:<u>start</u>:length)

On the right-hand side of an expression, returns a substring from a string, starting at the given location for the specified length. On the left-hand side of an expression, assigns a value to a substring within a field.

<u>**String**</u>   Character string from which to extract substring.

<u>**Start**</u>   Starting position of substring.

Length   Length of substring. Defaults to rest of string.

SUBST Substring

Free-form: Not supported

Factor 1		Factor 2	Result	HI	LO	EQ
Length to extract	SUBST(EP)	<u>Base string</u>: start	<u>Target string</u>		ER	

Calculates a substring from a string, starting at the given location for the specified length; assigns the substring to a target result.

Length to extract   The field must be numeric, and it can contain one of the following: an array, an array element, a subfield, or a table element. If no Factor 1 is specified, the length of the string from the start position is used.

(P)   Pad result with blanks.

<u>**Base string:start**</u>   Character string from which to extract substring; you can optionally specify a starting position (numeric with no decimal positions).

<u>**Target string**</u>   Must be a character field, and must contain one of the following: a field name, an array element, a data structure name, or a table name.

ER or **(E)**   Set on if an error occurs during SUBST operation.

Note: *Obsolete.* Use %SUBST function instead.

TAG Tag

Free-form: Not supported

Factor 1		Factor 2	Result	HI	LO	EQ
Label	TAG					

Creates a label that identifies the destination of a GOTO or CAB*xx* operation.

> **Label**   The label must be an unique symbolic name that is specified in Factor 2 of a GOTO operation or in the result field of a CAB*xx* operation.

Note: Conditioning indicators are not valid.

TEST Test date/time/timestamp

Free-form: TEST(EDTZ) date-time-format <u>tested-field</u>

Factor 1		Factor 2	Result	HI	LO	EQ
	TEST(E)		Tested field		ER	
Date format	TEST(ED)		Tested field		ER	
Time format	TEST(ET)		Tested field		ER	
	TEST(EZ)		Tested field		ER	

Tests the validity of date, time, or timestamp fields before using them.

> **Date format/**   A specific value that indicates the type of date or time format to be used.
> **Time format**

>> **(D)**   Test for valid date.

>> **(T)**   Test for valid time.

>> **(Z)**   Test for valid timestamp.

> **Tested field**   Field to be tested for validity. If the TEST operation does not contain an extender, the tested field must be a date, time, or timestamp field. Otherwise, the tested field must be a character or numeric field that represents a date, time, or timestamp.

> **ER or (E)**   Set on if the content of the tested field is not valid.

TESTB Test value of bit field
Free-form: Not supported

Factor 1		Factor 2	Result	HI	LO	EQ
	TESTB	Bit numbers	Character field	OF	ON	EQ

Compares the bits identified with the corresponding bits in the field named as the result field.

Bit numbers	The bits to be tested are identified by the numbers 0–7 (0 is the leftmost bit). You must enclose the bit numbers in apostrophes (').
Character field	One-position character field.
OF	Set on if all bits specified are set off.
ON	Set on if some bits specified are set on.
EQ	Set on if all bits specified are set on.

TESTN Test numeric
Free-form: Not supported

Factor 1		Factor 2	Result	HI	LO	EQ
	TESTN		Character field	NU	BN	BL

Tests a character result field for the presence of zoned-decimal digits and blanks.

Character field	Character field to be tested.
NU	The test field contains either numeric characters or a one-character field that consists of a letter in the range A–R.
BN	The field contains both numeric characters and at least one leading blank.
BL	The field contains all blanks.

TESTZ Test zone

Free-form: Not supported

Factor 1		Factor 2	Result	HI	LO	EQ
	TESTZ		Character field	AI	JR	SZ

Tests the zone portion of the leftmost character in the result field.

Character field Character field to be tested.

  AI Set on if the character is & (ampersand), A–I, or any character with the same zone as the character A.

  JR Set on if the character is – (minus), J–R, or any character with the same zone as J.

  SZ Set on for characters with any other zone.

 Note: You must specify at least one of the above indicators.

%THIS Class instance for native method

Function: %THIS

Returns an object value referring to the class instance on whose behalf a native method is being called.

%TIME Convert to time

Function: %TIME(expression:format)

Converts expression (numeric, character, or timestamp data type), returning a time in *ISO format.

 Expression Expression to be converted. If omitted, %TIME returns the current system time.

 Format Time format of character or numeric expression (%TIME always returns time in *ISO format). Do not specify for timestamp expression.

TIME Time of day
Free-form: Not supported

Factor 1		Factor 2	Result	HI	LO	EQ
	TIME		<u>Field</u>			

Accesses the system time of day and, if specified, the system date at any time during program processing.

> **Field** Must be a 6-, 12-, or 14-digit numeric field (no decimal positions), or a date/time/timestamp field, into which the time of day and system date can be written.

Note: *Obsolete.* Use %DATE, %TIME, or %TIMESTAMP function instead.

%TIMESTAMP Convert to timestamp
Function: %TIMESTAMP(expression:format)

Converts expression (numeric, character, or date data type), returning a timestamp.

> **Expression** Expression to be converted. If omitted, %TIMESTAMP returns the current system time.

> **Format** Time format of character or numeric expression. Only *ISO or *ISO0 (for character expressions) is allowed; do not specify for timestamp expression.

%TLOOKUP*xx* Look up element in a table
Function: %TLOOKUP*xx*(search-argument:table:alternate-table)

Searches a table for a specific element; returns *ON if the lookup is successful, sets the current table element to the found element, and optionally sets the current table element of an alternate table to the same element (or returns *OFF, if the search is unsuccessful). The *xx* in the %TLOOKUP*xx* function can be

(Blank)	Find an exact match to search argument.
LT	Find element closest to but less than search argument.
LE	Find exact match, or element closest to but less than search argument.
GE	Find exact match, or element closest to but greater than search argument.
GT	Find element closest to but greater than search argument.

Search argument	The search argument can be a character or numeric literal, a named constant, an array element, a data structure name, or a field name.
Table	The name of the table that is to be searched.
Alternate table	The name of the alternate table to set, if any.

Note: %TLOOKUP*xx* will *not* set the value of the %FOUND or %EQUAL function. %TLOOKUP does not apply to arrays; use %LOOKUP*xx* to search an array.

%TRIM*x* Trim blanks
Function: %TRIM*x*(string)

Returns a character, graphic, or UCS-2 string without leading and/or trailing blanks. The *x* in the %TRIM*x* function can be

(Blank)	Trim both leading and trailing blanks.
L	Trim left (leading) blanks only.
R	Trim right (trailing) blanks only.

String	Character string to trim.

%UCS2 Convert to UCS-2
Function: %UCS2(expression:ccsid)

Converts a character, graphic, or UCS-2 expression to UCS-2 format.

Expression	Expression to evaluate and convert.
CCSID	Character set identifier.

UNLOCK Unlock a data area or release a record

Free-form: UNLOCK(E) dtaara-record-file

Factor 1		Factor 2	Result	HI	LO	EQ
	UNLOCK(E)	Data area, record, or file name			ER	

Unlocks a data area or releases a record.

Data area, **record**, or **file name**	The name of the data area to be unlocked, the name of an update disk file or record, or the reserved word *DTAARA.
ER or **(E)**	Operation not completed successfully.

%UNS Convert to unsigned integer format
%UNSH Convert to unsigned integer format with half-adjust

Function: %UNS(numeric-expression)
%UNSH(numeric-expression)

Converts a numeric expression to unsigned integer format (optionally with half-adjusting).

Numeric expression Expression to convert.

UPDATE Modify existing record

Free-form: UPDATE(E) file-format-name data-structure

Factor 1		Factor 2	Result	HI	LO	EQ
	UPDATE(E)	File name or record format	Data structure		ER	

Modifies the last record retrieved for processing from an update file.

File name or **record format**	File or record format name.
Data structure	Data structure name for program-described files.
ER or **(E)**	Operation not completed successfully.

WHEN When true then select

Free-form: WHEN(MR) <u>logical-expression</u>

Factor 1		Extended Factor 2
	WHEN(MR)	<u>Logical expression</u>

Performs the operations controlled by a WHEN operation in a SELECT group when the expression in Factor 2 is true.

(M/R) Use *MAXDIGITS or *RESDECPOS precision rules when evaluating expression.

<u>Logical expression</u> Must be a logical expression.

Note: Conditioning indicators are not valid.

WHEN*xx* When true then select

Free-form: Not supported

Factor 1		Factor 2	Result	HI	LO	EQ
<u>Compare value 1</u>	WHEN*xx*	<u>Compare value 2</u>				

Performs the operations controlled by a WHEN*xx* operation in a SELECT group when the relationship between Factor 1 and 2 is true. The *xx* relationship can be

GT   Factor 1 > Factor 2
LT   Factor 1 < Factor 2
EQ   Factor 1 = Factor 2
NE   Factor 1 <> Factor 2
GE   Factor 1 >= Factor 2
LE   Factor 1 <= Factor 2

<u>Compare value 1</u> Must contain a literal, a named constant, a table name, an array element, a data structure name, or a field name.

<u>Compare value 2</u> Must contain a literal, a named constant, a table name, an array element, a data structure name, or a field name.

Note: Conditioning indicators are not valid. *Obsolete.* Use WHEN instead.

WRITE Create new records

Free-form: WRITE(E) <u>file-format-name</u> data-structure

Factor 1		Factor 2	Result	HI	LO	EQ
	WRITE(E)	<u>File name</u> or <u>record format</u>	Data structure		ER	

Writes a new record to a file.

File name or **record format**	The name of the file or external record format to be written.
Data structure	Data structure from which the record is written (valid for program-described files only).
ER or **(E)**	Operation not completed successfully.

%XFOOT Sum array expression elements

Function: %XFOOT(<u>array-expression</u>)

Returns the sum of all the elements of an array expression.

Array expression	Expression containing array(s) to crossfoot.

XFOOT Sum the elements of an array

Free-form: Not supported

Factor 1		Factor 2	Result	HI	LO	EQ
	XFOOT(H)	<u>Array name</u>	<u>Sum</u>	+	−	Z

Adds the elements of an array together and places the sum into the field specified as the result field.

(H)	Result will be half-adjusted (rounded).
Array name	Name of the array.
Sum	The summation of the XFOOT operation.
+	Set on if the result field is greater than 0.
−	Set on if the result field is less than 0.
Z	Set on if the result field is equal to 0.

Note: *Obsolete.* Use the %XFOOT function instead.

%XLATE Translate

Function: %XLATE(from:to:string:start)

Translates characters in a string according to the From and To strings and returns the resulting string.

From	The string containing characters to translate from.
To	The string containing characters to translate to. The From and To strings can contain one of the following: a field name, an array element, a named constant, a data structure name, a literal, or a table name.
String	Source string to be translated.
Start	Location in string at which to start translation. Defaults to beginning.

XLATE Translate

Free-form: Not supported

Factor 1		Factor 2	Result	HI	LO	EQ
From:To	XLATE(EP)	String:start	Target string		ER	

Translates characters in a source string according to the From and To strings and places them into a receiver (target) string.

From:To	The string containing characters to translate from, followed by a colon, followed by the string containing characters to translate to. The From and To strings can contain one of the following: a field name, an array element, a named constant, a data structure name, a literal, or a table name.
(P)	Pad the result with blanks.
String:start	Must contain either the source string or the source string followed by a colon and the start location. The string must be a character, and it can contain one of the following: a field name, an array element, a named constant, a data structure name, a literal, or a table name.
Target string	Character field, character array element, data structure, or character table to hold the translated string.
ER or **(E)**	Operation not completed successfully.

Note: *Obsolete.* Use %XLATE function insead.

%YEARS Number of years
Function: %YEARS(number)

Converts a number to a duration representing a number of years that can be added or subtracted to a date or timestamp.

> **Number** Number to be converted to years.

> **Note:** You can use %YEARS only on the right-hand side of an assignment expression. The result must be a date or timestamp.

Z-ADD Zero and add
Free-form: Not supported

Factor 1		Factor 2	Result	HI	LO	EQ
	Z-ADD(H)	Addend	Sum	+	–	Z

Adds the addend to a field of zeros and places the sum in the result field.

> **(H)** Result is half-adjusted (rounded).

> **Addend** The field must be numeric, and it can contain one of the following: an array, an array element, a field, a figurative constant, a literal, a named constant, a subfield, or a table name.

> **Sum** The summation of the Z-ADD operation.

> **+** Set on if the result field is greater than 0.

> **–** Set on if the result field is less than 0.

> **Z** Set on if the result field is equal to 0.

> **Note:** *Obsolete.* Use free-form expression instead.

Z-SUB Zero and subtract

Free-form: Not supported

Factor 1		Factor 2	Result	HI	LO	EQ
	Z-SUB(H)	Subtrahend	Difference	+	–	Z

Subtracts the subtrahend from a field of zeros and places it in the result field.

(H)   Result is half-adjusted (rounded).

Subtrahend   The field must be numeric, and it can contain one of the following: an array, an array element, a subfield, or a table element.

Difference   Must be numeric, and it can contain one of the following: an array, an array element, a subfield, or a table name.

+   Set on if the result field is greater than 0.

–   Set on if the result field is less than 0.

Z   Set on if the result field is equal to 0.

Note: *Obsolete.* Use free-form expression instead.

Appendix B

Status Codes

This appendix lists the file and program status codes that you can check using the %STATUS built-in function (BIF) discussed in Chapter 8. The same codes apply to file exception subroutines (INFSR), program exception subroutines (*PSSR), and file feedback data structures (INFDS).

Normal Conditions (%ERROR = *OFF)

00000	No error.
00001	Called program returned with *INLR on.
00002	Function key pressed.
00011	End of file (%EOF = *ON).
00012	Record not found (%FOUND = *OFF).
00013	Write to full subfile.
00050	Conversion resulted in substitution.

Error Conditions (%ERROR = *ON)

00100	String operation, value out of range.
00101	Negative square root.
00102	Divide by zero.
00103	Intermediate result too small to contain result.
00104	Float underflow. Intermediate value too small.
00112	Invalid date, time, or timestamp value.
00113	Date overflow or underflow.
00114	Date mapping error.
00115	Invalid length for variable-length field.
00120	Table or array out of sequence.
00121	Invalid array index.
00122	OCCUR value out of range.
00123	RESET attempted during initialization.
00202	Call to program or procedure ended in error.
00211	Error occurred while calling program or procedure.
00221	Called program tried to use unpassed parameter.
00222	Pointer or parameter error.
00231	Called program returned with halt indicator on.
00232	Halt indicator on in this program.
00233	Halt indicator on when RETURN operation run.
00299	RPG dump failed.
00301	Error in method call.

continued ...

Error Conditions *Continued...*

00302	Error converting Java array to RPG parameter when entering Java native method.
00303	Error converting RPG parameter to Java array when exiting RPG native method.
00304	Error converting RPG parameter to Java array when preparing Java method call.
00305	Error converting Java array to RPG parameter/return value after Java method call.
00306	Error converting RPG return value to Java array.
00333	Error on DSPLY operation.
00401	Data area not found.
00402	*PDA not valid for non-prestart job.
00411	Data area types/lengths do not match.
00412	Data area not allocated for output.
00413	I/O error while processing data area.
00414	Not authorized to use data area.
00415	Not authorized to change data area.
00421	Error while unlocking data area.
00425	Requested storage allocation length out of range.
00426	Error during storage management operation.
00431	Data area previously allocated to another process.
00432	*LOCK for data area not granted.
00450	Character field not enclosed by SO and SI.
00451	Cannot convert between two CCSIDs.
00501	Sort sequence not retrieved.
00502	Sort sequence not converted.
00802	Commitment control not active.
00803	Rollback failed.
00804	COMMIT error.
00805	ROLBK error.
00907	Decimal data error.
00970	Compiler/runtime level check.
01011	Undefined record type.
01021	Record already exists.
01022	Referential constraint error.
01023	Trigger program error before operation.
01024	Trigger program error after operation.
01031	Match field sequence error.
01041	Array/table load sequence error.
01042	Array/table load sequence error.
01051	Excess entries in array/table file.
01071	Record out of sequence.
01121	No Print Key DDS keyword indicator.

continued ...

Error Conditions *Continued ...*

01122	No Page Down Key DDS keyword indicator.
01123	No Page Up Key DDS keyword indicator.
01124	No Clear Key keyword indicator.
01125	No Help Key DDS keyword indicator.
01126	No Home Key DDS keyword indicator.
01201	Record mismatch detected on input.
01211	I/O operation to a closed file.
01215	OPEN issued to already open file.
01216	Error on implicit OPEN/CLOSE.
01217	Error on explicit OPEN/CLOSE.
01218	Unable to allocate record.
01221	Update/delete operation without a prior read.
01222	Referential constraint error.
01231	Error on SPECIAL file.
01235	Error in PRTCTL space or skip entries.
01241	Record number not found.
01251	Permanent I/O error.
01255	Session or device error.
01261	Attempt to exceed maximum number of devices.
01271	Attempt to acquire unavailable device.
01281	Operation to unacquired device.
01282	Job ending with controlled option.
01284	Unable to acquire second device.
01285	Attempt to acquire an allocated device.
01286	Attempt to open shared file with SAVDS or SAVIND.
01287	Response indicators overlap SAVIND indicators.
01299	I/O error detected.
01331	Wait time exceeded for WORKSTN file.
09998	Internal failure in RPG compiler or in runtime subroutines.
09999	Program exception in system routine.

Status Codes as Named Constants

The following definitions define named constants that map to the %STATUS codes. Including this code in an RPG program lets you check for errors using meaningful names instead of the actual codes. For example, you can code

```
IF %STATUS = errRcdLocked
```

instead of

```
IF %STATUS = 01218
```

to detect a locked record.

To use these definitions, code them in a /COPY member or in an error-handling procedure.

```
*.. 1 ...+... 2 ...+... 3 ...+... 4 ...+... 5 ...+... 6 ...+... 7 ...+... 8
DName++++++++++ETDsFrom+++To/L+++IDc.Keywords+++++++++++++++++++++++++++++++
 // 00000 No error.
D stsNoError       C                     00000
 // 00001 Called program returned with *INLR on.
D stsPgmRetLR      C                     00001
 // 00002 Function key pressed.
D stsFkeyPressed   C                     00002
 // 00011 End of file (%EOF = *ON).
D stsEOF           C                     00011
 // 00012 Record not found (%FOUND = *OFF).
D stsNotFnd        C                     00012
 // 00013 Write to full subfile.
D stsWrtSflFull    C                     00013
 // 00050 Conversion resulted in substitution.
D stsCvtSubst      C                     00050
 // 00100 String operation, value out of range.
D errInvalString  C                     00100
 // 00101 Negative square root.
D errNegSqrt       C                     00101
 // 00102 Divide by zero.
D errDivZero       C                     00102
 // 00103 Intermediate result too small to contain result.
D errResultOvflow C                     00103
 // 00104 Float underflow. Intermediate value too small.
D errFltUndflow    C                     00104
 // 00112 Invalid date, time, or timestamp value.
D errInvalDate     C                     00112
 // 00113 Date overflow or underflow.
D errDateOvflow    C                     00113
 // 00114 Date mapping error.
D errDateMap       C                     00114
 // 00115 Invalid length for variable-length field.
D errInvalVarLen  C                     00115
 // 00120 Table or array out of sequence.
D errArrSeq        C                     00120
 // 00121 Invalid array index.
D errArrIdx        C                     00121
 // 00122 OCCUR value out of range.
D errInvalOccur   C                     00122
 // 00123 RESET attempted during initialization.
D errInzReset      C                     00123
 // 00202 Call to program or procedure ended in error.
D errCallFail      C                     00202
 // 00211 Error occurred while calling program or procedure.
D errCall          C                     00211
 // 00221 Called program tried to use unpassed parameter.
D errParmNoPass   C                     00221
 // 00222 Pointer or parameter error.
D errPtrParm       C                     00222
```

continued ...

```
*.. 1 ...+... 2 ...+... 3 ...+... 4 ...+... 5 ...+... 6 ...+... 7 ...+... 8
DName++++++++++ETDsFrom+++To/L+++IDc.Keywords+++++++++++++++++++++++++++++++++
  // 00231 Called program returned with halt indicator on.
D errCallHalt       C              00231
  // 00232 Halt indicator on in this program.
D errHalt           C              00232
  // 00233 Halt indicator on when RETURN operation run.
D errHaltRtn         C             00233
  // 00299 RPG dump failed.
D errDumpFail        C             00299
  // 00301 Error in method call.
D errMthCall         C             00301
  // 00302 Error converting Java array to RPG parm entering Java native meth
D errCvtJavArrEnt  C               00302
  // 00303 Error converting RPG parm to Java array exiting RPG native method
D errCvtRpgPrmOut  C               00303
  // 00304 Error converting RPG parm to Java array preparing Java meth call.
D errCvtRpgPrmPrp  C               00304
  // 00305 Error cvting Java array to RPG parm/return value after meth call.
D errCvtJavArrAft  C               00305
  // 00306 Error converting RPG return value to Java array.
D errcvtRpgRtnVal  C               00306
  // 00333 Error on DSPLY operation.
D errDsply          C              00333
  // 00401 Data area not found.
D errDtaaraNotFnd  C               00401
  // 00402 *PDA not valid for non-prestart job.
D errInvalPsjPDA   C               00402
  // 00411 Data area types/lengths do not match.
D errInvalDara      C             00411
  // 00412 Data area not allocated for output.
D errDaraNoOut      C             00412
  // 00413 I/O error while processing data area.
D errDaraIO          C            00413
  // 00414 Not authorized to use data area.
D errDaraUseAut     C             00414
  // 00415 Not authorized to change data area.
D errDaraChgAut     C             00415
  // 00421 Error while unlocking data area.
D errDaraUnlFail    C             00421
  // 00425 Requested storage allocation length out of range.
D errInvalAlloc     C             00425
  // 00426 Error during storage management operation.
D errStorFail       C             00426
  // 00431 Data area previously allocated to another process.
D errDaraAlloc      C             00431
  // 00432 *LOCK for data area not granted.
D errDaraLock       C             00432
  // 00450 Character field not enclosed by SO and SI.
D errInvalSosi      C             00450
  // 00451 Cannot convert between two CCSIDs.
D errCvtCcsid       C             00451
  // 00501 Sort sequence not retrieved.
D errSortRtv        C             00501
  // 00502 Sort sequence not converted.
D errSortCvt        C             00502
```

continued ...

```
*.. 1 ...+... 2 ...+... 3 ...+... 4 ...+... 5 ...+... 6 ...+... 7 ...+... 8
DName++++++++++ETDsFrom+++To/L+++IDc.Keywords++++++++++++++++++++++++++++++++
 // 00802 Commitment control not active.
D errCmtNact      C                   00802
 // 00803 Rollback failed.
D errRolbkFail    C                   00803
 // 00804 COMMIT error.
D errCmt          C                   00804
 // 00805 ROLBK error.
D errRolbk        C                   00805
 // 00907 Decimal data error.
D errDecimal      C                   00907
 // 00970 Compiler/runtime level check.
D errCompLevChk   C                   00970
 // 01011 Undefined record type.
D errUndefRecTyp  C                   01011
 // 01021 Record already exists.
D errRecExists    C                   01021
 // 01022 Referential constraint error.
D errRefCst       C                   01022
 // 01023 Trigger program error before operation.
D errTrgBefore    C                   01023
 // 01024 Trigger program error after operation.
D errTrgAfter     C                   01024
 // 01031 Match field sequence error.
D errMatchSeq     C                   01031
 // 01041 Array/table load sequence error.
D errArrSeq       C                   01041
 // 01042 Array/table load sequence error.
D errArrAltSeq    C                   01042
 // 01051 Excess entries in array/table file.
D errArrOvflow    C                   01051
 // 01071 Record out of sequence.
D errInvalRecSeq  C                   01071
 // 01121 No Print Key DDS keyword indicator.
D errDDSPrtKey    C                   01121
 // 01122 No Page Down Key DDS keyword indicator.
D errDDSPgDn      C                   01122
 // 01123 No Page Up Key DDS keyword indicator.
D errDDSPgUp      C                   01123
 // 01124 No Clear Key keyword indicator.
D errDDSClrKey    C                   01124
 // 01125 No Help Key DDS keyword indicator.
D errDDSHlpKey    C                   01125
 // 01126 No Home Key DDS keyword indicator.
D errDDSHomeKey   C                   01126
 // 01201 Record mismatch detected on input.
D errInpMisMatch  C                   01201
 // 01211 I/O operation to a closed file.
D errIOClosed     C                   01211
 // 01215 OPEN issued to already open file.
D errAlreadyOpen  C                   01215
 // 01216 Error on implicit OPEN/CLOSE.
D errImplicOpnclo C                   01216
```

continued ...

```
*.. 1 ...+... 2 ...+... 3 ...+... 4 ...+... 5 ...+... 6 ...+... 7 ...+... 8
DName++++++++++ETDsFrom+++To/L+++IDc.Keywords+++++++++++++++++++++++++++++++++
 // 01217 Error on explicit OPEN/CLOSE.
D errExplicOpnclo C              01217
 // 01218 Unable to allocate record.
D errRcdLocked    C              01218
 // 01221 Update/delete operation without a prior read.
D errUpdNoRead    C              01221
 // 01222 Referential constraint allocation error.
D errRefCstAlloc  C              01222
 // 01231 Error on SPECIAL file.
D errSpecial      C              01231
 // 01235 Error in PRTCTL space or skip entries.
D errPrtCtl       C              01235
 // 01241 Record number not found.
D errRecNbrNotFnd C              01241
 // 01251 Permanent I/O error.
D errPermIO       C              01251
 // 01255 Session or device error.
D errSessDev      C              01255
 // 01261 Attempt to exceed maximum number of devices.
D errMaxDev       C              01261
 // 01271 Attempt to acquire unavailable device.
D errDevUnavail   C              01271
 // 01281 Operation to unacquired device.
D errDevUnacq     C              01281
 // 01282 Job ending with controlled option.
D errJobEndCtl    C              01282
 // 01284 Unable to acquire second device.
D errAcqAddDev    C              01284
 // 01285 Attempt to acquire an allocated device.
D errDevAlloc     C              01285
 // 01286 Attempt to open shared file with SAVDS or SAVIND.
D errShrOpn       C              01286
 // 01287 Response indicators overlap SAVIND indicators.
D errRespInd      C              01287
 // 01299 I/O error detected.
D errIO           C              01299
 // 01331 Wait time exceeded for WORKSTN file.
D errWait         C              01331
 // 09998 Internal failure in RPG compiler or in runtime subroutines.
D errIntRPGFail   C              09998
 // 09999 Program exception in system routine.
D errPgmExc       C              09999
```

Appendix C

DATECALCR Sample RPG IV Program

This appendix contains the code for a complete RPG IV program, DATECALCR. The program dabbles with RPG's date data-type support and is intended to be an instructional program to let you "play" with the date functions. You can enter a date (in *MDY format) and then add a duration to the date; when you press Enter, the program will return the "Add Duration" result in several different date formats, extract the portions of the resulting date, and display the day of the week for the resulting date. You can also press F10 to enter a mode that will exercise the "Subtract Duration" date arithmetic. Figure C.1 shows sample displays from DATECALCR.

In addition to its primary purpose of letting you practice date manipulation in RPG IV, program DATECALCR also uses several RPG IV concepts that we have talked about in this book:

- specification keyword notation
- D-specs for data definition
- basing pointers
- built-in functions
- procedures
- use of the OVERLAY keyword to "redefine" data
- free-form calculation specifications
- date manipulation opcodes
- use of the TEST opcode to check for valid dates

After reading this book, you should be able to easily understand program DATECALCR without further comment. The program has two components: a display file, DATECALCD; and the DATECALCR program itself. Figure C.2 shows the DDS code for the display file; Figure C.3 shows the RPG IV code for program DATECALCR. To create and run this program, follow these steps:

1. Enter the code into two source members. Use source type DSPF for display file DATECALCD, and use source type RPGLE for the DATECALCR program code.

2. Create the display file:

```
CRTDSPF  FILE(DATECALCD)
```

3. Create the RPG IV module:

```
CRTRPGMOD  MODULE(DATECALCR) DBGVIEW(*LIST)
```

4. Create the ILE program:

```
CRTPGM  PGM(DATECALCR) ACTGRP(*CALLER)
```

5. When you have created both objects, call the program:

```
CALL  PGM(DATECALCR)
```

FIGURE C.1
Sample DATECALCR Displays

```
                        Date Calculator (ADDDUR)

Type date, duration, press Enter.

    Date  . . . . . . .   01/15/97      (*MDY format)
    Duration  . . . . .           96
       Type  . . . . . .   o Months
                           • Days
                           o Years

    ADDDUR Results
      *MDY format . . :   04/21/97       *ISO format . . :   1997-04-21
      *DMY format . . :   21/04/97       *USA format . . :   04/21/1997
      *YMD format . . :   97/04/21       *EUR format . . :   21.04.1997
      *JUL format . . :   97/111         *JIS format . . :   1997-04-21

    EXTRCT Results
      Year  . . . . . :   1997
      Month . . . . . :   04
      Day . . . . . . :   21

    Day of week . . . :   Monday

    F3=Exit    F10=SUBDUR Mode
```

```
                        Date Calculator (SUBDUR)

   Type dates, press Enter.

     First date  . . . .   08/12/97      (*MDY format)
     Second date . . . .   08/12/48      (*MDY format)

     Difference
       In years  . . . :           49
       In months . . . :          588
       In days . . . . :        17897

     F3=Exit    F9=ADDDUR Mode
```

FIGURE C.2
DDS Source for Display File DATECALCD

```
*.. 1 ...+... 2 ...+... 3 ...+... 4 ...+... 5 ...+... 6 ...+... 7 ...+... 8
A                                              DSPSIZ(24 80 *DS3)
A                                              INDARA
A                                              CA03(03)
A                                              CA09(09)
A                                              CA10(10)

A          R DATECALC01
A                                            1 29'Date Calculator (ADDDUR)'
A                                              DSPATR(HI)
A                                            3  2'Type date, duration, press Enter.'
A                                              COLOR(BLU)
A                                            5  2'Date . . . . . . .'
A            INDATE      8A  B  5 24
A N98                                          DSPATR(HI)
A  98                                          DSPATR(RI PC)
A                                            5 41'(*MDY format)'
A  98                                        5 55'This date is not valid.'
A                                              DSPATR(RI)
A                                            6  2'Duration . . . . .'
A            INDURATION  9Y 0B  6 24DSPATR(HI)
A                                              EDTCDE(Q)
A                                            7  4'Type . . . . . .'
A            INDURTYPE   2Y 0B  7 24DSPATR(HI)
A                                              SNGCHCFLD
A                                              CHOICE(1 '>Months')
A                                              CHOICE(2 '>Days')
A                                              CHOICE(3 '>Years')
A                                           10  2'ADDDUR Results'
A                                           11  4'*MDY format . . :'
A            DMDY        8A  O 11 24
A                                           11 44'*ISO format . . :'
A            DISO       10A  O 11 64
A                                           12  4'*DMY format . . :'
A            DDMY        8A  O 12 24
A                                           12 44'*USA format . . :'
A            DUSA       10A  O 12 64
A                                           13  4'*YMD format . . :'
A            DYMD        8A  O 13 24
A                                           13 44'*EUR format . . :'
A            DEUR       10A  O 13 64
A                                           14  4'*JUL format . . :'
A            DJUL        6A  O 14 24
A                                           14 44'*JIS format . . :'
A            DJIS       10A  O 14 64
A                                           16  2'EXTRCT results'
A                                           17  4'Year . . . . . :'
A            EXTRYEAR    4S 00 17 24
A                                           18  4'Month . . . . . :'
A            EXTRMONTH   2S 00 18 24
A                                           19  4'Day . . . . . . :'
A            EXTRDAY     2S 00 19 24
A                                           21  2'Day of Week . . . :'
```

continued ...

FIGURE C.2 CONTINUED

```
*.. 1 ...+... 2 ...+... 3 ...+... 4 ...+... 5 ...+... 6 ...+... 7 ...+... 8
A              DAYOFWEEK      9   0 21 24
A                                   23  2'F3=Exit'
A                                       COLOR(BLU)
A                                   23 12'F10=SUBDUR mode'
A                                       COLOR(BLU)

A              R DATECALC02
A                                    1 29'Date Calculator (SUBDUR)'
A                                       DSPATR(HI)
A                                    3  2'Type dates, press Enter.'
A                                       COLOR(BLU)
A                                    5  2'First date  . . . .'
A              INDATE         8A  B  5 24
A N98                                   DSPATR(HI)
A  98                                   DSPATR(RI PC)
A                                    5 41'(*MDY format)'
A  98                                5 55'This date is not valid.'
A                                       DSPATR(RI)
A                                    6  2'Second date . . . .'
A              INDATE2        8A  B  6 24
A N99                                   DSPATR(HI)
A  99                                   DSPATR(RI PC)
A                                    6 41'(*MDY format)'
A  99                                6 55'This date is not valid.'
A                                       DSPATR(RI)
A                                    8  2'Difference'
A                                    9  4'In years  . . . .'
A              DIFFYEARS      9Y 00  9 24EDTCDE(Q)
A                                   10  4'In Months . . . .'
A              DIFFMONTHS     9Y 00 10 24EDTCDE(Q)
A                                   11  4'In Days . . . . .'
A              DIFFDAYS       9Y 00 11 24EDTCDE(Q)
A                                   23  2'F3=Exit'
A                                       COLOR(BLU)
A                                   23 12'F9=ADDDUR mode'
A                                       COLOR(BLU)
A
```

FIGURE C.3
RPG IV Program DATECALCR

```
*.. 1 ...+... 2 ...+... 3 ...+... 4 ...+... 5 ...+... 6 ...+... 7 ...+... 8
FDateCalcD CF   E            WORKSTN INDDS(Indicators)

     // ------------------------------------- Procedure interfaces
D DayName         PR            9
D                               D   VALUE

     // ------------------------------------- Indicator data structure
D Indicators      DS
D   Exit                   3       3N
D   F09Key                 9       9N
D   F10Key                10      10N
D   ErrDate1              98      98N
D   ErrDate2              99      99N
```

continued ...

FIGURE C.3 *CONTINUED*

```
*.. 1 ...+... 2 ...+... 3 ...+... 4 ...+... 5 ...+... 6 ...+... 7 ...+... 8
 // ----------------------- Miscellaneous definitions, structures
D                       DS
D DateIn                               D    DATFMT(*MDY)
D  InDate                                   OVERLAY(DateIn)
D DateIn2                              D    DATFMT(*MDY)
D  InDate2                                  OVERLAY(DateIn2)
D DateMDY                              D    DATFMT(*MDY)
D  DMDY                                     OVERLAY(DateMDY)
D DateDMY                              D    DATFMT(*DMY)
D  DDMY                                     OVERLAY(DateDMY)
D DateYMD                              D    DATFMT(*YMD)
D  DYMD                                     OVERLAY(DateYMD)
D DateJUL                              D    DATFMT(*JUL)
D  DJUL                                     OVERLAY(DateJUL)
D DateISO                              D    DATFMT(*ISO)
D  DISO                                     OVERLAY(DateISO)
D DateUSA                              D    DATFMT(*USA)
D  DUSA                                     OVERLAY(DateUSA)
D DateEUR                              D    DATFMT(*EUR)
D  DEUR                                     OVERLAY(DateEUR)
D DateJIS                              D    DATFMT(*JIS)
D  DJIS                                     OVERLAY(DateJIS)

D Mode             S         3
D DurMonths        C              1
D DurDays          C              2
D DurYears         C              3

 /FREE
 // -----------------------------------------------------------
 //
 //      Main Program Logic
 //

  InDurType = DurDays;
  Mode = 'ADD';
  DateIn = %DATE();

  DOU Exit;

    SELECT;
      WHEN Mode = 'ADD';
        EXFMT DateCalc01;
      WHEN Mode = 'SUB';
        EXFMT DateCalc02;
    ENDSL;
```

continued ...

Figure C.3 Continued

```
*.. 1 ...+... 2 ...+... 3 ...+... 4 ...+... 5 ...+... 6 ...+... 7 ...+... 8
     SELECT;
       WHEN Exit;
         LEAVE;
       WHEN F09Key;
         Mode = 'ADD';
       WHEN F10Key;
         Mode = 'SUB';
       WHEN Mode = 'ADD';
         EXSR AddDate;
       WHEN Mode = 'SUB';
         EXSR SubDate;
     ENDSL;

  ENDDO;

  *INLR = *ON;
  RETURN;

  // -----------------------------------------------------------
  //
  //     Subroutine - AddDate - ADDDUR Mode
  //
  BEGSR AddDate;

  TEST(E) DateIn;
    ErrDate1 = %ERROR;

  IF NOT ErrDate1;

    SELECT;
      WHEN InDurType = DurMonths;
        DateISO = DateIn + %MONTHS(InDuration);
      WHEN InDurType = DurYears;
        DateISO = DateIn + %YEARS(InDuration);
      OTHER;
        DateISO = DateIn + %DAYS(InDuration);
    ENDSL;

    DateMDY = DateISO;
    DateDMY = DateISO;
    DateYMD = DateISO;
    DateJUL = DateISO;
    DateUSA = DateISO;
    DateEUR = DateISO;
    DateJIS = DateISO;

    ExtrYear = %SUBDT(DateISO:*Y);
    ExtrMonth = %SUBDT(DateISO:*M);
    ExtrDay = %SUBDT(DateISO:*D);

    DayOfWeek = DayName(DateISO);

  ENDIF;

  ENDSR;
```

continued ...

FIGURE C.3 *CONTINUED*

```
*.. 1 ...+... 2 ...+... 3 ...+... 4 ...+... 5 ...+... 6 ...+... 7 ...+... 8
 // --------------------------------------------------------------
 //
 //      Subroutine - SubDate - SUBDUR Mode
 //
  BEGSR SubDate;

  TEST(E) DateIn;
    ErrDate1 = %ERROR;
  TEST(E) DateIn2;
    ErrDate2 = %ERROR;

  IF NOT ErrDate1 AND NOT ErrDate2;
    DiffYears = %DIFF(DateIn:DateIn2:*YEARS);
    DiffMonths = %DIFF(DateIn:DateIn2:*MONTHS);
    DiffDays = %DIFF(DateIn:DateIn2:*DAYS);
  ENDIF;

  ENDSR;

 /END-FREE


 // ------------------------------------------------------------
 //
 //      Procedure - DayName - Return Name of Day of Week for a Date
 //
P DayName          B
 // ------------------------------------------- Procedure interface
D                  PI          9
D ParmDate                     D    VALUE

 // ------------------------------------------- Local definitions
D WorkField        S           5  0
D Name             S           9    BASED(NamePtr)
D NamePtr          S           *    INZ(%ADDR(Names))

D Names            S          63    INZ('Sunday   Monday   Tuesday  Wedn+
D                                      esdayThursday Friday   Saturday '
 /FREE
 // ------------------------------------------------------------

  WorkField = %DIFF(ParmDate:D'1899-12-31':*DAYS);
  WorkField = %REM(WorkField:7);

  NamePtr = NamePtr + (Workfield * 9);
  RETURN Name;

 /END-FREE

P DayName          E
```

Index

(number sign), 3
$ (dollar sign), 3
& (ampersand), 114
* (asterisk), 4, 69, 133
+ continuation character, 31, 56
− continuation character, 31, 56
@ (at sign), 3
// (double slash), 4, 50

A

%ABS function, 77
ACTGRP keyword, 9, 154
Activation groups, 153–154
    defined, 153
    using, 153–154
    See also also Integrated Language
        Environment (ILE)
ADD opcode, 73
ADDDUR opcode, 51, 107, 109–110
    defined, 109
    use example, 109
%ADDR function, 77, 79, 127, 129
    defined, 94–95
    use example, 95
ALIGN keyword, 26
%ALLOC function, 77
ALLOC opcode, 52
ALT keyword, 26, 41
ALTSEQ keyword, 9, 26
ALWNULL keyword, 9
Application programming interfaces (APIs),
    126, 131–132
Arrays
    alternating, 41
    character string manipulation and, 175
    compile-time, 40
    defining, 39–41
    element specification, 62–63
    EVAL with, 69
    initializing, 39
    naming, 39
    pre-runtime, 41
    runtime, 39
    support, 39
AS/400 ILE Concepts, 155
ASCEND keyword, 26
AUT keyword, 9
Auto-report, 142

B

BASED keyword, 26, 127
Basing pointers, 127, 130
Binary data type, 125
Blank lines, 4
BLOCK keyword, 17
BNDDIR keyword, 9, 166
Bound procedure calls, 150–153
    bound-by-copy, 151
    bound-by-reference, 151
    execution, 150
    implementing, 151–153
Built-in functions (BIFs), 49, 77–97
    %ABS, 77
    %ADDR, 77, 79, 94–95, 127, 129
    %ALLOC, 77
    %CHAR, 77, 93, 114–116
    %CHECK, 77
    data-conversion, 92–93
    %DATE, 77, 79, 114–115
    %DAYS, 77, 79
    %DEC, 77, 92
    %DECPOS, 77
    defined, 77
    %DIFF, 77, 108
    %DIV, 77
    %EDITC, %EDITW, 77, 94
    %EDITFLT, 77
    editing expressions with, 94
    %ELEM, 77, 86–87
    for eliminating indicators, 87–90
    %EOF, 77, 79, 87–88
    %EQUAL, 63, 77, 79, 89
    %ERROR, 78, 91, 111, 112
    error handling with, 91–92
    %FLOAT, 78
    %FOUND, 78, 79, 88–89
    %GRAPH, 78
    %HOURS, 78
    %INT, %INTH, 78, 93
    learning to use, 79
    %LEN, 78, 85–86, 97
    list of, 77–78
    %LOOKUP, 63, 78, 89–90
    %MINUTES, 78
    %MONTHS, 78, 79
    %MSECONDS, 78
    %NULLIND, 78, 96
    %OCCUR, 78
    %OPEN, 78, 91–92
    %PADDR, 78, 79, 94–95, 128
    %PARMS, 78, 79
    for program self-examination, 84–87
    %REALLOC, 78
    %REM, 78
    %REPLACE, 78, 83–84
    %SCAN, 78, 82–83
    %SECONDS, 78
    %SHTDN, 78

%SIZE, 78, 84–85, 97
%SQRT, 78
%STATUS, 78, 91
%STR, 78
string manipulation using, 80–84
%SUBDT, 78, 79, 109
%SUBST, 78, 79, 81–82
%THIS, 78
%TIME, 78, 79, 114–115
%TIMESTAMP, 78, 79, 114–115
%TLOOKUP, 78, 89–90
%TRIM, %TRIML, %TRIMR, 78, 80
%UCS2, 78
%UNS, %UNSH, 78, 93
%XFOOT, 78
%XLATE, 78
%YEARS, 78, 79

C

CALL opcode, 149
CALLB opcode, 145
    for calling service program module, 151
    implementing bound procedure call, 150
    with PARM statements, 152
CALLP opcode, 51, 58, 145
    for calling service program module, 151
    E extender, 58
    implementing bound procedure call, 150
CCSID keyword, 9, 26
%CHAR function, 77, 114–116
    defined, 93, 115
    target for, 116
    use example, 117
    using, 93
    with variable-length fields, 124
Character fields
    converting, 119
    initializing, 30
    testing, 112
    See also Fields
Character string manipulation, 175–176
%CHECK function, 77
CLASS keyword, 26
CALLPRC (Call Procedure) command, 150
Columnar layout, 6
Comments
    // (double slash) beginning, 4
    end-line, 170
    using, judiciously, 169–170
COMMIT keyword, 17, 20
Commitment control, activating at runtime,
    20–21
Compile-time arrays, 40
Compiling
    procedures, 163
    RPG IV, 146
Conditional compiles, 147–148

CONST keyword, 27, 30

Constants
  declarations, 174
  defining, 30–31
  named, 175
  numeric, 31
  values, 30

Continuation characters, 31
  multiple-line arithmetic expressions and, 67–68
  requirement, 56
  use of, 56

Control specification. *See* H-spec

Conversion
  character field, 119
  with CVTRPGSRC command, 140–143
  data, 92–93
  data, functions, 92–93
  date, 115, 116
  packed decimal, 92
  problems, solving, 144–145

COPYNEST keyword, 9

COPYRIGHT keyword, 9

CRTBNDRPG (Create Bound RPG Program) command, 73, 146, 148
  ACTGRP parameter, 154
  DFTACTGRP parameter, 154

CRTDTAARA (Create Data Area) command, 14

CRTPGM (Create Program) command, 152–153
  ACTGRP parameter, 154
  BNDSRVPGM parameter, 153
  ENTMOD parameter, 153
  MODULE parameter, 152

CRTRPGMOD (Create RPG Module) command, 73, 146, 148, 163

CRTRPGPGM (Create RPG Program) command, 150–151

C-spec, 6, 49–63
  array element specification, 62–63
  defined, 5
  example, 49–50
  extended Factor 2, 52–57
  free-form specification, 49–50, 60–61
  layout, 49, 50
  Monitor blocks, 59–60
  opcodes, 51–52
  operation extender, 58–59

CTDATA keyword, 27, 40

CURSYM keyword, 10

CVTOPT keyword, 10

CVTRPGSRC (Convert RPG Source) command, 140–143
  CVTRPT parameter, 143
  defined, 140

EXPCPY parameter, 143
FROMFILE parameter, 142
FROMMBR parameter, 142
INSRTPL parameter, 143
LOGFILE parameter, 143
LOGMBR parameter, 143
messages, 144–145
parameters, 142–143
problems, 144
SECLVL parameter, 143
TOFILE parameter, 142–143
TOMBR parameter, 143
use example, 141

D

Data areas
  creating, 14
  IBM-supplied, 13
  user-defined, 13

Data Definition Specifications (DDS), 19

Data items
  global, 174
  identical, defining, 29–30
  indenting, 170

Data structures
  child, initializing, 36
  data-area, 37
  defining, 32–39
  externally described, defining, 38–39
  indicator, mapping, 37–38
  initializing, 35
  overlapping fields in, 34
  program status, 36
  special, 36–37
  subfields, 32–33

Data types, 6, 101
  binary, 125
  date, 99, 101, 106
  defining, 46
  indicator, 123–124
  integer, 125
  list of, 123
  new, 46, 123–133
  numeric, 125–126
  pointer, 126–128
  time, 100, 101, 106
  timestamp, 106
  unsigned, 125

Data-area data structures, 37

Data-conversion functions, 92–93

%DATE function, 77, 79, 114–115

Date data, 99–102
  defining, 99–100
  formatting, 100–102
  OS/400 storage of, 103
  types, 99, 101, 106

Date fields, 102, 103–114
  in calculations, 105–114
  initializing, 103–105
  keywords for formatting, 102, 107
  *LOVAL and *HIVAL values, 104
  testing, 111–114

Date formats, 12
  default, 102
  summary, 100–101
  TEST opcode support of, 113–114

DATEDIT keyword, 10, 102

Dates
  arithmetic, 106–108
  converting, 115, 116
  operating on, 176
  supporting, in display files, 121

DATFMT keyword, 10, 12, 17, 27, 103

%DAYS function, 77, 79

DEALLOC opcode, 52

DEBUG keyword, 10

%DEC function, 77, 92

DECEDIT keyword, 10

Declarations, centralizing, 170–171

%DECPOS function, 77

DESCEND keyword, 27

DEVID keyword, 17

DFTACTGRP keyword, 10

DFTNAME keyword, 10

%DIFF function, 77
  defined, 108
  interval calculations, 108
  return value, 108

DIM keyword, 27

Display files, date support in, 121

%DIV function, 77

DIV opcode, 73

*DMY format, 12

DO loops, 53–54

D-spec, 25–42
  data structure definition, 32–39
  defined, 5, 25
  definition keywords, 26–28
  layout, 25–26
  learning, 33
  named constant definition, 30–31
  standalone field definition, 29–30
  table/array definition, 39–41

DTAARA keyword, 27
  defined, 37
  use example, 37

Durations
  codes, 108
  defined, 105

E

%EDITC, %EDITW functions, 77, 94
%EDITFLT function, 77
%ELEM function, 77
   return value, 86
   using, 86–87
The Elements of Programming Style, 177
ELSEIF opcode, 56–57
ENBPFRCOL keyword, 10
ENDMON opcode, 52
ENDSR opcode, 52
%EOF function, 77, 79
   defined, 87
   notation documents, 88
   using, 87–88
%EQUAL function, 63, 77, 79, 89
%ERROR function, 78, 111, 112
Error handling, with BIFs, 91–92
E-spec, 5, 23
*EUR format, 12, 13
EVAL opcode, 51, 65–75
   with arrays, 69
   for assigning numeric values, 65–68
   for avoiding "column cram," 72
   for avoiding work fields, 71–72
   imprecision, 75
   with indicators, 69–71
   multiple operators and, 67
   numeric overflow with, 72–73
   precision rules with, 73–74
   result field and, 72
   rounding and, 65
   for setting indicator state, 172
   with string expressions, 68–69
EVALR opcode, 51
   defined, 74
   with %TRIMR function, 74
EXPORT keyword, 27, 160, 163, 174
EXPROPTS keyword, 10
   defined, 73
   use example, 74
EXTBININT keyword, 10
Extended Factor 2, 52–57, 175
   complex expressions creation in, 55
   multiple source lines and, 55
   opcodes using, 53
Externally described files, 38–39
   I-spec layout, 43–44
   O-spec layout, 135–136
EXTFILE keyword, 17
   defined, 18
   example use, 18
   files coded with, 19
   values, 18
EXTFLD keyword, 27, 38

EXTFMT keyword, 27
EXTIND keyword, 17, 41
EXTMBR keyword, 17
   defined, 18
   example use, 18
   files coded with, 19
   values, 18
EXTNAME keyword, 27, 38
EXTPGM keyword, 27
EXTPROC keyword, 27, 166
EXTRCT opcode, 51, 110–111
   with date/time format, 111
   defined, 110
   use example, 110

F

Fields
   date, 102, 103–114
   initializing, 30
   name length, 21
   overlapping, 33, 34
   renaming, 19, 46–47
   standalone, 29–30
   subfields, 32–33
   time, 102, 103–105
   variable-length, 96–97, 124
   work, 29–30, 71–72
File names
   length, 3, 16
   long, coding, 42
Files
   display, 121
   error processing, 22
   externally described, 38–39, 43–44, 135–136
   program-described, 44–45, 136–137, 176
   record address, 23
   specifying, at runtime, 18–19
   type specification, 17
FIXNBR keyword, 10
%FLOAT function, 78
Floating-point numbers, 125–126
FLTDIV keyword, 10
FOR opcode, 54
FORMLEN keyword, 17
FORMOFL keyword, 17
FORMSALIGN keyword, 10
%FOUND function, 78, 79
   LOOKUP operation with, 88–89
   opcodes working with, 88
   using, 88–89
Free-form expressions, 65–75
   date arithmetic in, 106–108
   using, 175

Free-form specification. *See* C-spec
FROMFILE keyword, 27, 41
F-spec, 15–23
   defined, 5, 15
   file keywords, 17–23
   layout, 15–16
FTRANS keyword, 10
Functions. *See* Built-in functions (BIFs)

G

GENLVL keyword, 10
%GRAPH function, 78

H

Header specification. *See* H-spec
*HMS format, 13
%HOURS function, 78
H-spec, 9–14
   control keywords, 9–11
   data area, 14
   date formats, 12
   defined, 5
   layout, 9
   multiline sample, 11
   time formats, 13
   using, 13–14

I

IGNORE keyword, 17, 20
IMPORT keyword, 27, 174
INCLUDE keyword, 17, 20
INDARA keyword, 19
INDDS keyword, 17, 37
   defined, 19
   use example, 38
INDENT keyword, 11
Indicator data type, 123–124
Indicator-less code, 172
Indicators
   conditioning, 172
   description, 172
   eliminating with BIFs, 87–90
   EVAL with, 69–71
   in logical expressions, 70
   predefined number, 69
   state, setting, 172
   use of, 172
INFDS keyword, 17, 36
   defined, 17
   use example, 22
INFSR keyword, 17, 22
%INT, %INTH functions, 78, 93
Integer data type, 125

Integrated Language Environment (ILE), 6, 13, 149–155
 activation groups, 153–154
 bound procedure calls, 150
 calling programs in, 149–151
 RPG and, 149–155
 separation from RPG IV, 155
 single runtime model, 155
INTPREC keyword, 11
INZ keyword, 28
 for data types, 103–104
 defined, 30
 for externally described data structures, 39
 for runtime arrays, 39
 use example, 30
 values, 30
*ISO format, 12, 13
I-spec, 6, 43–47
 defined, 5, 43
 layout (externally described files), 43–44
 layout (program-described files), 44–45
 name length support, 43

J

*JIS format, 12, 13
*JUL format, 12

K

KEYLOC keyword, 17
Keyword format, 6, 15
Keywords
 ACTGRP, 9, 154
 ALIGN, 26
 ALT, 26, 41
 ALTSEQ, 9, 26
 ALWNULL, 9
 ASCEND, 26
 AUT, 9
 BASED, 26, 127
 BLOCK, 17
 BNDDIR, 9, 166
 CCSID, 9, 26
 CLASS, 26
 COMMIT, 17, 20–21
 CONST, 27, 30
 COPYNEST, 9
 COPYRIGHT, 9
 CTDATA, 27, 40
 CURSYM, 10
 CVTOPT, 10
 DATEDIT, 10, 102
 DATFMT, 10, 12, 17, 27, 103
 DEBUG, 10
 DECEDIT, 10
 DESCEND, 27
 DEVID, 17
 DFTACTGRP, 10

DFTNAME, 10
DIM, 27
DTAARA, 27, 37
ENBPFRCOL, 10
EXPORT, 27, 160, 163, 174
EXPROPTS, 10, 73
EXTBININT, 10
EXTFILE, 17, 18
EXTFLD, 27, 38
EXTFMT, 27, 41
EXTIND, 17
EXTMBR, 17, 18
EXTNAME, 27, 38
EXTPGM, 27
EXTPROC, 27, 166
FIXNBR, 10
FLTDIV, 10
FORMLEN, 17
FORMOFL, 17
FORMSALIGN, 10
FROMFILE, 27, 41
FTRANS, 10
GENLVL, 10
guidelines, 177
IGNORE, 17
IMPORT, 27, 174
INCLUDE, 17, 20
INDARA, 19
INDDS, 17, 19
INDENT, 11
INFDS, 17, 22, 36
INFSR, 17, 22
INTPREC, 11
INZ, 28, 30, 103–104
KEYLOC, 17
LANGID, 11
LIKE, 28, 29–30
LIKEDS, 28, 35
MAXDEV, 17
NOMAIN, 11, 13
NOOPT, 28
OCCURS, 28
OFLIND, 17
OPDESC, 28
OPENOPT, 11
OPTIMIZE, 11
OPTIONS, 11, 28, 165
OVERLAY, 28, 121
PACKEVEN, 28
PASS, 17
PERRCD, 28, 40
PGMNAME, 18
PLIST, 18
PREFIX, 18, 19, 28, 47
PRFDTA, 11
PROCPTR, 28
PRTCTL, 18
QUALIFIED, 28, 35
RAFDATA, 18, 23
RECNO, 18
RENAME, 18, 21–22
SAVEDS, 18

SAVEIND, 18
SFILE, 18, 22
SLN, 18
SRTSEQ, 11
STATIC, 28
TEXT, 11
THREAD, 11
TIMFMT, 11, 13, 18
TOFILE, 28, 41
TRUNCNBR, 11
USROPN, 18, 23
USRPRF, 11
VALUE, 28, 166
VARYING, 28, 124

L

LANGID keyword, 11
LEAVESR opcode, 52
Legacy data, date operations with, 114–117
%LEN function, 78
 defined, 85
 use example, 86
 using, 85–86
 for variable-length fields, 97
Length notation, 170–171
LIKE keyword, 28
 defined, 29
 use example, 29
LIKEDS keyword, 28
 defined, 35
 for prototyped parameters, 35
 use example, 35
Lists, processing with pointers, 132–133
Local variables, 161
%LOOKUP function, 63, 78
 defined, 89
 examples, 90
 form, 89
 %FOUND/%EQUAL and, 90
 using, 89–90
 values, 89
LOOKUP opcode, 39
L-spec, 5, 20

M

MAXDEV keyword, 17
*MDY format, 12
%MINUTES function, 78
Mixed-case characters, 3
Modular programming
 skills, honing, 174
 techniques, 173–174
Monitor blocks, 59–60
 specifying, 60
 start of, 60

MONITOR opcode, 52, 60
%MONTHS function, 78, 79
MOVE opcodes, 117–119
  for converting character fields, 119
  defined, 117
  use examples, 118–119
%MSECONDS function, 78
MULT opcode, 73

N

Named constants, defining, 30–31
Names
  conventions, 171–172
  field, 21, 42, 46–47
  file, 3, 16
  variable, 3
Nested /COPY statements, 147–148
NOMAIN keyword
  defined, 11
  specifying in H-spec, 13
NOOPT keyword, 28
Null database values, 96
%NULLIND function, 78, 96
Numeric constants, 31
Numeric fields
  testing, 112
  values, 65–68
Numeric overflow, 72–73

O

Obsolescence, avoiding, 176–177
%OCCUR function, 78
OCCURS keyword, 28
OFLIND keyword, 17
Opcodes, 51–52, 73
  ADD, 73
  ADDDUR (Add Duration), 51, 107, 109–110
  ALLOC (Allocate Storage), 52
  CALL, 149
  CALLB (Call a Bound Procedure), 145, 150–151
  CALLP (Call a Prototyped Procedure), 51, 58, 145, 150–151
  DEALLOC (Deallocate Storage), 52
  DIV, 73
  ELSEIF, 56–57
  ENDMON (End a Monitor Group), 52
  ENDSR (End a Subroutine), 52
  EVAL (Evaluate Expression), 51, 65–75
  EVALR (Evaluate Expression, Right-Adjust), 51
  EXTRCT (Extract Date/Time/Timestamp), 51, 110–111
  FOR, 54
  LEAVESR (Leave a Subroutine), 52
  LOOKUP, 39

MONITOR (Begin a Monitor Group), 52, 60
MOVE, 117–119
MULT, 73
new, 51–52
not supported by free-form syntax, 61–62
obsolete, 176–177
REALLOC (Reallocate Storage with New Length), 52
renamed/deleted, 52
RETURN, 162
SUB, 73
SUBDUR (Subtract Duration), 51, 110
TEST, 106, 111–114
TIME, 119
using extended Factor 2, 53
OPDESC keyword, 28
%OPEN function, 78, 91–92
  defined, 91
  use example, 92
OPENOPT keyword, 11
Operation extenders, 58–59
  D, 112
  E, 58, 91, 172
  H, 58, 65–66, 71
  list of valid, 59
  M, 58, 73–74
  N, 58
  P, 58
  R, 58, 73–74
  T, 112
  Z, 112
OPTIMIZE keyword, 11
OPTIONS keyword, 28, 165
OS/400 System API Programming, 132
O-spec, 135–138
  defined, 5
  layout, externally described files, 135–136
  layout, program-described files, 136–137
  use examples, 138
Overlapping fields, 33, 34
OVERLAY keyword, 28, 121
  defined, 34
  use example, 34

P

Packed decimal, converting, 92
PACKEVEN keyword, 28
%PADDR function, 78, 79, 128
  defined, 94, 95
  return value, 95
  use example, 95
Parameter-passing methods, 164–165
  by read-only reference, 165
  by reference, 164
  by value, 164–165
  options, 165

%PARMS function, 78, 79
PASS keyword, 17
Pass-by-reference, 126
PERRCD keyword, 28, 40
PGMNAME keyword, 18
PLIST keyword, 18
Pointers, 126–133
  with APIs, 131–132
  basing, 127, 130
  defined, 126
  defining, 127
  initialization, 128
  for list processing, 132–133
  manipulation, 128–130
  manipulation example, 130
  procedure, 128
  support, 126–133
  testing, 130
  use of, 126
PREFIX keyword, 18, 28, 29
  defined, 19
  for renaming fields, 47
  syntax, 19
Pre-runtime arrays, 41
PRFDTA keyword, 11
Procedure pointers, 128
Procedures, 177
  calling, 162
  compiling, 163
  defined, 157
  example, 159
  interface, 161
  programs vs., 150
  specification layout, 161
  using, 162
  See also Prototypes
PROCPTR keyword, 28
Program status data structures, 36
Program-described files
  avoiding, 176
  I-spec layout, 44–45
  O-spec layout, 136–137
Programming Development Manager (PDM), 140
Programs
  calling, in ILE, 149–151
  compiling, 146
  converting, 139–145
  procedures vs., 150
Prototypes, 163–167
  appearance, 159
  C functions, 167
  compiler rules, 160
  declaring, 159–160
  defined, 158
  definition purpose, 159
  QCMDEXC, 166
  storing in /COPY members, 174

uses, 163–167
using for parameters and procedure
interfaces, 173
See also Procedures
PRTCTL keyword, 18
P-spec, 5

Q

QUALIFIED keyword, 28
defined, 35
use example, 35

R

RAFDATA keyword, 18
defined, 23
use example, 23
%REALLOC function, 78
REALLOC opcode, 52
RECNO keyword, 18
Record
address files, 23
formats, renaming, 21
%REM function, 78
RENAME keyword, 18
defined, 21
use example, 22
Renaming fields, 19, 46–47
%REPLACE function, 78
arguments, 83–84
defined, 83
using, 83–84
with variable-length fields, 124
RETURN operation, 162
RPG II, 7
RPG III, 2, 7
RPG IV
arithmetic operator support, 66
auto-report and, 142
blank lines, 4
changes, 2–5
comments, 4
date/time operations in, 99–121
defined, 1
ILE and, 6, 155
introduction to, 1–7
limit changes, 4–5, 16
mixed-case characters, 3
name changes, 3, 16
objectives, 2
programs, compiling, 146
reasons for, 1–2
as RPG dialect, 7
specification changes, 5
success, 6–7
syntax checker, 140
syntax conversion to, 139

Runtime arrays, 39
defined, 40
initializing, 39
See also Arrays

S

SAVEDS keyword, 18
SAVEIND keyword, 18
%SCAN function, 78
arguments, 82
defined, 82
multiple, 83
%SECONDS function, 78
Self-documenting code, 84
SFILE keyword, 18
defined, 22
use example, 22
%SHTDN function, 78
%SIZE function, 78, 84–85
arguments, 85
return value, 84, 85
for variable-length fields, 97
for writing self-modifying code, 84
SLN keyword, 18
Source Entry Utility (SEU) syntax
checker, 88
Source file members, 139–140
%SQRT function, 78
SRTSEQ keyword, 11
Standalone fields. *See* Work fields
STATIC keyword, 28
%STATUS function, 78, 91
%STR function, 78
String expressions
enclosing in apostrophes, 68
EVAL with, 68–69
manipulation, 175–176
Structured programming techniques, 173
SUB opcode, 73
defined, 110
use example, 110
%SUBDT function, 78, 79
defined, 109
use example, 109
SUBDUR opcode, 51, 110
Subfields, 32–33
initializing, 35
lengths, 32
overlapping, 33
renaming, 38
Subfiles, describing, 22
Subprocedures
coding, 160–162
defined, 157
source code for, 160
using, 165

See also Procedures
Subroutines, 157–158
%SUBST function, 78, 79
arguments, 81
defined, 81
using, 81–82

T

Tables
defining, 39–41
support, 39
TEST opcode, 106, 111–114
date/time fields, 111
defined, 111
numeric and character fields, 112
principle behind, 113
TEXT keyword, 11
%THIS function, 78
THREAD keyword, 11
%TIME function, 78, 79, 114–115
Time data, 99–102
defining, 99–100
formatting, 100–102
OS/400 storage of, 103
type, 100, 101, 106
Time fields, 102, 103–105
initializing, 103–105
keywords for formatting, 102, 107
*LOVAL and *HIVAL values, 105
testing, 111–114
Time formats, 13
default, 102
summary, 101
TIME opcode, 119
%TIMESTAMP function, 78, 79, 114–115
Timestamp
data type, 106
fields, testing, 111–114
format, 101
TIMFMT keyword, 11, 13, 18, 28
%TLOOKUP function, 78
defined, 89
%FOUND/%EQUAL and, 90
using, 89–90
values, 89
TOFILE keyword, 28, 41
%TRIM, %TRIML, %TRIMR functions, 78
return value, 80
stripping blanks with, 80
TRUNCNBR keyword, 11

U

%UNS, %UNSH functions, 78, 93
%UCS2 function, 78
Unsigned data type, 125

*USA format, 12, 13
USROPN keyword, 18, 23
USRPRF keyword, 11

V

VALUE keyword, 28, 166
Variable-length fields, 96–97
  %CHAR and %REPLACE functions with,
    124
  current length of, 124
  maximum length, 124
  for string handling, 175–176
  using, 124

Variables
  declaring, 170
  local, 161
  name length, 3
VARYING keyword, 28, 124

W

Work fields, 29–30
  avoiding with EVAL, 71–72
  defined, 71
WRKACTJOB (Work with Active Jobs)
  command, 166

X

%XFOOT function, 78
%XLATE function, 78

Y

%YEARS function, 78, 79
*YMD format, 12

Newest Books in the 29th Street Press® Library

FORTRESS ROCHESTER
The Inside Story of the IBM iSeries
By Frank G. Soltis

Go behind the scenes and get the story on the design and development of IBM's new eServer iSeries. Dr. Frank Soltis, IBM chief scientist for the iSeries, examines the five sacred architectural principles of the system, hardware technologies, system structure, enabling technologies, and e-business. Special chapters cover iSeries security, Java, Domino, and Linux. 400 pages.

STARTER KIT FOR THE IBM ISERIES AND AS/400
By Gary Guthrie and Wayne Madden

Starter Kit for the IBM iSeries and AS/400 provides essential information to help you understand the basic concepts and nuances of iSeries and AS/400 systems. The book is arranged in logical order from basic system setup information through important areas you need to know about to operate, program, and manage your system. Comprehensive sections cover system setup, operations, file basics, basic CL programming, TCP/IP, and Operations Navigator. Whether you're a programmer, a system administrator, or an operator, this book will help you develop a basic working knowledge of many key concepts and functions and apply what you've learned to make your iSeries or AS/400 environment more secure, productive, and manageable. An accompanying CD contains all the utilities and sample code presented in the book. 578 pages.

IMPLEMENTING AS/400 SECURITY, FOURTH EDITION
By Carol Woodbury and Wayne Madden

For years, AS/400 professionals have depended on earlier editions of *Implementing AS/400 Security* to learn and implement essential AS/400 security concepts. This latest edition not only brings together in one place the fundamental AS/400 security tools and experience-based recommendations you need but also includes specifics on the security enhancements available in OS/400 V4R5. In addition, you'll find expanded coverage of network, communications, and Internet security — including thwarting hacker activities — as well as updated chapters covering security system values, user profiles, object authorization, database security, output-queue and spooled-file security, auditing, contingency planning, and more. 454 pages.

ILE BY EXAMPLE
A Hands-on Guide to the AS/400's Integrated Language Environment
By Mike Cravitz

Learn the fundamentals of the AS/400's Integrated Language Environment (ILE) by following working examples that illustrate the ins and outs of this powerful programming model. Major topics include ILE program structure, bind by copy, ILE RPG subprocedures, service programs, activation groups, ILE condition handling and cancel handling, and more. A CD contains all sample programs discussed in the book, as well as a sample ILE condition handler to address record locks and ILE RPG software to synchronize system clocks using the Internet SNTP protocol. 165 pages.

SQL/400 DEVELOPER'S GUIDE

By Paul Conte and Mike Cravitz

SQL/400 Developer's Guide provides start-to-finish coverage of SQL/400, IBM's strategic language for the AS/400's integrated database. This textbook covers database and SQL fundamentals, SQL/400 Data Definition Language (DDL) and Data Manipulation Language (DML), and database modeling and design. Throughout the book, coding suggestions reinforce the topics covered and provide practical advice on how to produce robust, well-functioning code. Hands-on exercises reinforce comprehension of the concepts covered. 508 pages.

MASTERING THE AS/400, THIRD EDITION
A Practical, Hands-On Guide

By Jerry Fottral

The latest edition of this best-selling introduction to AS/400 concepts and facilities takes a utilitarian approach that stresses student participation. The book emphasizes mastery of system/user interface, member-object-library relationship, use of CL commands, basic database concepts, and program development utilities. The text prepares students to move directly into programming languages, database management, and system operations courses. Each lesson includes a lab that focuses on the essential topics presented in the lesson. 553 pages.

DOMINO R5 AND THE AS/400

By Justine Middleton, Wilfried Blankertz, Rosana Choruzy, Linda Defreyne, Dwight Egerton, Joanne Mindzora, Stephen Ryan, Juan van der Breggen, Felix Zalcmann, and Michelle Zolkos

Domino R5 and the AS/400 provides comprehensive installation and setup instructions for those installing Domino R5 "from scratch," upgrading from a previous version, or migrating from a platform other than the AS/400. In addition, you get detailed explanations of SMTP in Domino for AS/400, dial-up connectivity, directory synchronization, Advanced Services for Domino for AS/400, and Domino administration strategies, including backup strategies. 512 pages.

PROGRAMMING IN RPG IV, SECOND EDITION

By Bryan Meyers and Judy Yaeger

This textbook provides a strong foundation in the essentials of business programming, featuring the newest version of the RPG language: RPG IV. Focusing on real-world problems and down-to-earth solutions using the latest techniques and features of RPG, this book provides everything you need to know to write a well-designed RPG IV program. The second edition includes new chapters on defining data with D-specs and modular programming concepts, as well as an RPG IV summary appendix and an RPG IV style guide. An instructor's kit is available. 408 pages.

E-BUSINESS
Thriving in the Electronic Marketplace

By Nahid Jilovec

E-Business: Thriving in the Electronic Marketplace identifies key issues organizations face when they implement e-business projects and answers fundamental questions about entering and navigating the changing world of e-business. A concise guide to moving your business into the exciting world of collaborative e-business, the book introduces the four e-business models that drive today's economy and gives a clear summary of e-business technologies. It focuses on practical business-to-business applications. 172 pages.

INTRODUCTION TO AS/400 SYSTEM OPERATIONS, SECOND EDITION

By Heidi Rothenbuehler and Patrice Gapen

Here's the second edition of the textbook that covers what you need to know to become a successful AS/400 system operator or administrator. *Introduction to AS/400 System Operations, Second Edition* teaches you the basics of system operations so that you can manage printed reports, perform regularly scheduled procedures, and resolve end-user problems. New material covers the Integrated File System (IFS), AS/400 InfoSeeker, Operations Navigator, and much more. 182 pages.

CREATING CL COMMANDS BY EXAMPLE

By Lynn Nelson

Learn from an expert how to create CL commands that have the same functionality and power as the IBM commands you use every day. You'll see how to create commands with all the function found in IBM's commands, including parameter editing, function keys, F4 prompt for values, expanding lists of values, and conditional prompting. Whether you're in operations or programming, *Creating CL Commands by Example* can help you tap the tremendous power and flexibility of CL commands to automate tasks and enhance applications. 134 pages.

IMPLEMENTING WINDOWS NT ON THE AS/400
Installing, Configuring, and Troubleshooting

By Nick Harris, Phil Ainsworth, Steve Fullerton, and Antoine Sammut

Implementing Windows NT on the AS/400: Installing, Configuring, and Troubleshooting provides everything you need to know about using NT on your AS/400, including how to install NT Server 4.0 on the Integrated Netfinity Server, synchronize user profiles and passwords between the AS/400 and NT, administer NT disk storage and service packs from the AS/400, back up NT data from the AS/400, manage NT servers on remote AS/400s, and run Windows-based personal productivity applications on the AS/400. 393 pages.

JAVA AND THE AS/400
Practical Examples Using VisualAge for Java

By Daniel Darnell

This detailed guide takes you through everything you need to know about the AS/400's implementation of Java, including the QShell Interpreter and the Integrated File System (IFS), and development products such as VisualAge for Java (VAJ) and the AS/400 Toolbox for Java. The author provides several small application examples that demonstrate the advantages of Java programming for the AS/400. The companion CD contains all the sample code presented in the book and full-version copies of VAJ Professional Edition and the AS/400 Toolbox for Java. 300 pages.

DOMINO AND THE AS/400
Installation and Configuration

By Wilfried Blankertz, Rosana Choruzy, Joanne Mindzora, and Michelle Zolkos

Domino and the AS/400: Installation and Configuration gives you everything you need to implement Lotus Domino 4.6 on the AS/400, guiding you step by step through installation, configuration, customization, and administration. Here you get an introduction to Domino for AS/400 and full instructions for developing a backup and recovery plan for saving and restoring Domino data on the AS/400. 311 pages.

ESSENTIALS OF SUBFILE PROGRAMMING AND ADVANCED TOPICS IN RPG IV

By Phil Levinson

This textbook provides a solid background in AS/400 subfile programming in the newest version of the RPG language: RPG IV. Subfiles are the AS/400 tool that lets you display lists of data on the screen for user interaction. You learn to design and program subfiles via step-by-step instructions and real-world programming exercises that build from chapter to chapter. A section on the Integrated Language Environment (ILE), introduced concurrently with RPG IV, presents tools and techniques that support effective modular programming. An instructor's kit is available. 293 pages.

DDS KEYWORD REFERENCE

By James Coolbaugh

Reach for the *DDS Keyword Reference* when you need quick, at-your-fingertips information about DDS keywords for physical files, logical files, display files, printer files, and ICF files. In this no-nonsense volume, author Jim Coolbaugh gives you all the keywords you'll need, listed alphabetically in five sections. He explains each keyword, providing syntax rules and examples for coding the keyword. *DDS Keyword Reference* is a friendly and manageable alternative to IBM's bulky DDS reference manual. 212 pages.

SQL/400 BY EXAMPLE

By James Coolbaugh

Designed to help you make the most of SQL/400, *SQL/400 by Example* includes everything from SQL syntax and rules to the specifics of embedding SQL within an RPG program. For novice SQL users, this book features plenty of introductory-level text and examples, including all the features and terminology of SQL/400. For experienced AS/400 programmers, *SQL/400 by Example* offers a number of specific examples that will help you increase your understanding of SQL concepts and improve your programming skills. 204 pages.

OPNQRYF BY EXAMPLE

By Mike Dawson and Mike Manto

The OPNQRYF (Open Query File) command is the single most dynamic and versatile command on the AS/400. Drawing from real-life, real-job experiences, the authors explain the basics and the intricacies of OPNQRYF with lots of examples to make you productive quickly. An appendix provides the UPDQRYF (Update Query File) command — a powerful addition to AS/400 and System/38 file-update capabilities. CD included. 216 pages.

DDS PROGRAMMING FOR DISPLAY AND PRINTER FILES, SECOND EDITION

By James Coolbaugh

DDS Programming for Display and Printer Files, Second Edition helps you master DDS and — as a result — improve the quality of your display presentations and your printed jobs. The second edition offers a thorough, straightforward explanation of how to use DDS to program display files and printer files. It includes extensive DDS programming examples for CL and RPG that you can put to use immediately because a companion CD includes all the DDS, RPG, and CL source code presented in the book. 429 pages.

THE AS/400 EXPERT: READY-TO-RUN RPG/400 TECHNIQUES

By Julian Monypenny and Roger Pence

Ready-to-Run RPG/400 Techniques provides a variety of RPG templates, subroutines, and copy modules, sprinkled with fundamental advice, to help you write robust and effective RPG/400 programs. Highlights include string-handling routines, numeric editing routines, date routines, error-handling modules, and tips for using OS/400 APIs with RPG/400. The tested and ready-to-run code building blocks — provided on an accompanying CD — easily snap into existing RPG code and integrate well with new RPG/400 projects. 203 pages.

TCP/IP AND THE AS/400

By Michael Ryan

Transmission Control Protocol/Internet Protocol (TCP/IP) has become a major protocol in the AS/400 world because of TCP/IP's ubiquity and predominance in the networked world, as well as its being the protocol for the Internet, intranets, and extranets. *TCP/IP and the AS/400* provides background for AS/400 professionals to understand the capabilities of TCP/IP, its strengths and weaknesses, and how to configure and administer the TCP/IP protocol stack on the AS/400. It shows TCP/IP gurus on other types of systems how to configure and manage the AS/400 TCP/IP capabilities. 362 pages.

THE A TO Z OF EDI AND ITS ROLE IN E-COMMERCE, SECOND EDITION

By Nahid Jilovec

E-commerce expert Nahid Jilovec gives you the practical details of EDI implementation. Not only does this book show you how to cost justify EDI, but it also gives you job descriptions for EDI team members, detailed criteria and forms for evaluating EDI vendors, considerations for trading-partner agreements, an EDI glossary, and lists of EDI organizations and publications. The second edition includes new information about EDI and the Internet, system security, and auditing. 221 pages.

VISUALAGE FOR RPG BY EXAMPLE

By Bryan Meyers and Jef Sutherland

VisualAge for RPG (VARPG) is a rich, full-featured development environment that provides all the tools necessary to build Windows applications for the AS/400. *VisualAge for RPG by Example* brings the RPG language to the GUI world and lets you use your existing knowledge to develop Windows applications. Using a tutorial approach, *VisualAge for RPG by Example* lets you learn as you go and create simple yet functional programs from start to finish. The accompanying CD offers a scaled-down version of VARPG and complete source code for the sample project. 236 pages.

ESSENTIALS OF SUBFILE PROGRAMMING AND ADVANCED TOPICS IN RPG/400

By Phil Levinson

Essentials of Subfile Programming and Advanced Topics in RPG/400 teaches you to design and program subfiles, offering step-by-step instructions and real-world programming exercises that build from chapter to chapter. You learn to design and create subfile records; load, clear, and display subfiles; and create pop-up windows. In addition, the advanced topics help you mine the rich store of data in the file information and program status data structures, handle errors, improve data integrity, and manage program-to-program communications. An instructor's manual is available. 260 pages.

DATA WAREHOUSING AND THE AS/400

By Scott Steinacher

In this book, Scott Steinacher takes an in-depth look at data warehousing components, concepts, and terminology. After laying this foundation, Scott presents a compelling case for implementing a data warehouse on the AS/400. Included on an accompanying CD are demos of AS/400 data warehousing software from several independent software vendors. 342 pages.

CONTROL LANGUAGE PROGRAMMING FOR THE AS/400, SECOND EDITION

By Bryan Meyers and Dan Riehl

This CL programming textbook offers students comprehensive knowledge of the skills they will need in today's MIS environment. Chapters progress methodically from CL basics to more complex processes and concepts, guiding students toward a professional grasp of CL programming techniques and style. In this second edition, the authors have updated the text to include discussion of the Integrated Language Environment (ILE) and the fundamental changes ILE introduces to the AS/400's execution model. 522 pages.

BUILDING AS/400 CLIENT/SERVER APPLICATIONS
Put ODBC and Client Access APIs to Work

By Mike Otey

Mike Otey, a leading client/server authority with extensive practical client/server application development experience, gives you the why, what, and how-to of AS/400 client/server computing, which matches the strengths of the AS/400 with the PC GUIs that users want. This book's clear and easy-to-understand style guides you through all the important aspects of AS/400 client/server applications. Mike covers APPC and TCP/IP communications as well as the underlying architectures for each of the major AS/400 client/server APIs. A CD with complete source code for several working applications is included. 505 pages.

DEVELOPING YOUR AS/400 INTERNET STRATEGY

By Alan Arnold

This book addresses the issues unique to deploying your AS/400 on the Internet. It includes procedures for configuring AS/400 TCP/IP and information about which client and server technologies the AS/400 supports natively. This enterprise-class tutorial evaluates the AS/400 as an Internet server and teaches you how to design, program, and manage your Web home page. 248 pages.